Slavery in the
Upper Mississippi Valley,
1787–1865

Slavery in the Upper Mississippi Valley, 1787–1865

*A History of Human Bondage
in Illinois, Iowa,
Minnesota and Wisconsin*

CHRISTOPHER P. LEHMAN

McFarland & Company, Inc., Publishers
Jefferson, North Carolina, and London

Library of Congress Cataloguing-in-Publication Data

Lehman, Christopher P.
    Slavery in the Upper Mississippi Valley, 1787–1865 : a history of
human bondage in Illinois, Iowa, Minnesota and Wisconsin /
Christopher P. Lehman.
        p.   cm.
    Includes bibliographical references and index.

    ISBN 978-0-7864-5872-1
    softcover : 50# alkaline paper ∞

    1. Slavery—Middle West—History—19th century.   2. Slavery—
United States—Extension to the territories.   3. Middle West—
Politics and government—19th century.   4. Middle West—Social
conditions—History—19th century.   5. Middle West—Race
relations—History—19th century.   I. Title.
E415.7.L44   2011
305.800977—dc22   2011003416

British Library cataloguing data are available

Front cover images © 2011 Shutterstock

Manufactured in the United States of America

McFarland & Company, Inc., Publishers
  Box 611, Jefferson, North Carolina 28640
    www.mcfarlandpub.com

Table of Contents

Acknowledgments

ARCHIVISTS HAVE ASSISTED ME tremendously with this book. Some present and former staff members of the Stearns History Museum have assisted me throughout my seven years of research on Midwestern slavery. I offer my thanks to Charlene Akers, John Decker, June Kalla, Robert Lommel, Ann Meline, Cindy O'Konek, Jessica Paulsen, Steve Penick, Rosemarie Puerta-Curnutt, Diane Smith, Sarah Warmka, and Ken Zierden. I thank the staff of the Minnesota Historical Society; Don Parker of the Hancock County (Illinois) Historical Society; the Wilson County, Tennessee, Courthouse staff; Mary L. Kludy of the Virginia Military Institute; and the First Presbyterian Church of St. Cloud, Minnesota, staff.

I am thankful to St. Cloud State University for providing funding for my research over the past seven years and to the co-workers and staff of my department for their support.

Ambar Espinoza of Minnesota Public Radio was gracious to report on my work in May 2010. I am thankful to her for all of the assistance I have received from people who heard about my research from having listened to her radio interview of me.

My work would not have been possible without feedback from some of the descendants of the people I researched. Andrew Calhoun and Paul Calhoun helped me understand the development of slavery in Minnesota better. Lynne Bie and Marque Henson were similarly helpful with slavery in Iowa. Barry Cannedy, Lisa Canterberry, Billie Dewey, Karen Smith-Clopton, and Mary Tomcsanyi assisted me with slavery in Wisconsin. Kathleen Schott helped me with slavery in Illinois.

I am eternally grateful to my family for their support. My parents gave me the tools to conduct research. My children, Imani and Erik, inspired me to write the book so that they would know the long-standing presence of African Americans in the Midwest. My wife, Yolanda, has encouraged me to continue working on my most tired days, and I appreciate her endless enthusiasm.

Introduction

THE UPPER MISSISSIPPI RIVER VALLEY is an unlikely setting for a book about slavery in the United States. The land was unsuitable for the plantations that characterized slavery in the South, in large part because of the extremely cold climate in the Northwest Territory. Very few people with slaves lived there. Most importantly, the region was officially free. The federal government prohibited slavery in the territory in 1787, upon the passage of the Northwest Ordinance. Also, when states formed from Northwest Territory, they followed Congress' lead in banning slavery in their state constitutions.

Still, African American slavery in the Upper Mississippi existed from before the Revolutionary War to the end of the Civil War. Moreover, the practice in that region played a significant role in the development of the United States. As the Founding Fathers drafted the Constitution, they debated the legality of forbidding the trafficking of unfree labor into the territory. To protect the slaveholding that had persisted in the Northwest as the politicians argued, the country then fought wars against the British, the indigenous, and ultimately itself for over half a century.

Local and national politicians, including presidents from George Washington to James Buchanan, manipulated the meaning of the ordinance according to political expedience. Whenever they tried to appease antislavery leaders, executive officials promoted the Upper Mississippi as free from slavery. On the other hand, whenever placating the slaveholders and supporters of slavery, the executives allowed exceptions to the ban on human bondage in the territory. Thomas Jefferson and James Madison paid explorers allowances for their slaves.

Federal appointees defied the prohibition of slavery in the Upper Mississippi, often with the blessings of the presidents. Among the earliest violators were soldiers whom presidents allowed to bring slaves with them from the South or to occasionally purchase African Americans from other soldiers in the Northwest Territory. The federal government gave the officers stipends

1

for their slaves, too. In addition, governors appointed by presidents to lead subsequent territories in the area received permission to take their human chattel with them. Some of the governors, in turn, appointed southerners to territory offices, and they followed the federal government's lead in refusing to enforce the Northwest Ordinance. Whenever a new territory formed in the Upper Mississippi, each one — Illinois, Wisconsin, Iowa, and Minnesota — experienced this extralegal slavery.

Caught in the crossfire were the slaves themselves. They were at the mercy of the capriciousness of the federal government and the southern migrants who brought them to the Northwest. Some African Americans sued in courts to become free by virtue of their forced migration into an officially free land. Others lived similar lives to their southern counterparts. Slave-holders identified most female slaves as servants or domestic servants. In addition, Upper Mississippi slaves experienced painful auctions and sexual abuse at the hands of the slaveholders, just like any slave living below the Mason-Dixon Line.

Nevertheless, African American slavery in the Upper Mississippi was significantly different from southern slavery. The institution in the Northwest Territory never became central to the agriculture of the region. Slavery consequently never became crucial to the economy there. In addition, southern migrants brought very few slaves up the Mississippi River. The slave population in the new land was too small for slaveholders to politically benefit; the three-fifths compromise, which mandated that slave populations count toward representation among southern states in the federal government, made little impact in the Upper Mississippi Valley. These factors led to critics of slavery giving nearly all of their attention to the practice in the South and virtually ignoring the practice in the Northwest.

The present work discusses the existence of African American slavery in the Northwest Territory from Congress's passage of the Northwest Ordinance to the end of the Civil War. The book analyzes the effects of the federal government's appointments of proslavery southerners to offices in the Upper Mississippi. The book also examines the encouragement of slavery in that region by migrants from the East Coast who came to the Upper Mississippi to profit from the patronage of vacationing southern slaveholders by building hotels and starting various other businesses. The various laws from Congress concerning slavery over those eight decades and their influence upon slavery in the Upper Mississippi also receive attention. In addition, the book looks at the lives of the slaves, whose labor did not create the economy of the region, as in the South, but who nonetheless joined their southern counterparts in suffering family separation, sales, and identification as a white man's property.

For the purposes of this study, the Upper Mississippi Valley refers to counties and towns bordering the Mississippi River above the 36° 30' parallel. The Northwest Ordinance (1787) and later the Missouri Compromise (1820) were federal laws forbidding slavery north of that parallel. The slaveholding soldiers stationed there barely enforced the laws, and the federal government turned a blind eye as long as the soldiers effectively protected the region from attacks by the indigenous people there. After steamboat travel improved to allow wealthy and powerful southerners to travel upriver, even less incentive existed for executive-branch officeholders to enforce the ban. Bonded African Americans made round trips from slave states to free areas and back to slave states, and their time in the Upper Mississippi did not emancipate them.

The book is written as a chronological narrative. It starts with a discussion of how the federal government weakened its own ban on slavery in the Upper Mississippi Valley through vague legislation and allowing slaveholders to settle in the area. The first chapter focuses on slavery in the Northwest in the first decade following the passage of the Northwest Ordinance. The following chapter illustrates how the United States protected slavery there by fighting the War of 1812 and by sending executive officials and military officers and their slaves to protect the land from the indigenous. Meanwhile, the Territory of Illinois—the first from the Upper Mississippi to become a state—ushered in many of the legal and extralegal methods of defiance of the Northwest Ordinance that characterized slavery in the Northwest, including federal financial support to slaveholders utilizing African American slave labor in mines.

The next three chapters explore how slavery influenced the transition of three territories—Wisconsin, Iowa, and Minnesota—into states between the 1830s and 1850s. Wisconsin followed the lead of Illinois in employing slaves in mines, but anti-slavery migrants successfully petitioned the state and its communities to stop doing so before the end of the 1830s. Iowa, on the other hand, developed some communities of slaveholders and their slaves, and the population of both groups increased in Iowa over time. Moreover, the federal government sent slaveholders there to serve in political offices, which in turn made Iowa Territory more attractive to owners of African Americans. The residents of that state were especially resistant to the emancipating of local slaves, and they banned free African Americans from Iowa's borders for years. Minnesota, despite being the last territory of the region to receive statehood in 1858, still carried on the traditions of hosting federal slaving appointees and developing slave-operated businesses. Its migrants were mostly temporary residents either obeying military orders while stationed in a new land or spending vacations there. Some migrants came from beyond the South to capitalize on the vacationers by developing hotels that catered to a slaveholding clientele.

The final portion of the book is about the transition of the federal government from nonchalance about slavery to fierce opposition to slavery. Following the chapter on Minnesota, the sixth chapter analyzes the influx of southern migrants and their domestic slaves to the Upper Mississippi after the Supreme Court ruled that a slave remained a slave even in free land. The final chapter illustrates the decline of slavery in the Upper Mississippi due to the Civil War and its polarizing effect upon proslavery communities in the region.

Several early histories of the Upper Mississippi Valley and, more specifically, Minnesota, mention the existence of slavery there. Such authors as Gertrude Gove of St. Cloud, Minnesota, identify some of the people who left the South with a few of their slaves to serve the federal government in the Midwest. Prominent soldiers stationed at forts and governors appointed to territories by presidents receive the most attention from the authors. Most of the literature does not divulge the names of the slaves. Many of these books, however, feature anecdotes from survivors of the antebellum era who candidly discussed the attempts by various people to create proslavery communities.

More recent secondary literature about the Northwest Territory and the formation of the states Illinois, Iowa, Wisconsin, and Minnesota focuses on the effects of slavery in the Upper Mississippi upon slavery in the United States as a whole. Among the slaves Dred Scott receives the most attention because the Supreme Court's denial of his freedom despite his years spent in free Minnesota divided the nation in 1857. Authors provide substantial information about slave Eliza Winston, because a Minnesota court declared her free three years later — a clear break from the Supreme Court's verdict on Scott. The newer books identify few other slaves unless they either belonged to prominent politicians or became emancipated in the Upper Mississippi. Specific slaveholders also receive little attention, unless they either freed their slaves or used the legal system to keep them.

Very few books give much examination to the presence of slavery in the Upper Mississippi. Most authors of state histories treat slavery as tangential to their narratives. Similarly, history books about African Americans in these states offer a few names of slaves but tend to focus on free African Americans. Such books ignore the relevance of slavery to the development of the states and to the United States. *Slavery in the Upper Mississippi Region, 1787–1865* seeks to illustrate the historical importance of slavery in the Upper Mississippi in relation to the economies and politics of the states that emerged in that region, the role of the federal government in the practice of slavery there, and the effects of the region's slavery upon not only the slaves but also local and national ethnic relations.

CHAPTER ONE

Slavery in the Northwest Territory

THE PRESENCE OF THE ENSLAVED African in the Upper Mississippi River area began at the dawn of the sixteenth century. In 1526, nine years before Cortez came to California, Governor Panfilo de Narvaez of Spain called for an exploratory expedition of the New World. The five ships of Álvar Núñez Cabeza de Vaca and his crew of six hundred departed from the port of San Lucar de Barameda with a royal mandate to conquer and rule the provinces extending from the river of the Palms to the cape of the Floridas. One of the people on the voyage was a man of African descent named Estevanico, an Arab from Azamore on the Atlantic Coast of Morocco. He survived the many mishaps that the crew experienced. For example, a West Indian hurricane crushed many of the ships, and some of the indigenous people on the land to which they traveled killed a large number of the surviving members of the exploration party. Estevanico, however, was not one of the fatalities.

Still, the party continued to shrink in number as time progressed every year. By the expedition's ninth year, only four people — three Spaniards and Estevanico — remained from the original six hundred. They soon found evidence of other Europeans in the area. Cabeza de Vaca noted that "having positive traces of Christians and becoming satisfied they were very near, we gave thanks to God our Lord for redeeming us from our sad and gloomy condition." When he decided to look for them, Estevanico played a role in the search. Cabeza de Vaca recalled, "I took with me the Negro and eleven Indians, and, following the trail, went in search of the Christians."[1]

Cabeza de Vaca used Estevanico not only as a traveling servant but as a messenger. The Spaniard mentioned that he and Estevanico were the first people of the expedition party to arrive at the west coast of Mexico from Florida. Upon arrival they met Diego de Alcaraza, an officer of Nueno de Guzman. He sent Estevanico with a group of horsemen and fifty Indians to retrieve

Dorantes and Castillo, the remaining members of the party. Five days later they joined Cabeza de Vaca, returning in company with Estevanico and his indigenous travelers.

Estevanico later contributed to the Spanish exploration of the southwestern area of North America. He started two return trips to Spain with Cabeza de Vaca, but as they sailed each time in separate boats, a storm sent them back to port. After the second attempt, Estevanico chose to stay on the continent. Meanwhile, Viceroy Mendoza, the then ruler of Nueva Espana, wanted to explore it and recruited Estevanico for the job. The ruler sent Estevanico with some indigenous people to explore with Friar Marco de Mica and Friar Vasquez de Coronado, governor of Nueva Galicia, to the city of Saint Michael of Culiacan.[2]

Estevanico's relations with the indigenous peoples separated him from his fellow travelers. He quarreled with the friars, taking the women given to him by the indigenous. He had better relations than the friars had with the indigenous they encountered, because the locals had seen him before. For this reason the viceroy sent him to pacify the indigenous as he explored, so that when any explorers came along after him, they only had to record the things for which they sought. Another aspect of Estevanico's success with the indigenous lay in the resources he used when encountering them. As he traveled he carried a cross in one hand and a "gourd rattle" in the other. Some of the indigenous peoples considered the rattle a sacred object, used only during such events as rituals, religious feasts, and shamanistic performances. According to the sign languages of the plains, the sign for rattle was the foundation of all signs demonstrating anything sacred.[3]

By the eighteenth century, although African slavery remained in the Northwest, France had become the dominant European power in that area. Within North America the country created the colony of Louisiana Territory, extending France's control over the entire Mississippi River Valley. Because France permitted slavery, it existed in the territory, too. In 1717 the Compagnie de l'Occident took control of Louisiana Territory and soon began importing slaves there. In 1719, France brought five hundred Africans from Guinea for enslavement in the southern part of the territory. That same year Philip Francis Renault imported five hundred other slaves into northern Louisiana, which later became the Northwest Territory of the United States. So many of the French expatriated Africans to North America that by 1750, along the Mississippi River, they had created five new slavery-based settlements known as Kaskaskia, Kaokia, Fort Chartres, St. Phillipe and Prairie du Rocher.

Thirteen years later a transfer of power facilitated slavery's decline in the Upper Mississippi. At the time a significant number of African slaves still lived and labored in the Northwest Territory. However, in 1763 the French transferred control of the land to the British. Still, the transfer alone did not cause the decline, because the British did not call for the end of slavery there. Rather, many of the French colonists decided to leave the territory, because they did not want to be under the rule of the new power. The slave population did not increase again until settlers from Britain's thirteen colonies in North America began bringing their Africans to Louisiana Territory at the end of the eighteenth century.[4]

From the start, slavery in the Northwest Territory was unique among slave communities in the Americas. In the lower portion of Louisiana Territory, the strict enforcement of the Slave Code made the lives of African slaves almost unbearable. In contrast, the slaves of the Northwest Territory experienced slightly more agency. Their owners did not witness much enforcement of the rules by a mayor-commandant appointed by the governor of New Orleans. As a result the first slaveholders of the Upper Mississippi exerted relatively autonomous control over the management of their plantations. In addition, because few planters in the area owned as many as four Negroes, slavery in the Northwest Territory was little more than a patriarchal enterprise. Most slaveholders there fed their slaves well. Master-slave relations were generally not violent. The owners gave their slaves special privileges on every Sunday and holiday, and enslaved children received instruction on the catechism according to the ordinance of Louis XIV in 1724, which mandated that all masters teach their slaves in the Apostolic Catholic religion and provide baptisms for them. Slaveholders worked alongside male slaves, and female slaves accompanied their mistresses to matins and vespers. The owners allowed the slaves to participate in various festivities, as well.[5]

Twenty years after the British assumed control of the Northwest, newly independent residents in New England began arguing for the banning of slavery in northern Louisiana. The Revolutionary War had just ended after eight years, and the new United States government sought to govern its land on its own terms—including the Northwest. Timothy Pickering, an antislavery quartermaster general of the war, wrote the first antislavery proposition for the exclusion of slavery in the Upper Mississippi on behalf of a group of disbanded New England war veterans who in 1783 requested a land grant in that region for settlement. Although Congress ignored his idea, his notion that the country needed to prohibit the expansion of slavery to the northwest soon gained support from other U.S. citizens. For the next eight decades, antislavery activists and anti-expansionists took up his cause.[6]

The immediate legacy of Pickering's proposal, however, consisted of political compromise. In contrast to Pickering's sense of urgency, the following year Thomas Jefferson proposed delaying the banning of slavery in the Northwest Territory for sixteen years. Jefferson called for punishments for people engaged in "slavery [and] involuntary servitude" after the year 1800. He did not approve of slavery there and gambled that in a decade and a half, the residents there would end slavery themselves. Southern legislators, however, helped defeat the proposal, and slavery remained. Meanwhile, under the fourth of the thirteen Articles of Confederation, the governing document of the United States at the time, slaveholders had permission to take their slaves from one state to another without emancipating them in the process.[7]

The differences in the proposals from Pickering and Jefferson — particularly the former's call for immediate emancipation versus the latter's delaying — reflected each person's familiarity with the Northwest Territory. Pickering had lived in that land for a considerable time and knew of the impracticality of the expansion of slavery there. Jefferson, on the other hand, had never set foot there when he promoted gradualism. Nevertheless, both men established the political debate on slavery in the territory for the next eight decades, and rarely did people break the patterns they created. U.S. settlers in the territory increasingly preferred free land, but U.S. presidents and other federal officials out to the eastern seaboard perpetuated slavery in land over one thousand miles away.

Congress squelched attempts from within to drastically change Upper Mississippi slavery. Pickering urged Congressman Rufus King to agitate for an antislavery law concerning the region. On March 16, 1785, King acquiesced and introduced a motion to prohibit slavery in the Northwest Territory. After a split vote between northern and southern congressmen halted the bill's progress, a committee altered it by reinstating Jefferson's idea of a delayed ban until 1800 and calling for the territory's return of fugitive slaves from New England to their owners. The bill still died, but the government's watering down of King's proposal for an immediate ban indicated its investment in keeping slavery intact in the Northwest Territory. In addition, the votes from southern legislators against restrictions of the institution proved especially formidable to opponents of its expansion.[8]

Just as Pickering's time in the Northwest Territory moved him to push for slavery's restriction, a group of people with specific designs on the region also wanted no sign of the institution there. Some men from New England formed the Ohio Company and wanted Congress to give them at least six million acres of the Northwest Territory. The business offered to buy a significant portion of the land from an indebted Congress and to organize the land. Congress, awed by the wealth of the company's members, desired to sell the area. The New Englanders, however, refused to purchase it if the federal government permitted slavery.[9]

Congressmen Nathan Dane and Melancton Smith from the East and Richard Henry Lee from the South drafted a groundbreaking compromise. After the aforementioned streak of failed antislavery proposals, their idea eventually became the first successful federal legal restriction of slavery since the United States had revolted against Britain. In addition, their proposal extended the boundary of north and south — and the political differences both regions had concerning slavery — to the West. The authors called for the exclusion of slavery from the northern part of the territory, which appealed to the Ohio Company and antislavery politicians. They also proposed to permit slavery in the territory to the south and to call for the return of fugitive slaves to their home states. As a result of the bill's passage, the West collectively formed a political mirror image of the eastern United States; slavery eventually divided the territory's inhabitants along sectional lines as severely as it split the sections among the states. Congress accepted the proposal on July 13, 1787, as the sixth article of the Northwest Ordinance, which read,

> There shall be neither slavery nor involuntary servitude in the said territory, otherwise than in the punishment of crimes whereof the party shall have been duly convicted: *Provided, always,* That any person escaping into the same, from whom labor or service is lawfully claimed in any one of the original States, such fugitive may be lawfully reclaimed and conveyed to the person claiming his or her labor or service as aforesaid.

Although the federal government limited the enslaving of African Americans, the sixth article of the ordinance by no means signaled an early demise to the institution. On the contrary, it was about to become a fundamental part of federal law. After Congress passed the ordinance, Dane himself recalled that he had considered the idea a lark, saying, "I had no idea the states would agree to the sixth article, prohibiting slavery, as only Massachusetts of the eastern states was present [for the vote.]" He had a point about the unlikelihood of Congress' acceptance of a restriction to slavery. The same day that the ordinance became law, the three-fifths compromise became part of the Constitution of the United States. It called for each state to count each slave as three-fifths of a person toward the population, so that sparsely populated slave states would receive comparable representation to their northern neighbors for representatives in the House and for electors for president. The following night the Ohio Company bought one and a half million acres north of the Ohio River. When the Northwest Territory became divided into territories and states over the years, the government paid special attention to the size of each partition so as not to upset the northern-southern representational balance. Indeed, the Mason-Dixon sectionalism had spread to the Upper Mississippi.[10]

The passage of the ordinance was an exchange of sorts. The New Englanders of the Ohio Company purchased the land they had wanted. They also restricted the number of new states from the Northwest Territory to five in order for the North to preserve its numerical majority in Congress. Meanwhile, the new law appeased southern legislators by not prohibiting slavery in land below the Ohio River. Only the northwestern slaves themselves were on the losing end of the deal, for the ordinance allowed the settlers already in the Upper Mississippi to keep their Africans enslaved, just as they had done for nearly eighty years.[11]

Still, debate continued among others. Some migrants thought that the new law banned slavery in the territory, but others declared slavery permissible. For some in the latter group, their proof lay in the language of the law. The ordinance mentioned "free inhabitants" and the "free male inhabitants of full size," and the distinguishing of free people meant to proslavery people that not all people in the jurisdiction of the law were to be considered free. In addition, the practice of slavery was not uniform in the territory because three kinds of slaves existed there. The French still in the area enslaved their Africans. The British, who came to the territory after the French, brought their own Africans. In both their cases, any ban of their slaves would have been retroactive. The fastest growing segment of slaveholders there, however, consisted of U.S. citizens migrating to the northwest, and the ordinance's ban on slavery applied directly to them.[12]

Not everyone in the federal government considered African Americans to ultimately be free there. Although Congress had passed the ordinance, at least one of its members sought to clarify that only certain kinds of slaves in the Northwest Territory received emancipation under the law. A congressional committee headed by James Madison concluded that Congress had not meant for the sixth article to totally ban slavery. Rather, the federal government granted the territory the authority to protect its residents' ownership of human chattel, "anything in the said Ordinance to the contrary notwithstanding." Madison, moreover, considered the migration of slaveholders and slaves to the northwest a crucial development in lessening not only racial tensions but also physical abuse of slaves and people's concerns about the aftermath of the freeing of slaves. As much as the expansion of slavery benefited the nation, Madison argued, slaves stood to benefit twice as much, concerning both "their prospects of emancipation" and "their condition in the meantime."[13]

European immigrants and their governments helped continue African slavery in the Northwest Territory despite the ordinance. Fewer French and British people settled there with their slaves after the United States had won the Revolutionary War. Their numbers further decreased after the ordinance took effect because they faced intense hostility from the growing number of antislavery migrants into the territory after the law's passage. The slaveholders who remained, however, established their permanence with settlements. The French residents of the northwest communities of Cahokia, Kaskaskia, and Vincennes along the Wabash River kept their slaves where they lived. The British Empire, meanwhile, supplied Canadians in the territory with African slaves.[14]

Although the ordinance protected their slaves, the French grew concerned for the safety of their human property. In 1789 Congressman Bartholomew

Tardiveau, who shared Thomas Pickering's familiarity with the people of the Northwest Territory, asked his fellow legislators to pass a constitutional amendment that specifically declared that the ordinance of two years earlier had not freed the slaves of the territory. Tardiveau shared little else with Pickering, however. Pickering's antislavery proposal reflected his dealings with U.S. settlers, but Tardiveau represented the proslavery interests of the French settlers already with their African slaves.

The bickering about slavery in the Northwest Territory resulted in part from the federal government's absence of leadership on the issue. At the time, the Constitution had displaced all previous federal laws, including the Articles of Confederation. The new document did not specifically address the territory or slavery in it. As a result, the federal government had no official policy in operation concerning the institution in the Northwest Territory. Tardiveau sought to rectify the dilemma by having Congress draft and pass a definitive statement on where the federal government stood on the matter of slavery in the territory — especially a proslavery declaration. Congress made no statement at all.

Still, on occasion, Congress honored the ordinance's prohibition of northwestern slavery over the next few years. Four residents of the Northwest Territory offered several arguments for the permitting of slavery there. They complained that no citizens of the territory contributed to the development of the ordinance. They arrogantly spoke on behalf of their fellow territorial settlers by claiming that no one living there would have agreed to have the federal government limit their ability to enslave others. Some of them mistakenly thought the new law banned the institution itself and argued against the ordinance as retroactive. They also asserted that the emancipation of any slave born to slave parents there compromised the rights of the slaveholders to own any property birthed by their property. Citing economic practicality, they said that keeping slaves cost less money than paying free laborers to work the land and that most of the settlers simply could not afford to not enslave. The congressional committee that received the petition did not agree that the four authors of the proposal spoke for the territory. Rather, the committee knew that the admittance of slavery stood to cause greater displeasure than pleasure among the residents. Congress ultimately turned down the request.

The legislators also stood firm on refusing the expansion of slavery even when petitioned by people who militarily contributed to the country's new independence. A group of slaveholding veterans of the Virginia Line of the Continental Army wanted to find their bounty lands on the Virginia Military Reservation. They asked Congress to give them leave to bring their slaves into the Northwest Territory. Congress surprised them by noting that the request conflicted with the ordinance, and the legislators turned down the soldiers.

The government also refused to entertain a second request, in which the veterans softened their original petition with more conciliatory language.

In 1789, two events allowed African slavery to become deeply entrenched in the Upper Mississippi over the next three-fourths of one century. First, Congress revised the Northwest Ordinance in order to assign the appointing of the governor of the Northwest Territory to the president of the United States. The change in the law meant that no local residents of the land had control over its governance; rather, the leadership came from afar and from someone who may not have stepped foot in the territory. Second, George Washington became the first president of the United States, and his lack of enforcement of the sixth article of the ordinance set a precedent followed by the next fourteen successors to the office. Both he and Secretary of State Thomas Jefferson deliberately allowed settlers to defy the article.[15]

Moreover, one of the slaveholding settlers of the Northwest Territory had traveled there by order of President Washington. Arthur St. Clair received Washington's mandate to go from the East to the territory to serve as the land's first territorial governor. The former president of the Congress held slaves at the time of his appointment. In addition, he continued to do so after the passage of the ordinance and conducted at least one transaction while on the job as territorial governor. He brought African slaves he had purchased in 1788 to the territory and kept them in bondage there. While governor, he enforced the ordinance's ban of slavery only as it pertained to Africans brought to the territory after 1787. He let the pre–Ordinance French and British residents retain their slaves.[16]

Washington and his successors, meanwhile, did nothing to discourage St. Clair's permissiveness of and participation in Upper Mississippi slavery. The governor served the entire duration of Washington's presidency (1789–1797). The second president, John Adams, kept St. Clair in the territory for another four years (1797–1801). Adams did not own slaves, and he did not use slave labor in his household. His retention of St. Clair, however, reflected earlier political decisions that supported the continuation of slavery. He had opposed the federal government's employing of slaves as soldiers during the Revolutionary War, and he approved of the silencing of any discussion in Congress about abolition. In his opinion, by avoiding the subject, the government could keep the national peace. "We have causes enough of jealousy, discord, and division," he rationalized. By reappointing St. Clair, President Adams kept the peace in the Upper Mississippi and, by extension, permitted slavery's unofficial extension there.[17]

The next president, Thomas Jefferson, followed suit and reappointed Governor St. Clair in 1801. The president and the governor were both slaveholders, and St. Clair's extended tenure reflected not only Jefferson's choice to maintain the status quo but also his own personal involvement in the institution. When he fired St. Clair after only one year, the decision did not involve slavery. Rather, St. Clair disagreed with Jefferson's desire to grant statehood to Ohio. Nevertheless, in the eleven years of St. Clair's leadership, slavery proliferated in the Northwest Territory.

In 1802 President Jefferson replaced St. Clair with a Virginian who shared his benefactor's inconsistency regarding the affairs of African Americans. Charles Willing Byrd supported the right of African Americans to vote. On the other hand, he argued for the retention of his brother-in-law's ownership of a slave in the Northwest Territory. Similarly, Jefferson's hesitancy toward enforcement of the ordinance in the late 1780s contrasted sharply with his earlier determination to have an antislavery clause included in the legislation. He tried unsuccessfully to propose the prohibition of slavery in the Northwest Territory. Jefferson, however, struggled with the politics of slavery throughout his political career. On the one hand, he believed in the necessity of the eradication of the institution; slavery denied African Americans their freedom and lured slaveholders toward "the most unremitting despotism," as he put it. On the other hand, he considered total and immediate emancipation impractical. He predicted that the coexistence of free African Americans and European Americans in the same country would only cause strife between them and, if unresolved, would end with "the extermination of one or the other race." However, he did not know how to expatriate the potential masses of freed slaves.[18]

Jefferson's conflicting thoughts about slavery soon permeated the Upper Mississippi to an even greater degree than before. His gubernatorial appointee, Byrd, remained in office only into the following year, when Ohio's statehood eliminated the Northwest Territory and, by extension, Byrd's job. Jefferson appointed new officers for the new territories— Illinois, Indiana, and Michigan —created from the old one, but Byrd was not one of them. The president now had the power to place proslavery officials into three territories instead of just one. Indeed, all three new territories wrestled with the question of slavery, and their debates served as local manifestations of the inner argument President Jefferson had with himself about the issue and his lack of consistent leadership on it.[19]

Michigan Territory immediately experienced its first court trial regarding the ordinance and its content on slavery. There, the judicial branch of the law interpreted northwestern slavery in ways that corresponded with the decisions Congress made about the institution. Two slaves of the territory petitioned for their emancipation by arguing that the ordinance had freed them. The court, however, sided with the slaveholder, who had argued that the ordinance did not free them because their presence in the territory predated the law's passage. The judge said that the ordinance banned only slave importation, not slavery itself. Still, the judge did acknowledge that any slave entering the territory after the enacting of the law on July 13, 1787, became emancipated as long as no foreign powers ruled the part of the land where the slave resided. England did not relinquish its ownership of Michigan Territory until June 16, 1796, which meant that the federal government allowed a foreign country to delay the enforcement of a congressional law by nearly a decade.[20]

As for the rest of the Upper Mississippi, the Louisiana Purchase of 1803 sealed the fate of the region as a land of popular sovereignty. The purchase's opening of North America to the west of the Mississippi River for European American settlers guaranteed conflict between the migrants and the indigenous inhabitants of the land. The conflict, in turn, required the federal government to station U.S. troops all over the new land to protect it and its settlers. The soldiers, therefore, determined whether slavery would take place there by deciding whether to bring their slaves with them — popular sovereignty by military action.

Some of the soldiers, however, took on the role of explorers of the new territory, and slavery shaped their experiences in the new land. President Jefferson asked Congress for $2,500 for a group of explorers to travel west and record their experiences. He wrote that the only expenses would be the travelers' "arms and accoutrements, some instruments of observation," "light and cheap presents for the Indians," and "a soldier's portion of land on their return." However, Meriwether Lewis and William Clark, who led the group,

William Clark, who traveled with his slave York across the Upper Mississippi. Courtesy Library of Congress.

included a slave in their expedition, and Congress allowed part of the funds to go to the slave's care and maintenance, too. Clark's African American servant, York, was slightly older than his master. He also had a tall stature and hefty physique. In terms of demeanor, Clark described York as "insolent and sulky" and sometimes threatened either violence upon him or his sale to another slaveholder.[21]

The relationship of the slave's family to Clark's family had spanned at least three generations by the time of the expedition. York was the child of two slaves owned by Clark's father. John Clark kept

Old York — a slave John inherited from his father — and Rose, and their child played with John's young son William. York's namesake was possibly the York River of the Chesapeake region, where the Clarks lived. Upon John's death in 1799, his son inherited Old York, Rose, and Young York — later known simply as York.[22]

The party put York to considerable and important use. Some of the duties the explorers assigned to York determined the very survival of the travelers. For example, he traversed problematic landscapes to gather food for the explorers. As a result, without his success in the endeavor, the explorers would have gone hungry. To be sure, the act itself of collecting food was not uncommon slave labor, for slaves planted and harvested on plantations all over the country. In the Upper Mississippi, however, York had no community of slaves working with him but rather had the sole responsibility of feeding several people. Moreover, because he traveled constantly with the party instead of settling on some land to cultivate it, his agricultural work in the territory largely consisted of scavenging. Approaching a "very bad" sandbar with the travelers, "York swam to the sand bar to geather greens for our Dinner and returned with a sufficient quantity wild Creases or Teng grass."[23]

York received considerable agency from Clark for an antebellum slave. Although serving as cook, he also hunted on the expedition — an unusual privilege, because most citizens of the United States did not permit African Americans to carry and operate guns. "I killed a deer which York packed on his back," said one journal entry of the exploration, while in another, "My boys each shot an elk." York also chose a campsite during part of the expedition at a time when African Americans — slave and free — did not vote. In addition, Clark's willingness to highlight the wisdom and accomplishments of his African American slave demonstrated that York's resourcefulness and skill did not undermine his status as a slave in his owner's point of view; Clark learned from York while considering himself York's superior without the slightest hint of irony or contradiction.[24]

The expedition occasionally took a physical toll on York in various forms over the next two years. On a couple of occasions, weather provided the hazards for him. In December 1804 he suffered frostbite on his feet and penis. Seven months later, he and four others were caught in a severe hailstorm while traveling by river. As the shower fell, "the Creek rose so fast," wrote one of Clark's men, "that he and those with him, had scarcely time to get out, before the Water was ten feet deep in that Creek." Another time his body simply gave out on him from wear and tear. In September 1805, while exploring on foot for hours, his feet gave him pain. A fellow traveler wrote, "Capt. Clarke's blackman's feet became so sore that he had to ride on horseback."[25]

Although York physically suffered during the trip, his owner and fellow travelers expected him to entertain them and the people they encountered.

For all his talents, his mere presence was enough to elicit excitement among the indigenous people the expedition encountered. He adjusted in part to their gawking by poking fun at their ignorance and awe of him. Lewis and Clark expressed that York did too well of a job in so doing. The explorers later recalled that the indigenous, upon meeting the bondsman, "had never seen a being of that colour." They surrounded him in order "to examine the extraordinary monster," as Lewis and Clark put it. To have fun at the expense of the indigenous, York told them the elaborate fiction that he had been a wild animal until tamed by Master Clark. The slave then demonstrated his supposedly former ways by displaying "feats of strength which, added to his looks, made him more terrible than we wished him to be," said the adventurers.[26]

Lewis and Clark tried to ease the apprehension of the indigenous towards York, using gifts to win them over. "We then made or acknowledged three chiefs, one for each of the three villages, giving to each a flag, a medal, a red coat, a cocked hat and feather, also some goods, paint, and tobacco, which they divided among themselves," the explorers later wrote. "After this the air-gun was exhibited, very much to their astonishment." The locals expressed as much surprise about the weaponry as about York's skin color and behavior. During a visit with the Ricara tribe, "York was here again an object of astonishment; the children would follow him constantly, and if he chanced to turn towards them run with great terror."[27]

Some of the indigenous people thought that York's skin color was a disguise. With the slave's indulgence, the people studied him and mildly tested the durability of his pigment. Even then, they were not completely convinced that York wore no disguise. "In the course of the conversation," Clark wrote, "the [grand chief of the Minnetarees, who is called by the French Le Borgne] observed that some foolish young men of the nation had told him there was a person among us who was quite black, and he wished to know if it could be true." The explorers answered affirmatively and brought York to the chief for observation. "The Borgne was very much surprised at his appearance, examined him closely, and spit on his finger and rubbed the skin, in order to wash off the paint," Clark remembered, "nor was it until the negro uncovered his head, and showed his short hair, that he could be persuaded that he was not a painted white man."[28]

The sexual freedom York experienced on the expedition differed sharply from the strictness of the social mores that repressed his sexual behavior in the United States. European American slaveholders frequently forced themselves upon their slaves, but free and enslaved African Americans were forbidden from initiating any sexual contact with European Americans. Among the indigenous, however, York suffered no restrictions. Lewis and Clark later wrote that the Ricara tribe they encountered had the custom of men offering their wives or sisters to visitors for sexual purposes as a gesture of civility or thanks. Moreover, the men received gratification from the attention visitors paid to the women. The explorers bragged at having "withstood their temptation," but they also acknowledged that "such was their desire to oblige that two very handsome young squaws were sent on board this evening, and persecuted us with civilities." They freely disclosed, on the other hand, that "York participated largely in these favours." They stated that the indigenous were so amazed by the novelty of York's skin color that they gave him "additional advantages from the Indians, who desired to preserve among them some memorial of this wonderful stranger." The explorers recalled that a Ricara man had invited York to his house, offered his wife, and then went out of their presence. "While there one of York's comrades who was looking for him came to the door," the adventurers recalled, "but the gallant husband would permit no interruption before a reasonable time had elapsed."[29]

Near the end of the expedition, even when York was presented an opportunity for emancipation literally from the heavens, he decided to remain a slave. A heavy downpour had begun falling on the explorers in late June. The water rose rapidly to fifteen feet, and an accompanying intense current nearly drowned them. They found a safe plain and later reunited with York, who had ventured independently before the storm for a buffalo hunt. The loyal slave had not used the storm and his absence from his owner to flee for freedom.[30]

Clark's preferential treatment from the federal government did not end when the expedition came to a close. Not surprisingly, he decided to keep York as a slave after the expedition. Despite the servant's tenure in the free Northwest Territory, the federal government supported Clark's decision. Just as the government had paid for Clark to travel with his slave, Congress awarded Clark an allowance for his "black waiter" York as a reward for conducting the expedition. As a result, the Northwest Ordinance became null and void *de facto* by the very branch of government that had crafted it.[31]

In addition, by facilitating the funding of a person's enslavement in the South, Congress took the unusual step of using public moneys to finance the luxury of a private citizen in a region where all other slaveholders had to pay for their own provisions for their bonded Africans. Up until that time, only soldiers and federal politicians had that privilege. Whether appointed to northern or southern forts or territories, presidents permitted their designees to hold slaves wherever the president sent them, and the slaveholders received funding during their terms of service. Now, however, slave allowances became a new carrot for the federal government to dangle in front of private citizens in exchange for the stick of a presidential assignment. Such bribes were few and far between, but they were effective; and each person taking the bait helped establish the institution's permanence in the Upper Mississippi.[32]

Moreover, the federal government now enabled civilians to bring slaves into free lands. This new development partly reflected President Jefferson's views on emancipation; he did not know where, if freed, ex-slaves should live, but York's federally financed servitude in the Upper Mississippi meant that the former Northwest Territory was not the place Jefferson desired to expatriate them. Heretofore, leftover European settlers and presidential appointees had comprised the slaveholding population of the Northwest Territory. Now William Clark joined that population but as someone retired from public service instead of as an active government official. He received this privilege only a few years after Congress had denied Revolutionary War veterans the same luxury. One factor influencing the treatment accorded to him was that the executive branch, not the legislative, approved slave importation for him. The president's undercutting of the policies of the courts and Congress kept northwestern slavery in a state of flux. Once again, the federal government lacked consistency concerning the legality of the institution there. Meanwhile, within a few short years, many migrant slaveholders followed Clark's example by venturing to the Upper Mississippi.

Clark's return of York to more traditionally restrictive slavery also damaged the pair's relationship. Their relationship barely survived the transition from the casual tone of the Upper Mississippi trip to the more formal master-slave pattern of the southern plantation. Master Clark forced his slave to relinquish his increased agency from the expedition, but York balked at doing so. Consequently, Clark threatened to sell him. In 1809 he wrote, "Since I confined York he has been a good fellow to work; I have become displeased with him and Shall hire or Sell him, on the 5th of next month I [shall] Set him off on a boat to wheeling as a hand, on his return to the falls, I wish much to hire him or Sell him."[33]

Clark never did sell York. Rather, he allowed his slave to travel as the driver of a wagon for a new transporting business. He performed rather mundane labor, however, by simply loading and unloading goods each day. The work was a far cry from the various responsibilities given to him as part of the expedition. Still, during York's employment as driver, his master finally freed him. York failed to generate income on his own and sought reconciliation with and re-enslavement to Clark before dying of cholera.[34]

By approving Clark's post-expedition allowance for enslaving York, President Jefferson directly contradicted the antislavery policy for which he had pushed for years. Jefferson inferred that a slave's time spent in a free territory did not make the slave free. Indeed, the president's action corresponded with Madison's idea that the federal government was obligated to protect slave property — no matter where an owner took that property. Moreover, although he had originally argued for slavery to end in the Northwest Territory by 1800, he allowed Clark to travel through the land with York in 1803 — three full years after the president's deadline. Jefferson never distinguished whether he now considered northwestern slaves enslaved or whether he merely considered York a lone exception to the rule of northwestern freedom.

Jefferson's actions regarding Clark's holding of York adhered to the tendency of people unfamiliar with the Northwest Territory to advocate for slavery there. The local courts and local legislatures repeatedly decided against introducing the institution there, just as Thomas Pickering had done two decades ago. Even Congress took the feelings of the territory's residents into consideration when refusing to discuss the expansion of slavery. In the nearly twenty years since his proposal for gradual emancipation, however, Jefferson remained as removed from the territory as ever.

When the 1810s began, the westward expansion of the United States hit a snag when the country entered another war against England—the War of 1812. The former mother country armed the indigenous peoples of the Northwest Territory to fight U.S. soldiers. As a result, the United States had to win the war in order to totally wrest the land from English control. Moreover, by keeping the territory in U.S. control, the country would continue to govern it as before, which meant further undermining of the Northwest Ordinance. Therefore, a major outcome of the U.S. victory in the war was the preservation of African American slavery in the territory. James Madison, Jefferson's successor to the presidency and a fellow slaveholder, led the military's efforts toward that outcome.

President Madison prioritized military protection of the Mississippi River. As a result of keeping the body of water out of British hands, he enabled the continued exploration and eventual settlement of the Upper Mississippi by southern slaveholders. He asked for some troops from Congress in order for them to take the eastern half of West Florida. The troops would then prevent the British from using it to seize the river through New Orleans. Congress granted his request in 1813, and General Andrew Jackson and his forces began defending the river at New Orleans later that year. For example, he placed cannons atop bales of cotton to keep the weaponry from sinking into the soft terrain. He also positioned his troops and gunboats strategically in order to force British vessels to directly confront the U.S. forces. After the skirmish ended, the British had lost over two thousand servicemen, but U.S. fatalities totaled thirteen.[35]

In an ironic twist of fate, African Americans indirectly contributed to the continuation of slavery via military participation. Continuing the precedent set in the Revolutionary War, President Madison authorized African Americans to fight in this new war. On September 21, 1814, General Jackson issued a call to the free African Americans of Louisiana to enlist. He subsequently organized five hundred of them into two battalions. These battalions were among the U.S. troops in the Battle of New Orleans. He enticed the African

Americans to serve by avoiding discriminatory treatment of them on the basis of skin color; they even reportedly received the same pay as their European American counterparts received. One month later four times the number of African Americans went to defend Sackett's Harbor in New York. The government, therefore, paradoxically used equal treatment to save the institution of slavery and ensure its growth in the Upper Mississippi.[36]

The victories that the United States achieved through Jackson's nondiscriminatory recruitment efforts did not inspire equality on a permanent basis. Rather, the U.S. military did not treat African Americans this way again until well after the desegregation of the armed forces in 1948. After the War of 1812, the government focused its African American recruitment efforts on slaves. The military lured bondsmen into service by promising them emancipation. As a result, in many communities more slaves entered combat than free African Americans did. Because they were not enslaved, freedmen did not have to fight for liberation; therefore, many of them chose not to fight. Moreover, the absence of freedmen from the military encouraged the institution to discriminate against vulnerable slaves, many of whom enlisted in order to emancipate themselves. The segregation continued after the end of slavery, because African Americans continued to see the military as a means to escape the perpetual debt peonage of sharecropping and other post-bellum adaptations of enslavement.

A sizable number of African American sailors served in the navy during the War of 1812. They comprised around one-tenth of the crews that operated the ships on the Great Lakes. They participated in every battle of the Great Lakes, most notably in the Battle of Lake Erie. An artist later immortalized the wartime African American serviceman by placing an African American sailor among U.S. fighters in an illustration of that battle.[37]

In addition to artistic renditions, officers produced documentation that celebrated the military contributions of African Americans during the war. Some papers revealed commanders' respect for African American service that rivaled their admiration for the work of European American servicemen. Commodore Isaac Chauncey told Captain Oliver Perry in a letter that the fifty African Americans on his ship were among his best fighters. Perry had previously complained to Chauncey of "having no one to command the 'Niagara,' and only one commissioned lieutenant and two acting lieutenants, whatever my wishes may be, going out is out of the question." He grumbled about having received "a motley set — blacks, soldiers, and boys." Resigned, he concluded, "I cannot think you saw them after they were selected. I am, however, pleased to see any thing in the shape of a man."[38]

Commodore Chauncey defended the quality of the African Americans' service in his response. Acknowledging Perry's feelings, Chauncey noted, "I regret that you are not pleased with the men sent you by Messrs. Champlin and Forrest." He then compared those servicemen to others favorably: "To my knowledge, a part of them are not surpassed by any seamen we have in the fleet." Most importantly, he echoed Jackson in minimizing the importance of difference of skin color by declaring, "I have yet to learn that the color of the skin, or the cut and trimmings of the coat, can affect a man's qualifications or usefulness." He then praised the service of his own African American sailors before complimenting Perry's:

> Those people you call soldiers have been to sea from two to seventeen years; and I presume that you will find them as good and useful as any men on board of your vessel; at least, if I can judge by comparison; for those which we have on board of this ship are attentive and obedient, and, as far as I can judge, many of them excellent seamen: at any rate, the men sent to Lake Erie have been selected with a view of sending a fair proportion of petty officers and seamen; and, I presume, upon examination it will be found that they are equal to those upon this lake.

Perry eventually agreed with Chauncey and acknowledged the bravery and good behavior of his African American servicemen. He especially remarked about their apparent insensibility to danger.

The compliments were not solely from the highest-ranking military officials. In January 1813, a private wrote of two African American fatalities in a celebratory manner. He first established the danger of the battle in which he participated: "Before I could get our light sails in, and almost before I could turn round, I was under the guns, not of a transport, but of a large *frigate!* and not more than a quarter of a mile from her.... Her first broadside killed two men, and wounded six others." He then remarked about the first African American casualty, whom he claimed should "be registered in the book of fame." The private continued, "He was a black man, by the name of John Johnson. A twenty-four-pound shot struck him in the hip, and took away all the lower part of his body. In this state, the poor brave fellow lay on the deck, and several times exclaimed to his shipmates: 'Fire away, my boys; no haul a color down.'" On the other casualty of color, he recalled, "The other was also a black man, by the name of John Davis, and was struck in much the same way. He fell near me, and several times requested to be thrown overboard, saying he was only in the way of others." He ended by remarking about how their bravery kept the country safe, saying, "When America has such tars, she has little to fear from the tyrants of the ocean."[39]

Despite the best efforts of the military to promote equality among the servicemen, the negotiations that took place between the United States and Britain upon the war's conclusion in 1815 only solidified the likelihood of continued African American slavery, especially in the Upper Mississippi. In addition, the enslavement of the African Americans led to enormous sacrifice on the part of the indigenous. Britain revealed during the deliberations that it wanted what are now parts of Illinois and Wisconsin and other states to collectively become land restricted to the indigenous. That land would not only exclusively comprise the indigenous but also serve as a protectorate for Canada against any invaders. The United States, however, refused to comply. The country would have faced the loss of a significant amount of land. Also, European Americans had already begun to settle that area by that time, and many of the settlers were southern slaveholders and their slaves. Thus, slavery in the area pushed the indigenous further west and robbed them of an opportunity for designated land.[40]

African American slaves began to migrate to the former Northwest Territory in earnest in the 1810s but without their owners and as fugitives. At the start of the decade, twenty-four slaves lived there. Military conflict served as an avenue by which many more of them found an opportunity to escape the South. After the War of 1812, fugitive slaves increasingly sought shelter and emancipation in the region. The towns and counties closer to the borders of southern states tended to tolerate the fugitives more than the places farther north along the Mississippi. In the borderlands communities of free African Americans formed and flourished. The northernmost settlements of European Americans, on the other hand, were more likely to not only contain slaveholders and their slaves but also to return fugitive slaves to their southern owners.[41]

The Missouri Compromise of 1820 had a negligible effect upon limiting slavery in the former Northwest Territory. The designation of land above the 36°30' parallel as free made the region free only by law, not by practice. As with the sixth article of the Northwest Ordinance, the federal government took several steps to weaken enforcement of the compromise. Presidents often appointed slaveholding politicians to govern the land there, especially after the territory was divided into smaller territories such as Wisconsin, Iowa, and Minnesota. Other governors did not own slaves but supported the extension of slavery into the Northwest Territory. They, like their slaveholding counterparts, simply ignored the settlers who violated the law by bringing their human property to their new northwestern homes.

Soldiers stationed in the Midwest not only protected the slave interests of the proslavery leaders—federal and local—in the territory but also guarded the slaves they were allowed to transfer. Around this time Captain Hugh Scott arrived at Fort Snelling with his company (G, Fifth Infantry) and remained stationed there for about two decades. The federal government considered him an effective soldier in the territory, for he served on special duty everywhere in the Northwest, from Pembina to Fort Dearborn and from Lake Michigan to the Missouri River. Accompanying him were usually one or more horses, a pack of hunting dogs, many guns, and an African American servant to supervise his animals.

He avidly hunted for sport from Prairie du Chien to Fort Snelling. In his constant hunting, he familiarized himself with the layout of the Northwest Territory. According to legends, he killed whole hecatombs of bear, deer, elk, buffalo, wolves, and other animals. A stream in Wisconsin received the name Bloody Run because of Scott. That stream was one of Scott's favorite hunting places, and he killed a significant number of animals along its banks.

Even in the sport of hunting, Scott had use for his slave in developing hunting skills. His bondsman, however, risked his life in training Scott. His contemporaries considered him a marksman of exceptional skill. Among his most common tricks with pistols was to throw two potatoes into the air and fire a bullet into each one before they reached the ground. More dangerously, however, he employed his slave for target practice by shooting a bullet into an apple atop the servant's head.

As with Lewis and Clark, Scott kept his servant in bondage after having taken him to the Upper Mississippi. The captain had acquired a living from the military, and the servant comprised only part of the indulgences the officer could now afford. He often donated his military pay to family members needing financial assistance. When he visited his boyhood home after years of service in the former Northwest Territory, he had an opportunity to make a spectacle of his wealth. In poverty he had left his hometown, and he wanted his friends and family to see his acquisitions. He rode a large white horse into town with his pack of twenty dogs, and his slave, wearing livery, entered town atop his black thoroughbred. His disguise proved effective, for no one in town knew who Scott was.[42]

Politicians unsuccessfully tried to stem the tide of southern migration to the Upper Mississippi. In December 1829 Senator Samuel A. Foot of Connecticut introduced a resolution to Congress, calling for the government to keep high the value of land on the East Coast and keep low the wages of laborers on that coast. He sought the result of the restriction of the sale of the public land in the West. Fellow senator Robert Y. Hayne of South Carolina opposed the resolution and asked for the South to have a low tariff. The resolution failed, the South received its low tariff, and the residents of the Northwest found sympathizers in their belief in an unrestricted policy concerning the sale of public lands.[43]

The migration continued well into the next decade, however, largely thanks to Andrew Jackson. The general had gained considerable political stock during the War of 1812, and he used it to help his candidacy for president of the United States. When he started his term, he began implementing Indian Removal policies that decimated the lifestyles and lives of numerous indigenous tribes. Moreover, by relocating the indigenous peoples out of their land, Jackson opened the land to European American settlement. Among those settlers were several southern slaveholders and their slaves.

By the middle of the nineteenth century, the presence of African American slaves in the Midwest had become so acceptable that writers published stories about it in literary magazines. In 1844 Charles Fenno Hoffman published his short story "A Prairie Jumbie," in which the narrator explains his introduction to a jumbie — a piece of music that "fasten[s] so perversely upon your memory that it kept gnawing there for days together" or "[rattles] in your ear, like a pebble in a calabash." The character reveals the location early in the story with the passage, "Many years since I found myself, one dismal autumn day, on the edge of one of the largest prairies of our Northwest Territory, debating with a fellow traveller the expediency of attempting to cross it so late in the season." He has very little positive commentary about the area, calling it "one dull, dead, unbroken monotony — an interminable dark level — an eyewearying waste — marked only, but not relieved, by that circular limpid shallow, reflecting an ashen sky; and sky, earth, and pool, all equally motionless, without the faintest shadow or one variety of tint, save the leaden hues of the same sombre colour." The narrator is in poor spirits because he dislikes that a recent prairie fire left the travelers with only the food they carry. In addition, he worries that in case of a snowstorm, no shelter is available, and they may lose their way or perish. Nevertheless, his companion decides that the journey should take place over his objections, and they start "on a clear November morning, on the long-limbed horses of the country, a negro servant, and a sumpter horse with the baggage."

Hoffman applied many of the nineteenth-century standards of African American characterization to the "negro servant" Frank. As a result, the story reinforces the history that took place in the Upper Mississippi. Just as a slave was a slave, no matter where the owner took him or her, the stereotypes for fictional slaves remained consistent, whether authors wrote of southern slaves or Midwestern ones. The story uses dialect to differentiate the ethnic identities of characters. Near the beginning, a European American character tells Frank, "'Tis full as well that we didn't find that spring last night, for it will be just the place to breakfast at." The slave's response features the misspellings and incorrect grammar that defined fictional African Americans then: "Better not look for him, massa; dat spring jumbie — prairie jumbie — jumbie all around us."

Hoffman's slave character also believes very deeply in superstitions — another common African American stereotype. When a character asks Frank about washing dishes in a certain pool of water, the servant responds that spirits inhabit not only that pool but the entire prairie itself. "Pool jumbie — jis as spring jumbie — prairie all jumbie — nebber get away from him," he declared. Then, referring to himself in the third person, he continued, "Frank tink — tink ob him all day long — tink ob him, nebber find him — but still can't help tink ob him. What dat but jumbie spirit trouble Frank so, massa?"

He then explains the different between the powers of the various sizes of spirits: "De little jumbie spirit always bad enough when he get hold of folks; but here we be on de back ob great big jumbie, who keeps sliding from under us all de while we tink ourselves moving, keeping us jes in de same, same spot, for ebber, for ebber." He then dramatically laments, "Oh, de poor nigger will nebber, nebber see the trees, nor de hills, nor de running water of Gorra Mighty's yarth; nebber see any ting but dis black jumbie-back, nebber, nebber more."

The European American characters, meanwhile, act amused by Frank in some cases but treat him with contempt in other situations. They laugh at his explanation of the concept of the jumbie. However, when his superstitious beliefs interfere with his servitude, his bosses take issue. While camping one night, the wind extinguishes a fire Frank has just started in order to make coffee for the others. He refuses to make any immediate moves, reasoning, "What make dat great wind but de jumbie-back?" However, his master rhetorically snapped, "What do you sit so stupidly there for, Frank?—why don't you light another match?"

Amid the feelings of superiority expressed by the narrator and his friend, they both find some commonality with Frank. As a result, they discuss a shared humanity rarely exhibited among fictional slaveholders and slaves in American literature of the early nineteenth century. Eventually, the longevity of the trip and the monotony of the surroundings begin to affect the European Americans to the degree that they start to validate Frank's feelings. "I began to share more or less the superstitious terrors which did unquestionably blanch his cheek," the narrator confesses.

Moreover, the European Americans start honoring the feelings of their servant, despite their disbelief in the validity of his statement about jumbies. At one point of the journey, rain falls so hard that the travelers cannot see at a great distance, and they decide to camp for the evening where they stand. The narrator says that the inclement weather annoys both him and his companion. "My friend, who was of a fine game spirit, attempted to jest both about our present discomforts and the almost appalling prospects of the morrow," he recalls. "But the terror of poor Frank, who besought him not to speak with such levity of 'Massa Jumbie,' soon made him desist; a deep sigh that came from the breast of his master, as he turned away from his supper without touching it, betrayed to me the pardonable affectation of the gallant fellow." Rarely does a slave character tell a master character what to do in literature of this period, and the obedience of the slaveholder character is even rarer.[44]

Whenever soldiers brought slaves to the Upper Mississippi, both northern and southern European American migrants benefited. Northerners received military protection of their new land. Southerners had military defense not only of land but also of slavery, especially because of the slaveholding practices of some of the soldiers. Moreover, the tendency for migrant slaveholders to bring only one or two domestic slaves instead of several field-hand slaves eased southerners' fears of a new slavery-based economy. European Americans who resented having to compete with slaves for employment in the South faced no such competition in the Upper Mississippi. Finally, the masters were able to partially retain their lifestyle of having African American property do their work.

The only people who faced disadvantages in relation to Upper Mississippi slavery were the slaves themselves. They faced hardships in the new land that resembled their sufferings in the old land. By staying with the owner, the slave continued to suffer whatever means of punishment the owner distributed. As property, the slave remained in the control of the owner and faced the possibility of sale at a moment's notice. Some hardships, meanwhile, were unique to slaves in the Northwest. Slaves chosen to travel from the South to the North with the owners experienced family separation without having been sold or leased to another person. More importantly, owners took slaves that had lived in free land back to the enslaved South to sell them to other owners on occasion. Owners also found other owners in the Upper Mississippi to buy or sell slaves, without ever traveling south. Thus, the slaves suffered purchases and ownership transfers in a free territory.

The potential for military conflict also distinguished slaves' lives in the Upper Mississippi from the lives of southern slaves. Before the Civil War, most slaves below the Mason-Dixon Line lived with their owners on private lands, far away from forts. Whatever violence they experienced came at the hands of their owners and overseers. In contrast, the slaves of transplanted soldiers in the Northwest Territory faced not only corporal punishment from the masters within the forts but also attacks by indigenous people outside of the forts. The refusal of the federal government to arm African Americans, especially slaves, with weapons left them especially vulnerable in times of military conflict.

The partitioning of the territory into smaller territories that later became states did not help the slaves of the Upper Mississippi. Instead, more president-appointed governors and other officeholders appeared in the region, which meant more people to undermine the ordinance and the compromise. Then, when each territory entered statehood, each state's own public servants neglected to curb slavery and occasionally reinforced the practice. This turn of events took place in Illinois, Wisconsin, Iowa, and Minnesota over the next three decades.

CHAPTER TWO

The Politics of Indentured Servitude: Slavery in Illinois

IN ILLINOIS SLAVERY HAD EXISTED for six decades before the passage of the Northwest Ordinance. In 1712 France's King Louis XIV appointed Antoine Crozat to lead the area "from the edge of the sea [Gulf of Mexico] as far as the Illinois." Five years later, on September 27, 1717, Louisiana added "Illinois Country," which had formerly comprised part of Canada, to its territory. Meanwhile, Crozat's successor, John Law, supervised trade there. During his tenure the population of the Upper Mississippi increased, and its first businesses developed. The mother country's importation of African slaves to Illinois Country began at this time, as well. In 1721, French settler Philip F. Renault brought five hundred slaves there. Two years later, with a significant land grant, he started the village of St. Philip. Consequently, France had populated Illinois with Africans long before any European American settlement took place in the lower Louisiana Territory.[1]

Slavery in Illinois Country displayed remarkable stability for the next half-century. The institution was one of few constants as ownership of the land changed hands twice between the 1760s and 1770s. When France gave Illinois Country to England, nine hundred African slaves lived in the area. After the transfer of the land, some of the French settlers took their slaves with them west of the Mississippi River, leaving Illinois with at most 600 slaves by 1770. Slavery survived the Revolutionary War and the transfer of Illinois from England to the United States. The new owners placed no prohibitions on the ownership of slaves in Illinois. Even the passage of the Northwest Ordinance in 1787 had little effect upon the growth of the slaveholding population there, especially because of the willingness of Governors St. Clair and Byrd to permit the institution.

Slavery became the subject of intense debate in Illinois Country only after the federal government reconfigured the Northwest Territory. In 1800 the territory split into Ohio Territory and Indiana Territory, and Illinois Country comprised a portion of Indiana Territory. Some of Illinois' settlers asked the U.S. Senate to permit them to hold slaves in the new territory. They also requested permission to enslave their Africans forever. They proposed that any of their Illinois-born slave men become emancipated at thirty-one years old and that the government liberate slave women at twenty-eight years old. The proposal reflected the lack of clarity the federal government had provided on slavery in the territory for the past fifteen years and drew from both sides of the controversy of the ordinance. With the idea of permanent slavery for southern-born slave migrants, the settlers called for the same rights to enslave as the French and British residents had enjoyed under the ordinance. On the other hand, with the call for eventual emancipation of local chattel, the slaveholders recognized in part the ordinance's prohibition of slavery by U.S. residents.

The Senate gave no response to the proposal. The inaction of the legislators marked a significant difference from fifteen years earlier. Back in 1787 Congress was the part of the federal government that had created the ordinance. Since the law's passage, however, courts interpreted it, and governors enforced it as they saw fit. The lawmakers signaled through their silence that they were content to pass the responsibility of national discourse on Upper Mississippi slavery to the judicial and executive branches.

Undeterred by the Senate's negligence, the settlers then decided to push for their requests. They called for a convention in which the participants would discuss their proposals for slavery in Illinois Country. With the approval of Indiana Territory governor William Henry Harrison, the convention met in December 1802, in Vincennes. Delegates from each county gathered to propose that Congress suspend the ordinance's sixth article for one decade and allow slaveholders in the territory to keep their slaves in servitude. As part of their rationale, they tied the institution of human trafficking to the health of the territory—a new argument from supporters of Upper Mississippi slavery. They surmised that the population there would no longer decrease due to the ordinance's prohibition of slavery. Rather, anyone who wanted to migrate with their slaves to Illinois Country could do so without consequence.

The history of the Northwest Territory worked against the proponents. John Randolph chaired the committee that responded to the proposal. In the March 1803 reply, the committee noted that the population of Ohio had experienced rapid growth over the years but that the state forbade slavery. As a result, according to the response, a territory did not need slave labor in order to prosper. The committee did acknowledge, on the other hand, the potential for some territorial residents to feel oppressed by the prohibition. Nevertheless, the committee turned down the proposal. Tying the survival of the territory with enforcement of the ordinance's sixth article, Randolph wrote that "the committee deemed it highly dangerous and inexpedient to impair a provision, wisely calculated to promote the happiness and progress of the northwest country and add strength and security to that extensive frontier."[2]

As time progressed and more antislavery migrants moved northwest, the ideas from proslavery settlers began to reflect willingness to compromise with opponents. Indiana Territory refrained from directly challenging the ordinance's sixth article by instead implementing a "Law Concerning Servants." The law addressed servants regardless of ethnicity. It required any European American, African American, Native American, or mulatto entering the territory as a contracted servant to honor the contract. The new legislation permitted slaveholding migrants to set foot into the territory with their slaves, but the owners had to free the slaves and then contract their former slaves to lifetime service in order to maintain as close a facsimile to the old master-slave relationship as possible. Although Governor Harrison kept alive the tradition of territorial governors like Arthur St. Clair supporting mandatory lifetime service-labor, he differed from them by differentiating such labor from slavery itself. Because of the previous failed attempts to legitimize northwestern slavery, rebranding the institution constituted a more practical means for proslavery residents to achieve a legislative victory.[3]

The slaveholders, however, capitalized on their victory by pushing for legalized slavery instead of contracted servitude. The Indiana Territorial Assembly capitulated in part by passing "an act concerning the introduction of negroes and mulattoes into this Territory." The proponents did not receive the lifelong slavery they had originally requested, but they at least were able to hold slaves without punishment for an extended period of time. The new law required any migrant to the territory who held a slave under fifteen years old to record the name and age of each slave in a court of common pleas. The territory then allowed the owner to keep a male slave until he reached the age of thirty-five or the girl until she became thirty-two years old. Any slave arriving in the territory at age fifteen or older was an adult slave, according to the law. Within the first month of arrival, the owner of an older slave had to arrange with the slave the number of continued years of their master-slave relationship, and the law required a court of common pleas to witness the contracting. If the parties did not reach an agreement, the law forced the slave to leave the territory within two months of his or her arrival.[4]

The passage of the statute marked one of the first instances of popular sovereignty concerning slavery in the United States. The federal government permitted the people of Indiana Territory to decide how to define and enforce slavery and emancipation. Thomas Jefferson was the president of the United

States when the bill became a law in 1808, and the territory's circumventing of the Northwest Ordinance's sixth article comprised a portion of the extralegal slavery that took place in the Upper Mississippi under his administration. Unlike his authorization for William Clark to bring York to the Northwest, President Jefferson had no direct involvement with Indiana Territory's decision. Consequently, the territory's popular sovereignty resulted primarily from his distancing himself from the slavery debate there.

The supporters of slavery in Illinois were fighting against time in 1808, for that year the federal government had begun to limit the institution. The United States banned participation in the African slave trade. As a result, no new slaves came into Illinois from the African continent unless by illegal means. In Illinois as in other proslavery locations, slaveholders now legally received slaves either from purchasing them, claiming ownership of newborn slaves, or inheriting slaves.[5]

Another reconfiguration of the Upper Mississippi made the victory of the slaveholders short-lived. On March 1, 1809, the federal government detached Illinois Country from Indiana Territory and renamed that section of land Illinois Territory. The antislavery residents of the smaller Indiana Territory had more political influence there than they had enjoyed in the territory's formerly larger size. As a result, they persuaded Indiana Territory's legislature to repeal the indenture law in 1810. Meanwhile, in Illinois Territory, the "Act Concerning Servants" and the "Act concerning the introduction of negroes and mulattoes into this Territory" remained in place. As a result, African American slavery — albeit a more temporary version of the institution — took place in the new territory from the start.[6]

At this time the proslavery laws of Illinois Territory had little impact outside of a few towns of the southern part of the territory. Of the 7,147 people who lived there, only 128 were bonded African Americans. Moreover, 500 free African Americans resided in the territory, which demonstrated not only how little the citizens relied upon slavery but also how willing they were to relate to African Americans in a capacity besides a master-slave relationship. The places where people held slaves in Illinois Territory bordered the lower part of Louisiana Territory to the east across the Mississippi and the slaveholding states of Kentucky and Tennessee to the north. Although the territory extended north to border the Great Lakes to the west, the 1810 census recorded no slaveholders in that portion of the land, which largely consisted of St. Clair County. Meanwhile, in the proslavery towns of Kaskaskia, Springfield, and Grand Tower, the number of slaves per slaveholding household was almost always a single-digit number. Grand Tower resident M. Barbeu possessed the largest holding of slaves in the territory that year — twelve.

The first governor of Illinois Territory was a slaveholder. President James Madison appointed Ninian Edwards to rule the territory. While in office he held forty-year-old Antony, young adults Jesse and Rose, and adolescent girl Maria. He used his position as a bully pulpit, speaking out in favor of indentured servitude. Despite the growing opposition in the state to the institution, he called servitude "beneficial to the slaves, and not repugnant to the public interests." President Madison allowed the governor to complete his term despite his breaking of federal law by keeping slaves in federal territory. With the executive branches of local and national government demonstrating tolerance of "unfree labor" in a free land, several people soon tested the authorities.[7]

The next president, James Monroe, implemented policies toward the development of Illinois that served as the foundation of slavery there for the next two generations. He reappointed Edwards to the governorship, thus keeping a slaveholder in charge of the territory's executive branch. He also arranged for the federal government to fund the expansion of slavery to northwestern Illinois. In addition, he did not strongly enforce the Missouri Compromise, which he himself had signed to ban the practice from the Midwest. Through these decisions, he did for the institution in Illinois what Washington and Jefferson had done for it in the entire Upper Mississippi.

By the time Illinois Territory applied for statehood in 1818, the demographics and the slavery-related politics had dramatically changed. More migrants settled in the northern part of the territory during the previous eight years. The territorial government rechristened the westernmost portion of St. Clair County, bordering the Mississippi to the east, as "Madison County." That year a local census recorded 4,486 people in the county — seventy-seven of whom were slaves. Thus, in less than one decade, the northern part of the territory acquired nearly three-fifths the number of slaves as the territory's entire slave population of 1810. In addition, in Madison County, only thirty-three African Americans were free. As a result, while the county still had little use for slaves, the European American residents preferred their company to that of free African Americans. Indeed, throughout the 1810s slaves entered Illinois with owners mostly from Kentucky and Tennessee but also from North Carolina, South Carolina, Maryland, Virginia, Georgia, and Louisiana. A majority of the arrivals lived in the parts of Illinois that bordered the slave territory of Missouri — formerly Louisiana Territory. Most of the others resided in the town of Galena.[8]

Class issues separated Illinois from the rest of the slaveholding Upper Mississippi. Most of the state's slaveholders were southern yeoman farmers. They were poor European Americans. Their economic status contrasted sharply with the slaveholding populations in Western Michigan Territory. However, because the state bordered the slave states of Missouri and Kentucky, masters did not have to travel as far with their families and slaves to Illinois as to Western Michigan. The state's wealthiest slaveholders came from

Kentucky, Tennessee, and Virginia. They did not differ from the yeoman farmers, however, in how they fashioned slavery in Illinois. The rich owners still brought only one or two slaves with them and largely charged them with domestic responsibilities.[9]

When Illinois Territory became a state in 1818, it treated slavery much like the federal government had with the Northwest Ordinance. The state constitution, like the sixth article of the ordinance, banned slavery and emancipated all slaves except the French chattel whose presence in the state had preceded statehood. The state government followed the federal government's lead in declining to make emancipation retroactive. Also, by modeling the antislavery provision after the ordinance in order to appease the state's antislavery majority in the population, the state government ironically tried limiting slavery with the same vague language of the Ordinance that had fueled the debate on slavery in Illinois. As a result, the problem of slavery persisted in the new state over three decades after the passage of the ordinance.

The government of Illinois went one step beyond the ordinance by using the language of the old law to legitimate the continuance of pre-statehood slavery. As a gesture to the antislavery residents, the state legislature limited indentured servitude for African American men to one year and forbade the indenturing of boys past their twenty-first birthday and of girls turning eighteen years old. In keeping with the ordinance's anti-retroactive spirit, however, the state government declined to make the new ban apply to pre-statehood servitude contracts. Consequently, the African Americans who, before 1818, had agreed to work for periods ranging from two years to ninety-nine years had to honor their commitments.[10]

After only one year of statehood, Illinois took a drastic measure to address the problem of slavery. In the process the state differentiated free African Americans from European Americans. In 1819 the state prohibited African American immigration—an act implying that an African American could live in Illinois only as a servant to a European American. The ban comprised a portion of the state's Black Codes—laws targeting African Americans. The prohibition, in effect as of March 30, stipulated, "That from and after the passage of this act no black or mulatto person shall be permitted to settle or reside in this State, unless he or she shall first produce a certificate signed by some judge or some clerk of some court in the United States, of his or her actual freedom; which certificate shall have the seal of such court affixed to it." The law did address the culpability of slaveholding migrants and any other traffickers of African Americans: "That it shall not be lawful for any person or persons to bring into this State, after the passage of this act, any negro or mulatto, who shall be a slave or held to service at the time, for the purpose of emancipating or setting at liberty such negro or mulatto." However, the new law laid the onus ultimately on the African Americans to "register themselves together with the evidence of their freedom." Further delineating the state's second-class citizenship for African Americans, the laws stripped the ethnic group of judicial power by preventing its members from suing a person and testifying in court.[11]

As part of the unwelcome tone towards free African Americans, the Black Codes specifically noted that the act of setting foot in Illinois did not make a slave free. A similar principle regarding a slave's status as property across state lines had appeared in the Articles of Confederation nearly four decades earlier. An African American who lacked the means to prove his free status through such documentation as freedom papers faced possible arrest, imprisonment, and sale to service by the sheriff of the county for one year. The threat of sale also loomed for local slaves of poor owners, for the owners could legally sell or mortgage their slaves to settle debts. Any free African Americans who did not vacate Illinois within two months of either arrival or termination of indenture risked being sold as fugitives.[12]

The hostility of European Americans toward free African Americans had started well before Illinois became a state. However, after the state government passed the Black Codes, a growing vigilantism regarding the prohibition of free African Americans intensified. European Americans who were not part of law enforcement began kidnapping African Americans suspected of seeking employment, of running away from southern owners, or of not being in contracted service in Illinois. The kidnapping largely took place in the towns of Shawneetown and Illinoistown. The traffickers took their captives from these locations onto riverboats, sent them down the Mississippi, and delivered them to southern agents to have them sold. As early as 1816, Illinois Territory's legislature had tried to curtail the practice, but it was too lucrative. By the end of the decade, a seller typically received one hundred dollars for a healthy, workable slave.[13]

Eventually, captors developed a system which allowed them to circumvent anti-kidnapping laws by not directly sending them out of Illinois and selling them. Instead, the traffickers shuttled the African American detainees from county to county until bringing them to the state's border. At that point a resident of the neighboring slave state acquired the captives and prepared them for sale. By receiving money for their captives, the kidnappers participated in and profited from the slavery economy of the southern states. By spending that money where they resided, they also allowed the economy of Illinois to benefit from the purchases of human beings.[14]

African American slaves in Illinois had to obey the rules of not only their owners but also the State of Illinois. Moreover, the punishments mandated by the state government for the violators resembled those of slave states and slave-labor plantations. According to the law, no person could employ or hire any uncertified African American, and that slaves guilty of misconduct received a whipping for punishment. The law further legitimized slavery by calling for differential punishment, determining that as a free European American paid a fine as a punishment, a slave received a whipping "after the rate of twenty lashes for every $8." The state declared that African Americans venturing ten miles from the tenements of their owners without the permission of the masters could receive no more than thirty-five stripes. A similar law, except that the slave's offense was being on the land of another person besides the master, meant for the offending slave "ten lashes on his or her bare back." Even with the law prohibiting slaveholders from assembling at least three slaves "for the purpose of dancing or reveling either by day or night," the law mandated that only the slaves in assembly receive thirty-nine stripes "on his or her bare back."[15]

Despite the similarities of Illinois slavery to southern slavery, the new state's version of the institution had enough differences to offend potential slaveholding transplants. Southerners stopped migrating to Illinois, as did their money. The state then suffered an immediate and severe economic depression. Some local politicians wanted to woo the slaveholders back to the state. The proslavery citizens who remained made one final attempt through the electoral process to bring the slavery of the South to Illinois. They pressed for longer periods of African American indentured servitude, proposing a convention to change the state constitution. The electorate voted on the proposal in August 1824 and rejected it but only by a slim majority of 1,668 votes. The remainder of the existence of slavery in Illinois consisted of measures to restrict the practice instead of expand it.[16]

The debate over the convention, however, revealed how split the state had become over the institution. Disagreement existed in several diverse contexts. On the gubernatorial level, former governors Ninian Edwards and Shadrach Bond supported slavery, but current governor Edward Coles opposed the convention. In one of Coles' first messages as governor, he told the state legislators that he knew of slavery's persistence in spite of the Northwest Ordinance and wanted the practice abolished. In addition to rhetoric, he contributed his gubernatorial salary to the cause of abolition. Among the local media, the newspapers *Edwardsville Spectator* and *Illinois Intelligencer* spoke against the convention. Proslavery politicians, meanwhile, ran the periodicals that promoted slavery such as *Republican Advocate* and *Republican*.[17]

Although slavery did not advance further in the state, the government maintained a slave power of sorts. Shadrach Bond, who served as governor from 1818 to 1822, led the group. He was born in the slaveholding state of Maryland. The Black Codes began under his administration, and he supported the idea of a slavery convention. More importantly, he had received the support of the state's residents. He was the first governor to lead Illinois in statehood, which meant that instead of attaining the office through a presidential appointment, he had won an election.[18]

Fellow southerner John McLean also called for the slavery convention. He represented Illinois in Congress as a senator; he was born in North Carolina but raised in Kentucky. By the time of the last attempt to expand slavery in Illinois, he had gained considerable influence in the state. He eventually became a state Supreme Court justice with fellow supporters of the convention such as Theophilus W. Smith, Sidney Breeze, and Jesse B. Thomas.[19]

Elias Kent Kane, the secretary of state of Illinois from 1820 to 1824, was another member but was born and raised in New York. The proslavery governor Bond appointed him to serve in his administration. He followed his appointer's lead in publicly declaring his support of slavery. His periodical, the *Republican Advocate*, served as a forum for his views. On the other hand, he recognized the political volatility of his proslavery position in an increasingly antislavery state. For example, he tried unsuccessfully to distance himself from the convention in order to win the Senate election of 1820; instead, his incumbent antislavery opponent, Daniel Cook, won reelection. Like Ninian Edwards, Kane practiced slavery in his personal life, but he did so indirectly. He married a slaveholder named Felicite Peltier instead of holding slaves of his own. His views and practices did not hinder his political career, for the citizens of Illinois elected him senator in 1825.[20]

Although the slave power politicians failed to change the law to fit their desires, they had the agency to carry out the new law as they saw fit. In the most proslavery areas of the state, they saw fit not to do so. Slavery as it had existed when Illinois was a territory continued in statehood in spite of the new constitution. The state and local governments enforced only the portion pertaining to the registration of slaves with county officials. That way, the counties could keep track of which African Americans lived there legally — as slaves — and which ones — either free African Americans or fugitive slaves — were banned. The executive branch in Illinois neglected the remainder of the law, especially the restriction of contracts to one year. Rather, masters registered African American servants for terms of service spanning from as little as eighteen years to as long as one century. Owners circumvented the age limit of service for indentures by registering newborn baby migrants to contracts of service for twenty-one years. Some slaveholders brazenly assigned as many years of service to servants much older than a few months, and they suffered no reprisals.

The execution of the law also ignored the agency the state constitution assigned to the servants themselves. Owners circumvented the requirement that they negotiate terms of service with the indentures. Instead, the masters used intimidation to coerce the slaves to sign oppressive contracts. If any African American turned down an owner's offer, then the master could remove that slave from the state. At that point, the servant stood the nearly definite chance of returning to harsher slavery in the South and suffering a transfer by purchase to another slaveholder.

In places where the state and local governments loosely enforced the state constitution, indentured servitude flourished. One oversight of the law lay in its absence of a limit of the number of servants per owner. As a result, an owner could legally indenture new groups of African Americans on an annual basis. In the two decades since the formation of Indiana Territory, the number of indentured servants in Illinois quintupled from 168 in 1810 to 746 in 1830.[21]

The state's residents frequently sold and traded their African American servants, which meant that the servants sold in Illinois became uprooted more than once. To a degree, the Illinois slaves suffered with their southern counterparts the trauma accompanying dislocation from their transition from owner to owner. Moreover, the suffering from the sale in Illinois added to the pain the slave had already experienced from the earlier separation from the original slave community in the South in order to have lived in Illinois with the slaveholding migrant in the first place. Newspapers boldly trumpeted the offers, which resembled advertisements of slave sales in southern newspapers, for the notices lumped African Americans with household items and described the servants only in terms of their labor potential. "Sale of personal property, including two negro boys, of plantation utensils, furniture, horses, cattle, and several valuable servants of both sexes," read one item, and another announced, "For sale — a likely negro woman about 30 years of age, warranted perfectly healthy and an excellent house servant."[22]

The state government not only permitted these sales but participated in them. The state hosted frequent sales of slaves from sheriffs and executors of wills between 1816 and 1826. The executive branch sold away the African Americans it had caught disobeying the Black Codes and earned money from the transactions. Thus, the slave trade partly fueled the Illinois economy. As with the private sector notices, such local newspapers as the Illinois *Gazette*, the *Western Intelligencer*, and the Edwardsville *Spectator* advertised the state-sponsored sales. The sheriffs' sales took place as late as 1853.[23]

Money associated with slavery also exchanged hands in Illinois by other means. As a remnant of the days of the Articles of Confederation, such transactions happened when local citizens captured and returned fugitive slaves. Throughout the 1820s newspapers printed several notices of runaway servants. Most slaveholders promised rewards of between twenty-five and thirty dollars for the retrieval of their missing human property. Few successful returns took place in Illinois, however. In addition, local banks financially participated in slavery by allowing owners to use their slaves as collateral when lending them money. Finally, some masters who had little money rented their slaves to people who needed the labor.

Although some Illinois slaveholders parted from their property by sales, they rarely allowed their servants to leave them by emancipating them. The bonded laborers were too valuable to the households, especially because owners tended to bring only one or two of them to the Northwest. In addition, the state banned free African Americans. Therefore, if an owner had to lose a servant, the sale of the servant at least brought money to the owner's home. In the few occasions that owners freed their slaves in the state's early years, religion was usually the motivating factor.[24]

Not every slaveholder who relocated to Illinois sought to maintain slavery there. On the contrary, some masters brought their slaves with them in order to emancipate them. Although many of the Midwest's earliest prominent southern migrants kept their African Americans in bondage, Edward Coles of Virginia broke from tradition when he arrived in Illinois in 1819. A former private secretary of President Monroe, he had previously visited the state in 1815 and 1818. He took ten slaves with him when he left the East Coast for good in April 1819, when Monroe appointed him to the position of register of the land office. While en route to Illinois, he declared them emancipated, but they decided not to separate from him at that point. After arriving in Illinois, he gave one hundred acres of land to the head of each family of his former slaves.[25]

As the population of the state grew increasingly antislavery, its residents began electing people who endorsed those politics. Coles' generosity toward his slaves worked politically in his favor. He ran for governor in 1822, at a time when supporters of slavery still held tremendous political influence in Illinois. He won the election but with less than one-third of the popular vote. He received 2,854 votes, while his opponents won 2,687 (Joseph Phillips), 2,443 (Thomas Browne), and 622 (R. Moore) votes. Meanwhile, in other political races, candidates opposed to slavery began to make inroads in the proslavery hold on state politics that year. Daniel P. Cook ran for the Senate against McLean and won by a majority of 876.[26]

Four years later former governor Ninian Edwards attempted to regain the governorship. Unlike the days of his first administration, when the continuation of his tenure over Illinois Territory was a mere matter of presidential reappointment, he had to campaign and win the votes of the citizens of the state of Illinois. When he spoke to people while campaigning, he did not try to mirror them in appearance and behavior — no unkempt clothes, no drinking whiskey. Rather, he wore expensive, fashionable clothes. More importantly, part of his image involved fostering the appearance of practicing either slavery or indenture. He rode through the state in a carriage that an African American driver operated for him.

The state's slave power still loomed largely over state government, as evidenced by the two most prominent gubernatorial candidates. Running against slaveholder Edwards was Thomas Sloo, Jr., of Hamilton County. Sloo had served in the state senate since 1822, had supported the convention on local slavery, and had spoken publicly in favor of the institution. William Kinney, Sloo's running mate, won the lieutenant governor position over Edwards' partner, Samuel H. Thompson. Edwards, however, beat Sloo but only by seventy votes. The great extent to which the proslavery candidates monopolized the voting results of Illinois citizens signaled that state-level enforcement of antislavery laws was to remain delayed for the foreseeable future. Indeed, from the start of Edwards' first term in 1809 to the last year of his final term in 1830, the state's executive branch was led by slaveholders, and they neglected antislavery laws accordingly.[27]

Coles left the governorship in 1826 in a considerably weakened stature partly as a result of his treatment of his chattel. The state forced him to pay a fine of $2,000 for bringing his slaves into Illinois to free them. Although several other people brought bonded African Americans to the state, government officials who did not like Coles or his antislavery stance decided to enforce the law against him. The state legislature ruled that he did not have to pay the fine, but an anti–Coles circuit judge made void the lawmakers' decision. The Supreme Court, then, sided with the legislature and canceled the fine.[28]

State politicians had to be careful as to how they presented their views on slavery, especially because the economic climate determined in part the receptiveness of the citizens to the institution. In contrast to Edwards' ability to display opulence effectively for political advancement, Coles' wealthy lifestyle only further angered his detractors. As many local citizens labored on their own farms and suffered economic hardship in the mid–1820s, they groused about the governor's many farm employees. Moreover, he seemed hypocritical. For all of his work to end slavery in his own household and in the state, he remained a slaveholder while he served as governor. One of his slaves was his cook.[29]

Slavery continued in northwestern Illinois as European American settlers used human chattel to develop new businesses. The entrepreneurs who traveled to the territory did not permanently stay there. As a result, neither did their slaves. As a result, slavery was initially temporary in nature. Slaves either returned home with their masters after a brief period or stayed in the Upper Mississippi Valley as freed people. Slavery had permanence in the region only through the constant immigration of temporary entrepreneurs.

Excursions supported by President Monroe paved the way for slavery to gain permanence in Michigan Territory. In 1819 Colonel James Johnson of Kentucky—a government contractor for the U.S. Army—began a series of expeditions up the Mississippi River. President Monroe persuaded the federal government to fund Col. Johnson's trips. The explorer eventually made his way to the southwestern part of Michigan Territory. While there he obtained permission from the indigenous people of Galena, Illinois, to facilitate labor at lead mines there. He decided to use slave labor at the mines, which meant that such arrangements and treaties between European Americans and indigenous groups of the Upper Mississippi occasionally contributed to the northwest expansion of African American slavery.

Lead mining — the first Upper Mississippi business founded upon slave labor — began under Col. Johnson in 1822. As he brought in bondsmen, others from his state followed. John and Joseph Ward brought in between fifty and four hundred African American slaves. Several others also worked slaves in the mines. John Armstrong, who made a living by trading with the indigenous, arrived in Galena on July 10, 1822, over a week after Johnson, and he worked at various mines in Michigan Territory as well as in Illinois.[30]

The arrival of Johnson and his slaves marked another instance of the federal government supporting the expansion of slavery into the Upper Mississippi. In 1822 President Monroe ordered troops sent into the lead region specifically to protect Johnson and company. The soldiers secured the miners from attacks by indigenous groups. Monroe had the political capability of making these orders despite the illegality of bringing slaves to the region. Northwestern Illinois, where Johnson headed, had a sparse population. No sizable antislavery force existed there to effectively complain against Monroe's actions. As mining eventually brought wealth to that part of the state, critics of slavery had even less incentive to register any disagreement.[31]

The mining entrepreneurs ran efficient operations. Moses Meeker recalled that Col. Johnson had supervised the lead mines on Fever River, on the east side of the Mississippi. The day after Meeker arrived at St. Louis, he saw Anderson's keel-boat full of lead from the Dubuque mines. He told Meeker that the lead had come from an island in the Mississippi River, opposite the Indian village where he had set up his business. The indigenous people would not allow him to build upon the primary land where they had dug and smelted lead for a long time. Anderson, however, told the people about an efficient way for them to rid themselves of a significant amount of waste from their furnaces. He bought the waste and smelted it. He constructed a log furnace on the island, and purchased the by-products from their furnaces. By compensating the indigenous in goods, he paid a much lower price for the materials than he could have acquired it by mining. He spoke to Meeker very favorably about the mines of Fever River and of the east side of the Mississippi.[32]

Meanwhile, President Monroe devised a plan that, although dependent upon slave labor for success, did not benefit the African Americans providing the labor. He advertised in newspapers that he intended to lease one-half of a section of land on the Upper Mississippi lead mines to U.S. citizens. The lessee received a bond and security for ten thousand dollars, to be approved by a U.S. district judge. He then obtained the use of timber and stone on the half section for the purposes of smelting. Moreover, the federal government benefited from the slave labor there, because the lessee had to pay the government one-tenth of all the lead made. Of all the people receiving money from mining, only the slaves lacked access to the wealth which they were responsible for producing.[33]

Just as African American servicemen ironically had enabled the country to protect slavery in the Upper Mississippi during the War of 1812, African American slaves of soldiers stationed in the Upper Mississippi indirectly contributed to the expansion of slavery to a new part of that region. Col. Johnson and his fellow travelers approached Fever River in early July 1822. Predicting that the indigenous people would oppose his presence there, he requested and received federal soldiers from the region to protect him against any indigenous attack. The troops came from the Upper Mississippi's military commander — Col. Willoughby Morgan. His order to supply Johnson, meanwhile, had come from President Monroe's secretary of war. Troops from Fort Edwards, Fort Armstrong on Rock Island, and Fort Crawford at Prairie du Chien — Col. Morgan's headquarters—came to Johnson's defense. The large number of troops and their slaves overwhelmed the Sac and Fox tribes at Fever River, and the indigenous people decided to establish peaceful relations with the miners and troops.[34]

The Monroe administration's decision to protect Johnson with U.S. troops showed how valuable the federal government considered both the mining venture and the slaves transported for the mining labor. At the time, the government had kept troops at the aforementioned forts because it wanted to protect the interests of the nation's citizens in the Upper Mississippi. Transferring soldiers to Fever River meant decreasing the security of the forts. Either the Monroe administration left the forts with sufficient numbers of troops to keep the forts safe, or the executive branch considered the possible wealth from lead mining by slave labor worth risking the losses of the forts to attacks and left too few soldiers at the stations. Regardless, the forts survived, and the federal government continued to sponsor and protect the expansion of African American slavery to Fever River.

Most slaves settled with their slaveholders in the Upper Mississippi, but one of the first slaves of the Upper Mississippi to receive emancipation there did not remain with Col. Johnson but rather identified with the indigenous people. This person, James P. Beckwourth, was one of four slaves who traveled with Johnson. Although born in Virginia on April 26, 1798, Beckwourth relocated with his master, who was also his father, to Missouri by the Mississippi and Missouri rivers. He performed farm labor for several years before becoming a blacksmith's apprentice. He eventually grew annoyed with remaining an apprentice and sought opportunities to travel. His owner's permissiveness towards his slave's wishes enabled the servant to not only engage in travel but also meet the indigenous people with whom he related very well.[35]

At the time that he left for Col. Johnson's expedition, Beckwourth was still a slave. His father, in allowing him to go on the trip, thus demonstrated an unusual amount of trust in a master-slave relationship. "My father then wished me to set up in business in his settlement," Beckwourth recalled, "but I expressed disinclination, and declared a growing wish to travel. Seeing my determination, my father finally consented to my departure. He admonished me with some wholesome precepts, gave me five hundred dollars in cash, together with a good horse, saddle, and bridle, and bade me God speed upon my journey." He then bade his friends farewell and boarded the vessel."[36]

Beckwourth's experience as an Illinois slave resembled those of earlier Upper Mississippi slaves, showing that the institution in that region had hardly evolved from the immediate days following the Louisiana Purchase. Just as York's service to Meriwether Lewis and William Clark indirectly enabled the growth of slavery to the Midwest, Beckwourth's participation in Johnson's trip indirectly led to slavery's rapid expansion in northern Illinois. He served as the hunter of the group, not unlike York's role to Lewis and Clark two decades earlier. Also, like York, part of Beckwourth's enslavement involved interaction with the indigenous people. Johnson had the mission of negotiating a treaty with the Sac and Fox Indians so that he would have their permission to work the lead mines, which they owned at that time. Beckwourth remembered that for the expedition about one hundred men sailed on between six to eight boats. They traveled for twenty days before arriving in Galena. Numerous Sac and Fox members awaited their appearance, for they already knew why the travelers had come there. Despite wearing armaments and looking formidable, the indigenous people welcomed the voyagers without violence.[37]

Unlike York, who remained a novelty to the indigenous people he encountered, Beckwourth identified with the Sac and Fox. Moreover, they welcomed him more warmly than they had received his master. By the time Johnson and the indigenous people completed the treaty, Beckwourth had gotten along with the Sac and Fox so well that he stayed with them and hunted on their land for eighteen months. While there he deeply studied their culture. As a result, the indigenous people recognized his sensitivity to them and treated him kindly in return. Although the tribes of the area were wary of the arrival of the European Americans, they demonstrated a considerable amount of hospitality to Beckwourth. He noted, "The Indians soon became very friendly to me, and I was indebted to them for showing me their choicest hunting grounds. There was abundance of game, including deer, bears, wild turkey, raccoons, and numerous other wild animals." He and the indigenous people not only lived together but also were companions. "Frequently they would accompany me on my excursions (which always proved eminently success-ful)," he recalled, "thus affording me an opportunity of increasing my personal knowledge of the Indian character."[38]

Beckwourth's Upper Mississippi enslavement, especially his experiences with the Sac and Fox, laid the foundation for his lifetime of exploration of the western United States as a freedman. Having later spent the majority of his life among indigenous peoples, he reflected upon common traits among the various tribes. "I find their habits of living, and their religious belief, sub-stantially uniform through all the unmingled races," he began. "All believe in the same Great Spirit; all have their prophets, their medicine men, and their soothsayers, and are alike influenced by the appearance of omens; thus leading to the belief that the original tribes throughout the entire continent, from Florida to the most northern coast, have sprung from one stock, and still retain in some degree of purity the social constitution of their primitive founders."[39]

Beckwourth had comparatively more agency over his own life than other slaves—including those of the Upper Mississippi—enjoyed over their own lives. Due to the nature of the enslavement—an expedition with minimal rations—he was allowed to carry a gun in order to serve as hunter. In addition, most slaves of the region lived there temporarily with their owners before returning with them to the South as property. For many, emancipation after the completion of work in Illinois simply did not exist as a viable option. Beckwourth, on the other hand, related to his master in an unusual manner. Regardless of whether the owner's dual role as father of the slave influenced the generosity, he allowed Beckwourth to work at his own discretion in the mines and to keep his earnings for himself. The servant remembered, "I remained in that region for a space of eighteen months, occupying my leisure time by working in the mines. During this time I accumulated seven hundred dollars in cash, and, feeling myself to be quite a wealthy personage, I deter-mined upon a return home." In 1824, shortly after his return home, his father emancipated him.[40]

Interestingly, the federal government and Illinois' government had little to do with Beckwourth's emancipation process. Rather, the slave's entire period of mining labor violated both state law and federal law. Although he belonged to his father, he worked for Col. Johnson. However, Beckwourth's recollection of having left the mines on his own volition meant that neither Beckwourth's father nor Johnson contracted him to a specific term of service. Under the constitution of Illinois, Beckwourth, as a slave, was not allowed in the state without a contract. However, no employer could have legally arranged for Beckwourth's unfree labor there. Arriving in Illinois at age twenty-four, he was too old to be contracted to indentured servitude, according to the state constitution. Still, the Northwest Ordinance had prohibited slavery altogether in the state thirty-five years earlier. And because Johnson was a new migrant instead of a French settler, he had no legal exemption from the law.

The federal government soon spread slave labor and the slave trade itself northwest through other ventures besides mining. In 1823, a year after Johnson took Beckwourth to Galena, President Monroe authorized the military itself to extend African American servitude throughout the Upper Mississippi. Major Stephen Long underwent an expedition from Pennsylvania through the Midwest, and several soldiers accompanied him. Moreover, Long acquired an African American servant while in the region in the free state of Ohio. Recording the events of the trip in his journal on May 14, 1823, the major said of the extralegal transaction, "We dined at St. Clairsville, where we procured a black man as a servant, whose name is Andrew." The sentence was the only one in Long's journal to call attention to Andrew Allison's skin color, vocation and first name.[41]

Despite Allison's traveling with the others in the expedition and sharing their experiences, Long rarely identified him in any other contexts besides skin color and servitude in the documents pertaining to the journey. The major did not refer to Allison by surname at all and, after June 12, not by his first name either. One week after procuring him, the soldier dubbed him, in anonymous fashion, "the black boy." Then, he signified ownership of Allison when noting the start of a trip from Fort Crawford at Prairie du Chien, Michigan Territory, on June 25; Long called him "our black-boy." Near the end of the trek, on September 10, the officer acknowledged the adulthood of his servant but continued possessive language by identifying him as "our black man."[42]

More migrants and their slaves poured into the region. In 1823, between 100 and 150 slaves existed in Jo Daviess County, which meant at least a twenty-five-fold increase from the previous year's four slaves Johnson had taken with him. An influx of people seeking fortune in the Galena mines arrived as Johnson left for good in 1826. The new wave of prospectors was just as dedicated to finding wealth through lead as their predecessors had been. In the next year, many of the migrants of 1826 remained in or near Galena, operating their mines and running their farms. Calls for the policing of the trafficking of African American slaves to the area were few and far between. Galena and the mines of surrounding towns made too much capital from slave labor for local governments to seriously consider any such demands from antislavery residents.[43]

At least one local occasion for an antislavery protest came from a Galena slave during this time. In April 1827 James A. Duncan took his Virginia-born slave, thirty-one-year-old Swanzy Adams, aboard the steamboat *Shamrock* and sailed from Kentucky to Illinois. Duncan then hired Adams out to a Captain Comstock for mining labor. Because of his age, his enslavement violated the state constitution. On the other hand, he was able to use his wages from the work to emancipate himself for $1,500. He himself knew that his rare status as an Upper Mississippi slave increased his value; he later remarked, "Good boys like me could be bought in Kentuck for $350." Nevertheless, his fundraising and the transaction that took place to liberate him demonstrated that an economy based on slavery had reached well beyond the Missouri-bordered counties, up to the northern-most places in Illinois along the Mississippi.[44]

Meanwhile, slavery in the Galena area slowly began to change. In the 1830 census, more slaves were women than men. This shift in gender reflected not only the sustained political strength of the local advocates of slavery but also the decline of the mining industry. Among the slaveholders in Jo Daviess County that year, the majority of those who held only one slave owned a woman instead of a man. Most of those who owned more than one slave held both men and women and, among them, kept more women than men. Some households of multiple servants contained only women among the servants. Regardless of gender, the slaves were young, which demonstrated that Jo Daviess slaveholders tended to follow the law. Most of the county's slaves were under twenty-five years old, and among them the majority had not yet reached the age of ten.

The federal government, meanwhile, continued to undermine the free status of the westernmost portion of Michigan Territory by subsidizing the spread of slavery there, as long as the local population allowed it. For example, slaveholder James M. Kane was among a group of local residents to whom the federal government gave a charter to build a railway in the vicinity. Meanwhile, John and Joseph Ward brought their bonded African Americans to the mines, but the Wards stayed in the area for a temporary period. By the late 1820s, most of the new arrivals to the mines were of diverse European origins; the Irish, Cornish and Welsh had begun to migrate there. A German American started a boardinghouse business nearby. Among the forty Irishmen living in five miners' cabins in Shullsburg, several residents had mining claims.[45]

Despite the new laws constructed by the state about slavery over the years, different people interpreted the laws in diverse manners. In addition, the State of Illinois allowed the haphazard enforcement to continue unchecked. French settlers, for example, still kept their slaves without consequences over four decades after the Northwest Ordinance and ten years after the state constitution's rules about indenture. Southerners expressed resentment over the preferential treatment they perceived from the state towards the French. Both groups of people had in common antagonism towards northern migrants who opposed slavery and sought to eliminate it from the Midwest.[46]

The tension intensified as new developments in interstate travel allowed unprecedented numbers of northerners and southerners to resettle in Illinois. In 1823 the steamboat *Virginia* was the first to successfully travel upriver, reaching Fort Snelling, Michigan Territory and Winona before returning to St. Louis. Before then, steamboat travel had largely existed along the river among the southern states. From the very start of upriver steamboat sailing, however, southerners participated. A family from Kentucky was among the passengers of the *Virginia*. They disembarked near Galena, Illinois, to prospect for lead. Upriver travel meant that northwestern and southern states now stood the chance to enhance their businesses by trading goods with one another. To a certain extent, slaves were among those goods.[47]

Very few southerners enjoyed the ability to travel up the river over the next few years. As a result, few slaves entered the Upper Mississippi as well. Despite the success of that first Upper Mississippi trip by boat, upriver travel for the next two decades was hampered by rough rapids, especially near Keokuk, Iowa. Upriver towns, consequently, developed slowly. Only one or two annual trips to Fort Snelling took place in that time period. The upriver steamboats then included the *Otter*, the *Rock River*, and the *Lynx*.[48]

The mines of Galena and other locations along the Fever River were among the first beneficiaries of upriver steamboat travel. After 1823 vessels carried lead from the mines of northeastern Iowa, northern Illinois, and southwestern Wisconsin. The interstate commerce greatly enhanced the mining industry, which attracted more people to the region. The advent of the steamboat, however, also reinforced Upper Mississippi slavery, because as southerners continued to pour into the area, their slaves did, too. Moreover, the increase in bonded adult African Americans testified to the absence of federal and state enforcement of the legal guidelines of slavery.[49]

The Upper Mississippi states benefited from slave labor in other ways besides the wealth slaveholders earned from mining. Slaves ran many of the ships that carried goods to the upper states. Also, upper state businesses allowed masters the opportunity of bringing slaves to work there in hotels of the region. Passengers who remarked on the presence of slaves tended to focus on the appearances of the bondsmen instead of their labor. The author Herman Melville, better known for his novel *Moby-Dick*, wrote in *The Confidence Man* about "slaves, black, mulatto, quadroon" and "grinning Negroes" among the passengers aboard a riverboat.[50]

Upriver travel prospered through the 1830s and, at one point, was nearly indomitable. That decade ended with disasters that had the potential to curtail northern trips. For example, a boiler of the *Dubuque* exploded, killing twenty-two aboard in August 1837. Then, the economic panic of that same year devastated much of the United States. Still, migrants continued to flock upriver to the mines, and the Upper Mississippi region remained largely unaffected by the panic.[51]

A traveler to nearby Prairie du Chien took notice of the shared social space of European Americans and African Americans in February 1834, even as people observed the physical differences—especially skin color—among one another. Writing about a voyage for the New York *American* periodical, the passenger wrote of the vessel, "I entered a large barrack room, fitted up very neatly as a theatre by the soldiers themselves; the scenery, quite cleverly done, being all painted by them, and the lights ingeniously placed in bayonets, prettily arranged, a contrivance suggested by their own taste." Taking note of the segregation aboard the ship, the journalist said, "The seats, rising like the pit of a theatre, were so adjusted as to separate the audience into three divisions, the officers, with their families, furnished one, the soldiers another, and gumbos Indians, and a negro servant or two making up the motley third."[52]

Not every steamboat trip featured such orderly, albeit hierarchical, organization of the various ethnic groups. On the contrary, the controversy over slavery's existence also influenced early steamboat travel, as demonstrated in the Negro Riot of 1833. That June authorities in Michigan Territory arrested two fugitive slaves from Kentucky—Thomas Blackburn and his wife—and ordered their return home to their owner in the South. They went to jail in the territory while the steamboat remained in the region. Blackburn's wife, however, escaped from incarceration, and a mob of African Americans approached local sheriff John Willson as he brought Blackburn to the steamboat. Although the sheriff shot into the crowd with his gun, the mob overpowered him, liberated Blackburn, and sent the slave to Canada. The incident marked one of the earliest examples of open antislavery vigilantism taking place in the northwest part of the United States.

In the process of freeing the Blackburns, however, the riot resulted in further restrictions for African Americans in the area. The vigilantism of the African American mob inspired those sympathetic to the slaveholder to form their own vigilante horde. As alarm bells rang, men of various ages armed themselves with a diverse array of weapons and stormed the streets. The European American mob overpowered its victims in a similar manner that the African American mob had done. Some residents, on the other hand, used the law to bring about order but at the expense of African Americans. The city council held a special session, in which it passed a curfew ordinance to keep African Americans indoors after dark. The new law was certainly nowhere nearly as oppressive as the Black Codes in Illinois were, but both Michigan Territory and Illinois shared in common the relegating of African Americans—slave and free—to second-class citizenship.[53]

As for Illinois, not every slaveholder in the state was European American.

In the 1830s or 1840s, slave Mamie Thompson's mother was born in Cairo, Illinois, to a Cherokee slaveholder named Redman and an African American slave. Mamie's mother labored in Redman's field. Her European American overseer tried to rape her, but she successfully defended herself. The overseer requested that Redman whip her as a punishment, but she picked up a stick and threatened to kill her master. Redman then put her on an auction block, but his wife, Mary, warned that she would leave him if he sold Mamie's mother. Mary then made her slave a house slave — caring for the children and cleaning the house — instead of a field slave.[54]

In *Nance v. Howard* (1828), the Illinois Supreme Court declared that African Americans could be sold in the state.[55] The courts of Missouri significantly affected slavery in Illinois, for the courts in the neighboring slave state made judgments on whether the human property of Missouri's citizens would remain so in Illinois and, if so, to what degree. Four years into its statehood, Missouri experienced its first trial concerning slavery in the state's own Supreme Court. In *Winny v. Whitesides*, the court decided whether a slave taken from the South to Illinois received a legal entitlement to freedom. Twenty-five years earlier, the defendant and her husband migrated from the Carolinas to Illinois with their slave — the plaintiff. After a period of no more than four years of residence there, the couple relocated to Missouri and took the plaintiff with them in bondage. In the fall of 1824, the court sided with the plaintiff, noting that after a slave fulfills a contract of servitude in Illinois, the former servant became legally free and, therefore, not liable to re-enslavement in a slave state. The verdict marked the first time that a court from a slave state recognized and respected the terms of emancipation in a free Upper Mississippi state. In addition, the ruling was one of the first times that a slave state specifically mentioned which African Americans within its borders could not be enslaved.[56]

To be sure, *Winny v. Whitesides* had little influence on slavery in Illinois, because slaves continued to arrive with their owners for many more years. The next legal milestone came from state lawmakers, who followed Missouri's lead in specifying which African Americans could be freed without weakening slavery itself. On January 17, 1829, the state legislature passed an act that designated African Americans lacking documentation on their free status as "runaway slaves or servants." The law called for the arrests of the fugitives and, if no slaveholders claimed them, for the sheriff to hire them out "for the best price he can get" for one entire year. If still unclaimed after that year, they were able to have the sheriff vouch for their unclaimed status to the circuit court. That court, then, could declare the African Americans free unless "lawfully claimed by the owner or owners thereafter." Due to the constant threat of reclamation hanging over the undocumented slave like a cloud, such a servant was in perpetual limbo — not completely freed from the owner but allowed to live as free in the meantime. The new law's greatest significance lay in its further distinguishing of Upper Mississippi slavery from its southern counterpart, for in the South, unlike Illinois, a master could buy an unclaimed slave and keep the purchase for life.[57]

The law further differentiated Illinois slavery by ensuring that a case like Missouri's *Winny v. Whitesides* would not take place in Illinois. According to the law, each African American who was "the property of any citizen of the United States, residing without the State," had no right to sue in an Illinois court for freedom. The law further mandated that any state court immediately dismiss any such case. Whereas an Illinois slave had successfully sued for emancipation in Missouri, no slave from Missouri or any other state could sue for freedom in Illinois. Just as the Missouri court recognized the temporary nature of Illinois slavery, Illinois' legislature acknowledged the permanent nature of southern slavery.

On February 1, 1831, the lawmakers promised further protection of southern slavery while simultaneously limiting not only the institution but the presence of African Americans themselves in Illinois. First, fugitive slaves were prohibited from the state and sent back to the South. The new law ordered "that hereafter no black or mulatto person shall be permitted to come into and reside in this State" without having shown a certificate of freedom and having paid bond. The lawmakers also held liable any slaveholders possessing abolitionist sympathies. A fine of one hundred dollars awaited "any person who shall hereafter bring into this State any black or mulatto person, in order to free him or her from slavery, or shall directly or indirectly bring into this State or aid and assist any person in bringing such black or mulatto person to settle or reside therein." The legislation was one of the latter victories of the state's slave power.[58]

Sometimes in northwestern Illinois slaveholders developed legal loopholes instead of blatantly defying antislavery laws. In Galena, Abner Field emancipated his two slaves Arch and Cherry on June 30, 1830. Concerning Arch he wrote, "Know all men by these presents, that Abner Field, of the County of Jo Daviess, Illinois, and by these presents do liberate and set free a certain black man now an indentured apprentice, named Arch alias Arch Davis, hereby releasing and exonerating the said Arch from all further service." On the other hand, Field made the liberation conditional, stipulating that if Arch and his wife remained in his ex-master's household, then he "shall be compelled to work to the amount of at least two days in each week." In effect, he would have become re-enslaved. Field, in turn, proposed to supply Arch "with a sufficiency to eat, and to permit him to sleep in his kitchen, etc."

Field's treatment of Cherry demonstrated his lack of concern for the marriage of his slaves. His statement about her emancipation began similarly to his remarks about Arch: "Know all men by these presents, that I, Abner Field, do by these presents release and free an indentured woman of color now belonging to me, known and called Cherry alias Chaney." First, however, she had to labor for him "for one year from the date of this writing." Field then required her to agree to separate herself from her husband. The master proposed to remove her "to Kentucky or elsewhere" by his providing of "bond and security for her return."[59]

Despite the liberating of Arch and Cherry, several slaves remained in Jo Daviess County that year. George Davenport owned four slaves— a relatively high number of bonded people for a slaveholder uninvolved with the mining business. Known as Col. Davenport, he was a trading agent for the American Fur Company. He traded at Fort Armstrong. He operated a ferry. Robert A. Drummond, meanwhile, owned three slaves.

On occasion slaves of northwestern Illinois brought lawsuits for emancipation to the courts. A prominent local citizen named Charles D. St. Vrain had spent a few years in Illinois as a county election judge by 1830. That year he owned two slaves but sent them to the South soon after the census was taken. One of them subsequently asked a court for permission to sue him for her freedom. According to the abstract for her case, twenty-year-old Matilda claimed to have been born of a free African American woman named Sarah on March 16, 1810, in Illinois. She recalled that until St. Vrain took her to Missouri two months before the lawsuit, she had spent the entirety of her life in Illinois. Lamenting that the defendant "now holds your Petitioner in Slavery," she begged "that She may be permitted to Sue as a poor person to Establish her freedom that Counsel may be assigned to her that her mother Sarah may be appointed her next friend ... & that Such order may be made for her personal Security as her case requires & the Law provides." She brought her case to a Missouri court in March 1831, and a free African American woman named Sarah testified on Matilda's behalf.[60]

The controversy surrounding the case did not hurt St. Vrain's reputation. Rather, he received several opportunities for social advancement, thanks to the continuing rule of the state's slave power. In June 1832 Illinois governor John Reynolds wrote to Secretary of War Lewis Cass, asking him to appoint St. Vrain to the Indian Agency at Rock Island County, Illinois. Governor Reynolds himself was a Tennessean and held proslavery views. His petitioning for St. Vrain meant that a slaveholder now had state approval to extend slavery to another Upper Mississippi county in the state. The institution already had federal approval, because soldiers had brought slaves to Fort Armstrong for a generation. Rock Island never became an attraction for slaveholders as Jo Daviess had, but the president and governor had allowed that possibility.[61]

A few migrants to northwestern Illinois brought one slave, thus signaling a shift in migrants from using masses of African Americans for field work to keeping only a single domestic servant for housework. William Hempstead owned one slave. John Atchison owned one female slave in 1830. Arriving in Jo Daviess in 1827, he served as a federal collector of revenue. He was a member of the Masonic Lodge. He was also a steamboat captain, who navigated vessels from Galena up the Mississippi River for over twenty years. He owned the village of Old Belmont in Illinois.

In August 1834 Captain Thomas C. Legate, superintendent of lead mines, brought his servant Barney Norris to the state. He had been a government official during the presidency of John Quincy Adams from 1826 to 1828. According to Captain G. W. Girdon, Norris utilized several skills in his servitude. Concerning Norris' overall labor, Girdon recalled, "There is a gifted and talented lady among us, who, when at those wedding feasts, says that he reminds her of a 'butler of ye olden time.'" Girdon wrote of Norris' cooking and entertaining, "What wedding would be perfect without Barney Norris, the prince of caterers?" On cleaning, "And when spring-time comes, and house-cleaning is the order of the day, the over dreaded time when we, 'lords of creation,' are banished from 'the old arm chair,' the mother tells us that Barney Norris is coming to paper and whiten the parlor. And she has no anxiety, for Barney handles his brush with as fine a touch as a Landscer." For anyone interested in spending time fishing, "Tell Barney that at break of day you will be ready, and it will not be his fault if you do not bring home a heavy string of finest pike and bass." Norris developed a positive reputation for his fishing assistance, and some people asked for his service on more than one occasion. Girdon said that among "a trio of friends, fishermen of old, who for many years have made up a fishing party" were one person who became "younger and happier" after "returning from one of those day's fishing down at the 'cutoff' with Barney" and another who "would rather Barney would catch all the fish than not, so that he has a good day's recreation."[62]

Girdon further mentioned that Norris engaged in community service while owned by Legate. For three decades he labored at a local church. "He rang that old church bell, calling together the faithful flock to hear their honored shepherd read from Holy Writ, and in strains of eloquence divine soothe their sad and anguished hearts," Girdon wrote. The author attributed to the slave spiritual powers usually reserved for descriptions of the work of the clergy. "Full many a bereaved heart — a mother or a daughter, or perhaps a father or a son, has found hope and consolation there where Barney rings the bell," the author claimed. "Yes, full thirty years has the faithful Barney tolled the bell for some loved one who has gone, never more to return."[63]

Indeed, the writer depicted the slave as a religious symbol in Galena. Girdon's further comments about Norris' work at the church suggest that his deeds significantly helped to shape the religious life of a portion of Upper Illinois' population. The author associated Norris' bell-ringing with the decisions of some people to enter the ministry: "Many whose willing feet have hastened to the House of God when Barney rang the bell, have gone to the higher house above. Some who have occupied that pulpit have gone to their reward; others to other fields of labor." Girdon also celebrated the servant as the one constant of the church over the years, remarking that "Barney still remains faithful at his post, in sunshine or storm, opening the doors of God's house alike to rich and poor, neglecting no duty, and beloved by all."[64]

Overall, the description Girdon gave of Norris was on par with tributes that southerners tended to make of their slaves and indentured servants. When mourning the loss of a bonded African American laborer in an obituary or another kind of biographical salute, the slaveholding writer often talked about the servant only in terms of his labor and his relationships with European Americans. Rarely did a remembrance note of any family members or African American friends of the slave. Similarly, Girdon did not mention whether Norris had a wife or children. Rather, the author described him exclusively in the context of his labor for the European American community at large. "No Galenian will ever forget him," declared Girdon. "He still lives among us. Hale and hearty, although the frosts of many winters rest upon his faithful head. 'Faithful to duty' has been his motto ever, and ever will be, until he tolls that bell no more."[65]

Some Galena slaves received honors for their assistance to the soldiers who had brought them to the town in bondage. Girdon identified "old 'Uncle Isaac' and 'Aunt Edy'" among those servants. Adhering to stereotypes about the associations of color with morality, the writer juxtaposed the slaves' "faces of ebony hue" with their "hearts as white as the clothes they always wore." In addition, the slaves served during wartime: "When the fearful war-whoop of the Indian rang over the prairie, [the servants] did the washing for the defenders of the fort at Galena." On their absence, "They have gone, with many another busy actor in those stirring scenes, but they are not forgotten by those who remain."[66]

Not every local slave was remembered for labor. Girdon remembered one slave who embodied the generalizations about African Americans and their lack of inclination to work. By writing, "And 'old Tom Jasper' and his old roan horse; an old, old negro, whose highest ambition was to sit in the sunshine and sleep, beside his old nag as sleepy as he. What old settler will ever forget him?" Girdon helped bring the Sambo stereotype to the Upper Mississippi.[67]

The town's African American slaves had experienced very little change by the 1830s. In some instances the servitude became more inhumane, for some masters made their slaves perform labor more appropriate for animals. In 1834 a traveler to Galena remarked upon the interplay he saw between an African American adult and European American children. In this particular remembrance, the servant served as a mode of transportation in inclement weather. At the time ice had thawed, which "rendered the streams impassable," according to the traveler. As for the roads, "The mud is so deep that it is impossible to go afoot," he remarked before adding that "these steep hills are unfit for carriages." As one solution, schoolchildren passed by the writer's door on horseback. Another solution, however, placed an African American in the role of the horse, because the idea involved "three or four boys and girls sometimes being piled on before and behind an old negro." The traveler likened the slave to the "Old Woman Who Lived in a Shoe," joking that "the mass of heads, arms and legs belonging to the juveniles, makes the fabric look like the wood-cut in the nursery book of that celebrated ancient female's residence, who had so many children, 'she did not know what to do.'"[68]

Elsewhere in Illinois that same year, Sam Blow, later renamed Dred Scott, began part of his enslavement, which he later argued constituted his right to seek emancipation. Blow became an Upper Mississippi slave, which he saw as a contradiction because the Northwest Ordinance and the Missouri Compromise had banned slavery in that region. Dr. John Emerson, an army surgeon, was Blow's master and, with the government's blessing, brought him from the state of Missouri to a military fort at Rock Island, Illinois. Emerson did not free him there but rather kept him in servitude. In the spring of 1836, they left the fort upon Emerson's orders to relocate to another base further north in the Upper Mississippi, but the military permitted the doctor to take Blow with him to his new destination — Fort Snelling in Wisconsin Territory.[69]

By the end of the 1830s, the Illinois state government had developed other means of preserving slavery. The state assessed taxes against "indentured apprentices." Also, as of March 16, 1836, the state ordered a tax of one-half percent on several items. "Slaves; indentured and registered negro or mulatto servants" were only a portion of the taxable objects. The other property mentioned included "wheeled carriages, and sleighs; distilleries; all horses, mares, mules and asses and neat cattle above three years old; watches and appendages; clocks and household furniture, and all other property." Illinois not only reinforced its codifying of slavery into state law but now acquired a means to draw revenue from the ownership of human beings.[70]

As the 1830s drew to a close, the slave trade in Illinois still ran similarly to that of the southern states. New slaveholding migrants continued to register their servants, and the occasional purchase of African Americans took place on Illinois soil. Local authorities still neglected to prosecute participants in unlawful indenture. The slave "Uncle" Lewis Adams, for example, lived in the state from 1824 to 1839, when his owner sold him, his mother and two brothers to Col. Tom Dancy of Houston, Texas. Their owners in Illinois disobeyed the state constitution, for members of the slave family reached past the age limits of indentured servitude as defined by the government. Thus, the slaves were, most likely, not registered. In addition, as African Americans arriving in the state in 1824, their presence was a violation of the prohibition of new African American migrants from Illinois. Slave dealers Bob and John Kirkendaul transported the Adamses southward by covered wagon.[71]

The uppermost part of the state still had active slaveholders. As upriver steamboat travel improved over the years, more southerners had access to riverside counties and towns in Illinois beyond the border to the slave state of Missouri. As the 1840s began, Jo Daviess was still a prominent slaveholding county of northwest Illinois. On the other hand, the influx of antislavery migrants led to the weakening of the institution there. The number of slaves in the county had dramatically declined from the heady 1820s. Only three slaveholders lived there, according to the 1840 census.

One of the masters in the county had helped spread slavery to the Upper Mississippi by transporting other owners and their slaves upriver. John Atchison was the only Jo Daviess slaveholder of the previous decade who remained in the county. In the 1840s he was the captain of the *Lynx* and the *Highland Mary*. He no longer owned a slave girl but rather a slave boy in 1840.

In the 1840s slavery became a contentious issue in Illinois' judicial system. Many slaveholders and slaves brought cases to courts in order for judges to make definitive decisions about slavery. The Northwest Ordinance inspired contradictory interpretations from both state and federal government officials; the state legislature tried to preserve the institution, and various governors participated in it at times. Litigants wanted to know definitively where the state stood on the issue. For African Americans the court's verdicts meant the difference between emancipation and continued enslavement.

As the 1840s dawned, the courts tried to strike a balance between the right to carry property from one state to another and the freedom stipulated for African Americans in the Ordinance. In 1839 the estate of Nathan Cromwell sued David Bailey, who made a promissory note to Cromwell in order to buy a female African American named Nance. Cromwell's administrators won the first case, in which the court awarded them $431.97. The decision had significant relevance to the state's Upper Mississippi counties, because the case was deliberated in Tazewell County, only three counties directly east of Hancock County — the southernmost riverside county in Illinois that bordered the free Iowa Territory instead of the slave state Missouri. Even above the 36° 30' parallel, free Illinois courts still honored the existence of slavery. Congress ended slavery in the Upper Mississippi states and territories via the Missouri Compromise two years after Illinois had legalized indentured servitude, but the state's courts acted as if federal law did not take precedence over state law.

On appeal, Bailey argued that the promissory note was no longer valid, because Nance had become emancipated and consequently could not be sold. The Supreme Court agreed with Bailey this time, declaring that the state legally presumed an African American to be free and not available for purchase. The verdict set a new legal precedent. Any slave who previously sued for emancipation held the burden of proving his freedom. Now, from *Cromwell v. Bailey* onward, slaveholders had to provide sufficient evidence of an African American's status as a slave; otherwise, the African American was legally considered free.[72]

To be sure, *Cromwell v. Bailey* did not end the practice of slavery in Illinois. The state Supreme Court did not declare it unconstitutional, nor did it rule as illegal any of the requirements of slavery as outlined by the state constitution. Rather, the institution remained intact, and the case did not deter further slaveholders from settling in the state. The Supreme Court merely forced masters to formalize the practice with documents that explained the conditions of enslavement in no uncertain terms. The state's judges were now, at least, more willing to emancipate slaves that they had been in recent years.

Still, slaveholders occasionally won their cases in Illinois. As a result, the judicial branch of the state government not only deliberately kept some African Americans indentured but also reinforced the relevance of the slave power to Illinois politics. Slaveholder Andrew Borders, for example, used the courts to keep his African Americans under his ownership. He lived with his slaves in Randolph County, whose western boundary was the Mississippi River, which separated the county from the slave state of Missouri. According to the 1840 census, his household included five African Americans. Two of his slaves actively sought their emancipation. The judge upheld Borders' claim of ownership. Although Borders lived in the Lower Mississippi part of Illinois, the verdict affected all of Illinois, which included the Upper Mississippi counties.

In fact, members of the Upper Mississippi communities of Illinois figured significantly in Borders' case. An antislavery Presbyterian minister named John Cross was indicted in 1844 for preventing the slaveholder from retaking his slave Susan and for secretly quartering her at his home in Knox County, which was the direct southeastern neighbor of Mercer County, Illinois—an Upper Mississippi county. When authorities eventually apprehended Borders' fugitives and the Reverend Cross, the officers had found their suspects at Cross' house. While in prison Cross used his experiences to promote abolition. Later that year in the periodical *Western Citizen*, he wrote a vivid memoir of his treatment in jail. Its popularity led other periodicals to reprint it, such as *Voice of Freedom*, *Liberator*, and the Valparaiso, Indiana, *Ranger*. The Borders case marked one of the first times that slavery in the Upper Mississippi influenced the abolition movement on a national scale.[73]

In *Jarrot v. Jarrot*, the Illinois Supreme Court ruled in December 1845 that an African American could sue in courts and that all indentured servitude by African Americans was illegal. The latter point represented a shift in the state's interpretation of federal law ever since the days of "Illinois Country." The descendant of a slave sued his French master for wages. The lower court decided against the slave, but the state Supreme Court reversed the lower court's decision. After nearly six decades of politicians arguing that the pre-ordinance settlers had the legal right to keep their slaves, the court ruled that the prohibition of slavery in the sixth article of the ordinance was retroactive and that the law freed the property of French and British slaveholders of the former Northwest Territory from before 1787 as well as the human chattel of U.S. slaveholders from that year onward. The state government showed how dramatically the antislavery population had wrested power from proslavery forces by beginning to legally dismantle the institution that its own constitution had sanctioned when Illinois gained statehood.[74]

Three years later the state revised its constitution and further documented the legal demise of African American slavery. The 1848 constitution banned both "slavery" and "involuntary servitude" in nearly every context. The new law only allowed for the practices to continue "as punishment for crime, whereof the party shall have been duly convicted." Thus, with slavery transformed into a penal exercise, the judicial system now exclusively possessed the right to enslave, and convicted criminals were the only eligible potential slaves. Private citizens no longer could legally enslave or indenture anyone.

The outcome of the court case did not bring African American servitude to an immediate end in Illinois. Rather, masters continued to bring slaves into a few isolated areas of the Upper Mississippi portion of the state for over a decade. Few people lived in these locations, and some the slaveholders who moved there helped contribute to the growth and development of riverside counties and towns. As a result, they became indispensable to their new communities, and their slaving went unchallenged.

In the summer of 1850, John Atchison died of cholera. He was eulogized as "a fine business talent," "frank, generous, and amiable," and "the most obliging Captain of a boat, and the most patient of delays of any commander of a water craft, since the days of Capt. Wouter Van Twiller." A St. Paul newspaper remembered him as "always the first to greet us in the Spring ... with his little brass band, whose music echoed upon our waters, whenever that figure head of Mary, the Highland lassie, showed its face around the bend at Pig's Eye." Atchison's brother Mark commanded the *Highland Mary* for a final trip before the vessel left the Mississippi for good. Atchison's widow and children remained in Galena but gave quarter in their home to a European American man from Illinois instead of an African American slave girl or slave boy.[75]

By 1850 Hancock had replaced Jo Daviess as the dominant slaveholding county of northwest Illinois. Masters left the latter county as the mining industry in Galena went into sharp decline. They had brought slaves to the city three decades earlier in order to have a workforce for the mines. With the industry gone, owners had no reason to bring more bonded African Americans there. In the meantime, other nearby locations such as the city of Dubuque, Iowa, began to draw people away from Galena. Ironically, with the advent of steamboat travel, Galena had served as an important hub city, serving as a connection to vessels traveling as far north as Minnesota Territory or as far south as Missouri. By the 1850s more people sailing upriver from the South bypassed Galena for even more northern cities like St. Paul.[76]

Slavery survived in Hancock County partly because of the county's smallness. It had no city as major as Galena, nor was it a thriving port county like Jo Daviess. As a result, newcomers trickled into Hancock, as opposed to the droves that had come to Jo Daviess, and Hancock's slaveholders did not have to worry about a mass of antislavery migrants drawing attention to the continuation of slavery. On the other hand, even if abolitionists had done so, most local slaveholders adhered to the state constitution's regulations. Unlike Jo Daviess at its mining peak in the 1820s, Hancock had an overwhelming majority of female slaves, and a significant percentage was under ten years old. As a result, the servants fell within the age requirements of the state for indentured servitude.

One of the main differences between Hancock and Jo Daviess concerning slavery was that the former county consistently practiced a feminized version of the institution throughout the antebellum period. Because of the mining that masters wanted their workers to perform, they tended to bring male slaves instead of female ones to the latter county. In Hancock County, however, at least 75 percent of the servants were women. The masters did not require intense physical labor from their workers. No mining industry existed in that county as in Jo Daviess, nor did Hancock depend on a plantation economy as in the South. In addition, due to the absence of military posts, the owners did not call upon their servants to assist in military campaigns. Also, the slaveholders who came to Hancock had operated small farms in the South and knew how to do the same in Illinois. As a result, the bonded African American women who accompanied them largely performed domestic labor for the masters' families.

The masters brought slavery to Hancock County largely in order to maintain a lifestyle of African American service at home, not to have slaves work in mines. Many of them had received their "mammies" as gifts from the southern communities they departed for the Upper Mississippi. Residents of a migrant slaveholder's hometown pooled their money to purchase a female slave for the traveler, because they wanted him and his family to have some part of their southern lifestyle in the Midwest. Most of the Hancock migrants came from Virginia, Kentucky, and Maryland.[77]

Some members of the Grove family of Virginia migrated to Hancock County, and at least one of them brought a slave there. Samuel Grove brought an African American girl named Elizabeth when he moved to Hancock in 1835 with his wife and children and his son-in-law Jacob Brumback. Upon arriving, Grove and Brumback then bought farms in St. Mary's. By the 1850 census, Elizabeth still lived in the Grove household and worked for the family. That census was the first in which all free members of a household appeared by name, unlike the restriction to only the head of the household by name in previous censuses. However, in the Midwest, even slaves appeared by name in 1850, because the free states and territories did not have the South's separate slave schedule for masters to simply mark slaves by color, age, and sex. As of that year, she had yet to possess a surname, and her owners did not pass on the Grove name to her; the census simply identified her by her first name only — a common fate for slaves of the Upper Mississippi.[78]

The Swope family practiced slavery in a manner that blended Illinois' unique laws about servitude with traditional southern master-slave relations. The Swopes came from Kentucky to Hancock County during the 1840s. In 1850 they kept a nine-year-old African American girl from their home state. As a juvenile servant, she fell within the state's age requirements for indenture. However, she had similar issues of identity with the Groves' slave, Elizabeth. The name of the Swopes' slave in that year's census was Esther; no surname appeared with her first name.

Meanwhile, the Pierson family of Kentucky shared very little about the African American male slave who lived with them. The census did not identify Solomon, the bondsman, with a surname; nor was he given an age. The census merely divulged his first name and his birthplace of Virginia.

Well into the mid–1850s, new slaveholders kept coming into Hancock. Alfred Dickerson of Maryland brought his family and slave to the county at that time. The Dickersons' ownership of their Virginia-born servant, Letitia Laws, not only violated the new ban on slavery but would have defied the earlier laws of indenture. Laws was over forty years old at the time of her arrival — well beyond the legal limit of enslavement at the teenage years. The isolation of the county and the prestige of the slaveholders, however, likely kept abolitionists from effectively pressuring the family to emancipate their servant. Alfred, for example, was a man of means, owning $1,000 in real estate by 1860. Also, one of his female relatives in Maryland married a U.S. senator.[79]

The isolation of Illinois' counties along the Upper Mississippi fell away when transportation technology improved in Illinois in the 1850s. As more people outside of northwestern Illinois gained access to that part of the state, the area came under greater scrutiny. Some isolated cities rapidly declined, for example, when railroads emerged in northwestern Illinois. Galena lost business to Chicago.

In contrast to slavery's decline in Jo Daviess because of Galena's failing industry, the institution disappeared in Rock Island County as a result of a transportation-driven population boom. Work began in the 1850s on a railroad connecting Chicago to Rock Island. Its completion in 1854 turned Rock Island into a hub county not unlike Galena's role as a hub city. Chicagoans who wanted to travel to Minnesota Territory, for example, could now ride the rails to Rock Island and then take a steamboat upriver from that county. The influx of Midwesterners into the county made it less isolated than before, and African American servitude fell out of favor there as the county proved it could thrive without bonded African American labor.[80]

Although slavery in northwestern Illinois had spread beyond Jo Daviess to a few other counties along the Mississippi, fewer people were involved in the practice than before. The institution had diminished sharply from its peak in the 1820s, when state officials, the French, and southern miners dominated it. The wealthy and influential masters abandoned the practice as the politics of the state changed, and many of them retained their power as a result. By this time the remaining slaveholders were migrant yeomen who hid with their mammies in sparsely populated counties in order to maintain some semblance of their southern lifestyle without facing prosecution for having broken antislavery laws. Illinois, however, was not alone in winding down slavery in the Upper Mississippi. Wisconsin, its neighbor to the northwest, took as long to do so but for different reasons.

CHAPTER THREE

Miners and Soldiers:
Slavery in Wisconsin

In 1818, when Illinois became a state, part of it remained a territory — renamed the Western Division of Michigan Territory. As with the rest of the Upper Mississippi, Western Michigan struggled with the question of whether to allow slavery. It, however, became a strong antislavery land, and communities across the territory intensely and successfully resisted efforts by southern migrants to institutionalize slavery there. Although the small number of slaveholders in the territory retained the power to keep their slaves in the Upper Mississippi for decades, the antislavery sentiment kept new masters and mistresses from entering the territory with their slaves.

As the 1820s began, Western Michigan hosted very few slaveholders, in comparison to the number of those in Illinois. The new territory was not much different from the others of the Upper Mississippi in that federal appointees of slaveholders largely contributed to the proslavery sentiment that lingered in Western Michigan after the earlier French settlers had relocated. Also, as in Illinois, the proslavery migrants in the new territory were among the wealthiest and most politically powerful settlers in the Upper Mississippi. Some prominent dynasties of slaveholders called the southwest part of the territory (especially Grant County) home. The lead mines that southern migrants had first forced their slaves to excavate in 1822 continued to fill with unfree laborers for at least the next two decades. Illinois, however, was closer to the South than Michigan was, and fewer slaveholders migrated to Michigan than to Illinois.

One main reason for the absence of masters and slaves was the potential for conflict with the indigenous peoples. In late June 1827, Western Michigan was the scene of violence, and African Americans were among the casualties. Four members of the Ho-Chunk tribe — two of them named Red Bird and Wekau — sailed by canoe to Prairie du Chien, which had a sizable Creole

59

population. Just outside the town, they entered the home of one of the Cre-
oles— Red Bird's acquaintance Registre Gagnier. His mother was African, and
his father was French. The indigenous visitors fellowshipped and dined with
him, his European wife, their two children, and their servant, Solomon Lipcap. Then, suddenly, Red Bird killed Gagnier with a gunshot to the breast
and shot Lipcap dead, and Wekau scalped Gagnier's eighteen-month-old
daughter. Gagnier's wife grabbed a gun and aimed it at Wekau as she escaped
to Prairie du Chien with her ten-year-old son. The Ho-Chunk members then
escaped. Rescuers later found the daughter alive and successfully helped preserve her life.[1]

African Americans also participated in the conflict that ensued immediately following Gagnier's killing. Red Bird and Wekau met with at least thirty-
five other Ho-Chunk members by the mouth of the Bad Axe River. A few
days later they attempted an attack upon keel-boats bringing provisions to
U.S. troops at Fort Snelling. As the *Oliver H. Perry* came within thirty yards
of the shore, rifle shots fell upon the deck. The keel-boat crew and the indigenous people battled for hours, but the sailors kept the keel-boat afloat and
successfully sailed downstream. Red Bird himself was captured and died in
prison within one year. One of the few U.S. casualties of the attack was an
African American man named Peter. He died of a wound that had destroyed
one of his legs.[2]

Most of the southern families who settled in the southwest corner of
Western Michigan brought personal or house servants with them. One of
these was George Wallace Jones, whose father, John Rice Jones, was an advocate of extending slavery to Illinois. The younger Jones settled at Sinsinawa
Mounds, and had a considerable establishment where slaves were employed.
He was the first delegate to Congress from Wisconsin Territory and was a
well-known statesman of his time.[3]

George Wallace Jones once discussed fellow slaveholder Henry Dodge's
humane treatment of his slaves with a fellow congressman. He recalled to
Indiana senator Jesse Bright an incident in 1827, in which Dodge, his sons
and his slaves were to have cordelled a keel boat from southeast Missouri—
south of St. Louis— up the Mississippi to Galena's lead mines. "I overtook
him once early in the morning, between Dodgeville, Wisconsin, and Galena,
driving two ox-teams of five yoke each, to wagons loaded with lead," Jones
started. "I was on horseback, and sometime before I came up to him heard
him cracking his whip and hallooing to his oxen. When I remonstrated with
him for not making Joseph, his negro-slave, drive one of the teams, he replied:
'Joseph is broken down driving through the deep snow.' On the top of the
wagon was their bedding, blanket, and buffalo robes."[4]

Kentuckian John Hawkins Rountree came from a family of slaveholders.
He had spent his entire childhood in Warren County, Kentucky, but his rel-

atives practiced slavery in other areas besides Warren. Rountrees owned slaves all over the South. The masters of the family lived in the coastal states like the Carolinas, Deep South states like Georgia, Alabama and Mississippi, and Upper South states like Missouri and Tennessee. John Rountree was not even unique among his relatives in traveling to the Midwest. As he moved to Wisconsin, other Rountrees relocated to Illinois.

When he moved to the Upper Mississippi, Rountree continued to surround himself with African American slaves. Moreover, the slave labor facilitating the lead-mining business he eventually started in Galena became the foundation of his income in Western Michigan, for the mines made him rich and allowed him to expand into other business ventures. He moved to Montgomery County, Illinois, in 1824 and became deputy sheriff and then sheriff. At the age of twenty-one, he was elected sheriff of Montgomery County, which office he held until 1827, when, with several others, he arrived at the Galena lead mines with ox-teams. While living in a log cabin in Platteville, he facilitated his mining business with some success. In 1828 he built the first lead-smelting furnace in Grant County, Michigan Territory, while remaining in the mining business for many years.

From his success of his business came political opportunities. In part, the weak enforcement by the Jackson administration of the ban against slavery in the Midwest contributed to Rountree's rise to prominence. Around this time Lewis Cass, justice of the peace for Iowa County, nominated him for his first public office. Later, on March 10, 1829, W. S. Barny, postmaster-general of the United States, appointed him postmaster at Platteville. In 1831 he started a weekly mail route from Galena by Platteville to Prairie Du Chien. By this time he had already started practicing the peculiar institution in Michigan Territory, but he remained in a federal office despite his violation of a federal law.[5]

Rountree not only held slaves in the Upper Mississippi but also bought them there, too. His selection of humans, however, demonstrated that he had no interest in employing them in his mines. Rather, they had greater potential as his personal servants. In May 1830, while briefly in Galena, he purchased two African Americans from James W. Stephenson: a mulatto named Maria and her eighteen-month-old son, Felix. The new master paid three hundred dollars for both people. Despite the scarcity of slaves in the Midwest, Rountree received a low offer for them. With one of the unfree laborers as a woman and the other too young to work, they had very little market value outside of domestic labor.[6]

Two counties in Michigan Territory — Iowa and Crawford — attracted southern slaveholders. Those coming to the former county were entrepreneurs in the lead mining business. Iowa County additionally benefited from its position as the direct northwestern neighbor of Jo Daviess County, Illinois — the dominant mining location of the Upper Mississippi. Many people who had lived in Galena in the 1820s to work the mines relocated to Iowa County within a decade. The choice of men for upriver enslavement meant that the masters intended for them to perform intense physical labor but not to the extent that the owners wanted the reproduction of slaves for the purpose of maintaining a labor force for longer than one generation. Both William Malden and John Parkinson owned two male slaves each in Iowa County in 1830. James Morrison did have one female slave, but he relied more on male labor; he held five male slaves in Iowa County. Federal appointments, meanwhile, brought people to Crawford. All three counties were located by the Mississippi River in the southwest corner of the territory. As a result, they had the closest proximity to the slaveholding states of the South. Although Missouri was logistically closer than Kentucky to the territory, the majority of the territory's slaveholding migrants had come from Kentucky.

James H. Gentry owned two male slaves in Iowa County, Michigan Territory, in 1830. Gentry was one of the first residents of the area after the War of 1812. By 1829 he was in the lead-smelting business at Mineral Point. He most likely bought his slaves long after his arrival to the territory. Most historians credit James Johnson for bringing African Americans to the upriver mining region in 1822. Therefore, if those accounts are correct, Gentry did not bring any human chattel with him upon his initial arrival but instead bought slaves only after Johnson had migrated with his slaves. Also, by bringing only young adult male laborers, Gentry brought people more likely to do the demanding physical labor of mining instead of domestic servitude typically performed by older and female servants.[7]

Before the end of the 1820s, Crawford County became the dominant slaveholding area of Michigan Territory along the Mississippi. It was merely a small portion of the wilderness that characterized the upriver region. Buffalo still grazed on the few prairie lands that existed there. Northern Crawford consisted largely of lake, river and bog, with bits of land interspersed throughout the area. As a result of the topography and the harsh winter climate of the county, the slaves that soldiers brought were restricted to performing as domestic servants or body servants; the field labor that bonded people performed in the South was not feasible in Crawford. Consequently, the plantations of the South never materialized upriver but not because of a lack of slaves to do the work.[8]

Instead of plantations the environment of the Crawford slaves consisted of a fort and some trading posts. The servants were likely to interact with a diverse array of people in the county, whether indigenous tribespeople, European American settlers, or French Canadian trappers. The African Americans also became exposed to a different culture than what existed in the South, except perhaps for Louisiana. The language and civilization of upriver counties like Crawford blended French, English, and indigenous influences, not unlike the similar elements comprising Creole in southern counties such as Orleans, Louisiana.[9]

A slave who was bilingual in both English and an indigenous language was worth tremendous value. On at least one occasion, a slave's possession of that skill contributed to his liberation. In late 1835, the Rev. Alfred Brunson of Pennsylvania began missionary work on the Upper Mississippi, starting at Galena, Illinois, in September before moving upriver to Rock Island, Illinois, and arriving at Prairie du Chien in November. At Fort Crawford he was unprepared for his missionary work, especially because of his ignorance about the indigenous languages of the area. He soon, however, learned of an African American slave named Day at nearby Fort Snelling, who knew the Sioux language. Brunson accepted the soldier's offer of $1,200 for the slave. The minister then successfully raised the money via donations and purchased Day. Brunson then acquired Day's emancipation papers.[10]

Because Brunson needed Day as an interpreter, the clergyman's motives for freeing the slave were not entirely altruistic. Brunson still wanted Day to work for him but not in the context of a master-slave relationship. Still, the missionary's actions smacked of paternalism, especially after the lack of fruit the work arrangement bore. Day did not perform his job of interpreting well, and Brunson had no use for him as a result. The minister considered the money he spent on Day's freedom a loss. Brunson remained bitter about his misadventure with Day for years, and the reverend's critics made sport of the incident for a long time afterward, as well.[11]

African American slave migrants shared some commonalities with the indigenous of the Midwest. Just as slaves tended to live in small, poorly-constructed housing, the Ho-Chunk and other tribes resided in single-room huts made out of logs. However, the indigenous peoples built their homes as kinds of forts against both potential enemies and dangerous winter weather. In addition, just as many African Americans retained religious and cultural practices despite having been removed from the African continent, some of the indigenous peoples practiced their own religious beliefs. Some of them expected a relative to die if a rooster crowed at sunset, and they worried about the bad luck a rabbit could bring to a hunter if it hopped in front of him from right to left.[12]

Andrew Jackson was president of the United States at this time. Consequently, his decisions about which soldiers to assign to the Upper Mississippi and where in the region to station them dramatically influenced whether the land would become friendly or hostile to slavery. President Jackson's choices to assign slaveholders meant that at least during his tenure in office, slavery was acceptable by virtue of the servicemen's popular sovereignty. His own ownership of slaves while leading the nation made more likely his support of the expansion of slavery into the Upper Mississippi.

The ambiguity concerning slavery in Prairie du Chien reflected the status of the mission's commanding officer — Col. Zachary Taylor — as a slaveholder. He and his wife were unique among Upper Mississippi slaveholders in that their slaves performed agricultural labor, in contrast to the domestic work that most slaves in the new land performed. The Taylors brought two domestic slaves from the Louisville, Kentucky, to Wisconsin Territory when the president had appointed him to supervise military defense against the Ho-Chunk. The names of their slaves were Will and Sally, and they assisted Taylor's wife in her household duties. She directed them to help her skim milk and feed chickens, among other chores.[13]

Antoine Grignon's recollection of one of Taylor's slaves suggested that the servant had some agency in determining his reputation at the fort. In Grignon's presence, at least, Taylor's slave decided to forego the standard behaviors of docility and amiability. "I'll never forget his negro servant, whose skin was as black as tar," Grignon remembered. "I first saw him when I was a youngster some seven years old, and was nearly frightened out of my wits, and ran home as fast as my trembling limbs could carry me. My! but I was afraid of that black man, as I called him." As the slave learned of Grignon's fear, the servant made a sport of it by deliberately scaring him. Grignon said, "He used to take delight in frightening me when he found how afraid I was of him." The servant's status as a slave of a soldier in a remote Upper Mississippi fort enabled this interplay with the young Grignon. The great value of the servant's labor to Taylor in an area with few slaves almost ensured his employment. On the other hand, Taylor could take solace in not only being armed but also being surrounded by other armed troops; by outnumbering and out-arming the servant, any chance of slave revolt on his part was highly unlikely.[14]

In 1829 President Jackson appointed another slaveholder to Fort Crawford at Prairie du Chien. In a sense the slaveholder — a young solider named Jefferson Davis — was an appropriate choice. He constituted part of a new generation of slaveholders — a generation that saw slavery as migratory across regions of the United States. As a child he was acquainted with the slaves his father owned at home in Mississippi. During Jefferson's youth the country expanded with the Louisiana Purchase, which created the possibility for the founding of more slave state. Also, he had seen the first steamboats as a boy in New Orleans, which meant that he had watched people bring slaves aboard and therefore take slavery with them. Then, while alongside the Upper Mississippi at Fort Crawford in the late 1820s and early '30s, he witnessed the voyages of the first upriver boats. However, he owned only one slave — his first — at the time of his appointment to Fort Crawford, and that slave was a recent acquisition.[15]

Moreover, although the slave was in the Davis family for a while, Jefferson indirectly owed his personal acquisition of the slave to his military appointment. He had just finished his studies at West Point in 1828. The summer after his graduation, he left for his brother Joseph's home, in Warren County, Mississippi, where he experienced his first vacation in seven years. Their father had recently died, and their older siblings subsequently scattered to new locations along the Mississippi with their inheritances. Only their mother remained at the family home in Wilkinson County.[16]

The Davis family had no slaves bearing the Davis surname. Jefferson's brother Joseph had bought slaves bearing the surnames Montgomery, Pemberton, and Jones at public auc-

President Andrew Jackson, whose appointments of slaveholders to territorial governments helped strengthen Upper Mississippi slavery. Courtesy Library of Congress.

tion; the Davises were too new in the slave trade to have their own surnamed slaves. Joseph — the custodian of his brother's portion of the inheritance — chose a particular African American slave to accompany the solider. He chose a young male slave named James Pemberton to be at Jefferson's "beck and call." Pemberton and Davis had played together as children on father Samuel Davis' plantation, but now the slave served his playmate-turned-master.[17]

Joseph's pairing of his brother with Pemberton was also appropriate because of the absence of a significant slave population in Prairie du Chien. The slave was accustomed to service while traveling, for had accompanied Samuel Davis on his visit to Philadelphia in 1823 and to Harford, Maryland. Meanwhile, by performing military labor in a land with few slaves, Jefferson was continuing an avoidance of African Americans that had shaped much of his existence. By the age of twenty-eight, when he left the army, he had barely spent a decade — his childhood years— in the South and Southwest. He had dealt with African Americans only in passing. Pemberton, a gift from Davis's mother when they were both boys, was the first slave with whom he developed a substantial relationship. In the years that Davis served in the free land of Prairie du Chien, he did not express discontent with his master about his continued slave status.[18]

Although traveling to the North, Davis and Pemberton had ample opportunity to meet other slaveholders and slaves. After a cold voyage aboard a riverboat up the Mississippi River to St. Louis, Davis received orders to proceed to Fort Crawford, at Prairie du Chien. Before arriving there he stayed to meet with former West Point schoolmates Albert Sidney Johnston, George W. Jones, and Thomas F. Drayton. When he reached Fort Crawford, his commanding officer was fellow slaveholder and Jackson appointee Colonel Zachary Taylor, whose two slaves were older than Pemberton.[19]

The pain of family separation that slaves experienced on auction blocks after sales also took place when a federally appointed soldier took a slave with him, away from the slave's family and community. Pemberton was married at the time that he left for Fort Crawford with Davis. Whenever writing to Jefferson, his family asked about Pemberton and remarked about how Pemberton's wife, Julia-Ann, and their son fared. The soldier's brother-in-law David Bradford once wrote to him, "[Your] Mother says Jims wife and son are in good health also Aunt Charity and all his friends."[20]

Zachary Taylor, a slaveholding soldier stationed at Fort Crawford in Prairie du Chien, Wisconsin. Courtesy Library of Congress.

For all that Pemberton and his family suffered because of his relocation, Davis benefited tremendously from Pemberton's presence. Indeed, the servant enabled the soldier not only to do his work at the fort but also to exist altogether. As part of the experience of spending winter at the fort, Davis had to perform his duty in the deep snow of the Midwest. He consequently contracted pneumonia and nearly succumbed to it. Pemberton, however, remained constantly at his master's bedside, and he later received credit for preserving Davis's life. The slaveholder's body never fully recovered.[21]

Fort Crawford's combination of wet and freezing weather that winter permanently damaged Davis's health. His worsening incapacitation forced him to give directions to others from his sick bed. Among Pemberton's new duties with Davis's illness, the slave now carried him "from bed to window" and, as the officer's wife put it, "carried the arms, the money, and everything of value possessed by his master." His loyalty and dependability to his owner endeared him to the Davises as "tender and faithful as a brother."[22]

When soldiers brought their slaves from the South to the Upper Mississippi Valley, the federal government knew it and allowed it. More importantly, the government budgeted for it, using taxpayer dollars to defray the costs involved in keeping slaves at the forts. The General Accounting Office, for example, documented each payment the paymaster distributed to Davis. Typical of the records was one of the first of Davis' tenure at Prairie du Chien, on September 30, 1829: "Brevet Second Lieutenant Jefferson F. Davis, First Infantry, acknowledges that he has received $262 from Paymaster Major David Gwynne. Amount includes pay, and allowance for one servant, for June through September 1829." The document then specifically identifies the slave: "The servant is described as 'Jas. Pemberton dark,' five feet ten inches in height." Over the years the documents varied in their descriptions of Pemberton; sometimes he was "James a Slave," and other times he was "James Pemberton a Slave."

The use of public funds for lodging Pemberton at the fort demonstrated that the federal government financially invested in the expansion of slavery. The government's budgeting for the care of a slave showed its prioritizing of the comfort of the soldiers. Also taking top priority was the safety of the soldiers and European American settlers from attacks by indigenous peoples. If a slave helped keep a soldier in good health, as Pemberton did for Davis, then the officer had a better chance of effectively defending the fort.

Moreover, the government paid money to undermine one of its own antislavery provisions. Although very few opponents of slavery lived in the slaveholding areas of Michigan Territory, they still opposed the expansion of slavery into land that they believed the Northwest Ordinance declared free. Nevertheless, the allowances for slave care for troops in the Upper Mississippi came from the taxes of slaveholders and abolitionists alike Thus, the president forced the latter group to subsidize a practice in which they not only did not believe but also abhorred.

The military's holding of slaves at Fort Crawford transcended the rank of the officer. On the high end, Col. Willoughby Morgan owned three male slaves there in 1830, according to the year's federal census. At the time he commanded the fort, in charge of the First Infantry. It was not his first assignment to the Upper Mississippi, for he had served at Fort Snelling in the 1820s. Morgan, in fact, was the officer who had led the troops whom President Monroe assigned for the protection of James Johnson at Galena, Illinois, against any possible attacks by the indigenous peoples. He survived the 1830 census by only two years, dying on April 4, 1832.[23]

Somewhat lower in rank, Captain Stephen Watts Kearny arrived at the fort in 1828. He had lived for most of his life at that point in his home state of New Jersey. Like Morgan, Kearny had spent the 1820s in forts of the Northwest but only a small amount of time at Fort Crawford. He most likely acquired human chattel while on assignment at Jefferson Barracks in St. Louis briefly in the 1820s, because the location was in a legal slave state. Nevertheless, the chattel came with him to Michigan Territory until his reassignment to St. Louis in 1830.[24]

Even after Kearny left the Upper Mississippi, he still experienced personal connections to slavery in that region. His human property returned to the South with him in enslavement. In addition, upon his arrival to his new assignment, he began working with William Clark, who had brought his slave, York, on the Lewis and Clark Expedition. Soon afterward, Kearny married Clark's stepdaughter. As a result, he established a connection to the family of another former slaveholder of the Midwest.

Surprisingly the president who allowed Kearny to bring slavery to Fort Crawford was no champion of the practice. One year before Andrew Jackson began to open the territory to further exposure to slavery, John Quincy Adams had appointed Kearny to the fort. Adams followed in his father's footsteps by avoiding the ownership of slaves; they both lived without slaves throughout their lives, not merely during their respective presidencies. By appointing Kearny, Adams demonstrated an ability to place personal feelings about slavery secondary to military pragmatism. Adams, like his predecessors, was willing to undermine the Northwest Ordinance and the Missouri Compromise to get the number of soldiers he needed to guard Fort Crawford. That willingness included the migration of slaveholding troops and their slaves.

After Kearny left, enslavement continued at the fort. William A. Read owned one male slave in Crawford County in 1830. Also, Joseph Rolette provided one of the few remaining links to the territory's recent past of French settlement. He held one female slave, most likely a domestic servant, at the fort that year. He was a successful fur trader there. He had taken on the habits of the French predecessors on the land. Moreover, his political ascendancy complicated the legality of upriver slavery. In 1821 he had begun public service in Crawford County as an associate justice, and nine years later the slaver became the county's chief justice. He therefore embodied law and order while violating the Northwest Ordinance and the Missouri Compromise. In 1831, however, he decided not to purchase a "servant maid" from Pierre Choteau. He cited the illegality of slavery in Illinois.[25]

Traveler Caleb Atwater recalled the experience of being entertained by local slaveholders while visiting them in Crawford County. Among those he saw were Col. Taylor, Joseph Rolette, and Judge T. H. Lockwood — owner of a female slave there. Atwater enjoyed the fruit of labors most likely performed by the African American slaves his hosts owned. To him the comforts he received at the masters' homes were unavailable anywhere else at Fort Crawford. "When I was very unwell from exposure, miserable water, and the worst of cookery, and worn down too by fatigue of body and mental suffering," he began, "I always found sympathy, food that I could eat, and smiles and kindness which touched my heart, in the families I have named." He especially marveled at how long the officers and their wives had lived at the fort by the time of his visit and how the wives especially could stand to live among the indigenous people, whom he hardly considered the soldiers' social equals. As he put it,

> It is an interesting sight, to see such persons located as they are, in a fort, on the very verge of civilized life, educating a family of young children. The situation of delicate females, belonging to some of the best families in the nation, reared in tenderness, amidst all the luxuries and refinements of polished society, now living in a fort, calls for our sympathy, and admiration of their fortitude, which enables them to bear with all the ills, and overcome all the difficulties attendant on their mode of living.[26]

Atwater also indirectly and reluctantly revealed that European Americans there had some sexual relations with slaves, among other groups of people. He witnessed that activity for himself at a gathering he hosted for "all the respectable part of the people in the garrison and in the village." He noted that the invited guests were inside the council house during the party and consisted of "civilized ... persons of both sexes, as polished and as refined in their manners, as well bred, and educated as well too, as any persons in the United States." From outside the building, however, "a motley group of creatures" held its own party. He identified them ethnically as "a mixed breed, and probably more mixed than any other human beings in the world; each one consisting of Negro, Indian, French, English, American, Scotch, Irish, and Spanish blood." He acknowledged that French colonization of the Upper Mississippi led to the development of that particular community of people. The Negro, therefore, was most likely a reference to any African slaves the colonists owned. In addition, his reference to the outsiders as a group revealed that the sexual encounters had taken place often enough to have produced a community of people with the multiethnic heritage that so intensely repulsed Atwater. As with others of that time period who lamented miscegenation, he failed to mention the role played by the Europeans or European Americans in the forming of the "mixed breed."[27]

Despite the probability that some of the "motley" people shared ancestors with the "civilized" and "respectable" guests, Atwater refused to recognize the former group as people. "I can scarcely call them human beings," he sneered before joking, "I should rather suspect some of them, to be a little touched with the Prairie wolf." The end of his anecdote devolved into ethnic stereo-types, unfounded accusations, and hyperbole. He argued that they possessed "the vices and faults of each and all the above named nations and animals, without even one redeeming virtue" but failed to mention a single character flaw and to which nationality or animal it belonged. Returning to the theme of Prairie du Chien as an untamed land, he lamented that "we were on the very confines of civilized and savage life." His story clearly delineated which people lived which life, in his opinion.[28]

The various ethnic groups of Michigan Territory related to one another in ways other than the sexual ones to which Atwater alluded. President Jackson specifically called upon John Rountree and other slaveholders of the territory to participate in the expansion of the United States by taking control of indige-nous lands. As a result, the slaves who accompanied them on missions con-tributed at least indirectly to the acquisition of new territory. Jackson sent Rountree, Zachary Taylor and James H. Gentry to the area now known as Madison, Wisconsin, to try to persuade the Ho-Chunk tribe not to fight alongside the Sac in the Black Hawk War. By May 23, 1832, fellow slaveholder Dodge and Colonel Henry Gratiot, sub-agent of the Winnebagoes, established a military company of fifty mounted volunteers, and Captains Gentry and Rountree commanded them. They soldiered to the head of the Four Lakes, where, on May 25, they asked the indigenous people to state their inten-tions.[29]

The indigenous people were wary of the influx of southerners. Many of Black Hawk's fighters believed that the migrants would bring with them a "horde" of African American male slaves and breed them with the Sac and Fox women. The women would then give birth to African Americans, "raising the stock of slaves to supply the demand in this country where negroes are scarce," as Taimah told William Clark in mid–1832.[30]

The Black Hawk War of 1832 and its aftermath further cemented the practice of popular sovereignty by the settlers in the Upper Mississippi River Valley for the next thirty-three years. U.S. soldiers went to the valley to fight the Sac and Fox tribes. The troops remained in forts all over the Upper Mis-sissippi for years after the war. In addition, the government established mis-sion schools for the tribes, which resulted in civilians joining the troops in migrating to the area by order of the president. As with the servicemen, some of the civilians appointed to run the missions were slaveholders.

Soldiers were not the only Jackson appointees to bring slavery into the region. From the end of the Black Hawk War in 1832 to the end of his pres-idency in 1837, his appointments populated the Upper Mississippi with slaveholders from various walks of life. Some of them served as territorial administrators such as governors. Others labored as missionaries and educators to indigenous people. One of the latter was the Rev. David Lowry, a Cumberland Presbyterian minister from Princeton, Kentucky.

The Lowrys started as an unlikely family to experience Upper Mississippi slavery and even less likely to influence it. The Reverend Lowry came from extremely humble beginnings. Records of the Cumberland Presbyterian denomination document his birth in January 1796. His parents were members of the Presbyterian Church but possessed "little of this world's treasure." His suffering continued when, at age two, his parents died within two days of one another. The new orphan went to live with strangers described by church records as "reckless" and "intemperate." He worked as a bonded laborer to "a wicked man" until reaching the age of adulthood.[31]

He improved his life through ministry from young adulthood onward. He accepted his call to Christianity at eighteen years old in a Cumberland Presbyterian camp meeting. He rose to prominence in the Cumberland Presbyterian denomination after his ordination in 1822. He ministered for the Kentucky church but also started a Cumberland Presbyterian Church in Indiana. He also worked in the academic realm, holding a professorship at Cumberland College in Princeton.

Early in his ministry, he found a helpmate in Mary Ann Jones—a woman who, despite faring better in her early years than the Reverend Lowry in his youth, shared a bond with him. She was born in Kentucky to David and Rosanna Jones in 1800. The church records describe her parents as "respectable" and proponents of "religious training and parental restraint." Both raised Mary Ann and her nine siblings well into her teenage years. Unfortunately, she, like the Reverend Lowry, lost her father at a young age but at the much older age of sixteen. Still, she found in her husband a man living as a product of the "religious training" that her parents had favored for her. They produced their first child, Sylvanus, in 1823 and then Elizabeth four years later.[32]

As the Reverend Lowry started a family, however, the impact of his years as a bonded servant remained with him. When he was born, Kentucky was a forest-filled state full of wildcats, wolves, and bears. But by 1830 more Kentucky residents possessed African slaves, and the minister was among them. In that year he helped to make sure that the state would continue to associate bonded labor with black chattel slaves so that no additional white children would have to become bonded, as he had been. While settling his family and ministering in Caldwell County, Kentucky, he joined the local American Colonization Society (ACS) branch. The organization supported the transportation of emancipated African slaves to Liberia; hundreds of them left the state of Kentucky alone. For southerners like the Reverend Lowry, the removal of freed blacks meant that the South did not have to bother with treating any members of the racial group as American citizens with the same rights as white people. By shipping the ex-slaves to Africa, the only blacks in the South would, theoretically, always be slaves.[33]

The preacher, however, demonstrated a complex stance on slavery. In 1830 the minister himself owned a female slave whose age ranged between ten and twenty-four. That same year, however, he began work as an editor of the Cumberland Presbyterian newspaper, *The Revivalist*. For several years the periodical served as an antislavery forum and featured attacks on proslavery legislation from Congress. The denomination's propaganda failed to stir the slaveholding population of Tennessee. In the South most planters were but pious but rather skeptical of religion, and the region's churches generally failed to sway the public opinion of the population.[34]

A drastic change in the Reverend Lowry's life reportedly inspired him to make a clear antislavery stand. He liberated his own slaves upon receiving orders from President Jackson to start a school for Ho-Chunk Indians in Iowa in 1833. He was well supplied for the task except in a very crucial capacity. He and his family settled near Fort Crawford. The federal government gave the Ho-Chunk a 200-acre farm in order for Lowry to instill in the tribe of hunters a love of farming. The agricultural school received six agricultural specialists, twelve oxen, twelve plows, assorted tools, and a yearly budget of $3000. The entire operation consisted of a schoolhouse, Lowry's church, and eighteen dormitories for the tribe. Despite all these provisions, the endeavor failed because the government had the impractical hope that Lowry's lessons on farming and the English language would Americanize the Indians. Even worse, he was completely ignorant of Ho-Chunk culture.[35]

The Reverend Lowry arrived at Prairie du Chien on September 7, 1833. He was excited about starting a mission in a free territory. Wisconsin Territory had no protestant church at the time. "I never saw a place where the gospel was more needed," he remarked. He expected to see no African American slaves at his mission or in the territory itself. Upon his arrival he expressed joy that "no slavery can be admitted here."[36]

Not everyone in religious circles in Wisconsin Territory shared the Reverend Lowry's stance on slavery. As he founded his mission church, debate over slavery caused serious discord. Missouri slaveholder Andrew Cochrane came to Prairie du Chien in 1833 to take charge of the construction of a new fort. His desire to worship at the Reverend Lowry's church, however, put him at odds with at least one of the parishioners. Judge Joseph Trotter Mills vowed not to attend the house of worship if a slaveholder were to worship there, too. The feud between the two did not last long, for Cochrane left the territory by the completion of Fort Crawford within a year of his arrival.[37]

The Reverend Lowry eventually left Prairie du Chien with his family in 1834. The government pushed the Ho-Chunk westward, and the Lowrys moved with them to continue the mission work. He had contributed significantly to the religious culture of Prairie du Chien by successfully starting Wisconsin Territory's first protestant church. On the other hand, he could not change the proslavery politics of the town's settlers. By 1836 slaveholders still populated the town and held seventeen slaves at Fort Crawford. Thomas Street, for example, owned one female slave in Crawford County in 1836, as did the aforementioned Judge Lockwood.[38]

Missouri helped facilitate the beginning of the demise of slavery in Western Michigan, just as the state had done for Illinois. A Missouri court decided on a case concerning slavery in the territory, not unlike *Winny v. Whitesides*. Moreover, the court received the case about Western Michigan's slavery — *Rachel v. Walker* — in 1830, only two years after the Illinois case. Rachel had been a slave in Missouri, and her master — an army officer named Stockton — had purchased her there. Upon receiving an assignment to Fort Snelling, he relocated Rachel there with him, and she labored for him in bondage for one year. He then took her to Prairie du Chien for another of his appointments, and she worked as his slave for three years there. While there, she gave birth to her son, whom she named James Henry. Afterwards Stockton sent Rachel and James to Missouri to sell them as slaves to Joseph Klunk, who then made arrangements to sell them to slave-trader William Walker. At that point Rachel decided to sue on the grounds that her time spent in free land made her an emancipated person.[39]

The defendant claimed that he was within his legal rights to take his slave into free territory, because he served in the military while doing so. It was a reasonable argument, considering that so many other soldiers brought slaves to the territory's forts. The federal government's sabotaging of its own antislavery laws led the defendant to believe that the undermining of the law served, in effect, as a proslavery law. In short, the absence of an enforced ban on slavery made legal slavery in the Upper Mississippi a *fait accompli*.

In 1834, however, the court sided with Rachel, thereby upholding *Winny v. Whitesides* in the process. The verdict marked the second time in less than a decade that a southern state — in fact, the same southern state — restricted the expansion of slavery beyond the South. The court disagreed with Walker, saying that no law mandated his enslavement of anyone. The court asked, "Shall it be said, that because an officer of the army owns slaves in Virginia, that when, as officer and soldier, he is required to take the command of a fort in the non-slaveholding states or territories, he thereby has a right to take with him as many slaves as will suit his interests or convenience?" and then answered itself, "It surely cannot be law," as if the reply were obvious and should not have caused so much confusion in the Upper Mississippi for four decades. "If this be true, the court say, then it is also true that the convenience or supposed convenience of the officer repeals, as to him and others who have the same character, the ordinance and the act of 1821, admitting Missouri into the Union, and also the prohibition of the several laws and constitutions of the non-slaveholding states."[40]

Another important aspect of the case involved James Henry. Both sides associated the status of the child with that of the mother. Walker had wanted to purchase both Rachel and James, which meant that he considered James a slave. Neither side disputed that Rachel had given birth to her son in a free territory. Nevertheless, as far as Walker was concerned, Rachel gave birth while in slavery; therefore, her child was born in bondage. Rachel, in contrast, argued that her free status by virtue of living in Western Michigan made the son she birthed there free, as well.

The court's decision also settled the issue of the status of African Americans born in territories of the Upper Mississippi. By declaring James free, the court affirmed the legality of both the Northwest Ordinance and the Missouri Compromise. His freedom under federal laws took precedence over any state that may have sought his enslavement. Rachel's victory was no small accomplishment, because the free state of Illinois had already considerably circumvented the aforementioned federal legislation. Moreover, so did the federal government, as evidenced by the executive branch's sponsorship of the upriver enslavement of York Clark and James Beckwourth. In no small irony, through *Winny v. Whitesides* and *Rachel v. Walker*, a court from a slave state arguably adhered to the existing federal antislavery laws better than the presidents from Washington to Jackson had done.

Owners of slaves bankrolled the development of new communities in Western Michigan Territory, which made their money fundamental to the economy of the southwestern part of the territory if not the entire territory itself. After the Black Hawk War, Grant County formed from western Iowa County, and the new county's residents immediately started establishing its institutions. In 1835 the residents helped Rountree build a sizable log house, in which the locals could hold suitable school sessions and county meetings. His new home had cost one hundred and ninety-four dollars to build. Meanwhile, Richard Waller started an enterprise of constructing blast furnaces. Among those several residents who invested in the business with Waller were the local slaveholders Rountree and Atchison. Waller operated as the company's general agent, leading engineer and manager because only he was experienced in the making of blast furnaces. In 1835, the company constructed not only its first furnace but also the first one in the United States for the purpose of smelting lead ore. The smelters and the miners benefited financially from the new technology. The mine extracted the whole metal, which allowed Waller and company to pay about one-third more money to the miners while spending a third more in the manufacture. In addition, the smelters spent one-fourth less of their money, which enabled them to pay even more of an advance for the mineral. Rountree and Atchison's participation ended when

Waller reorganized the operation in 1838 with a new group of partners and greater redistribution of profits to the smelters.[41]

With the help of Andrew Jackson's successor to the presidency, Rountree continued to expand his wealth in Grant to the end of the decade. On August 1, 1839, President Martin Van Buren signed a parchment land warrant for eighty acres in Western Michigan Territory — recently reorganized as Wisconsin Territory — to Waller and Rountree. After over one decade there, the latter's ownership of slaves was well documented, especially in the previous federal census. Rountree, however, received Van Buren's warrant with no strings attached; for example, he did not have to emancipate his slaves before acquiring the land. Van Buren differed from his predecessors in that he did not give an Upper Mississippi master the money to care for slaves but instead gave him the land upon which he could acquire wealth and, therefore, afford to remain in the Midwest with his slaves and keep breaking federal antislavery laws.[42]

The federal government formed Wisconsin Territory from Michigan in 1836, but the new territory was no more able to prevent slavery than any of the other territories created from the former Northwest Territory. Inconsistency among the government branches about slavery led to much of the ineffectiveness. Congress originally designated Wisconsin Territory as free through the passage of the Wisconsin Enabling Act. The legislation gave all settlers there the rights designated to them by the Northwest Ordinance. In addition, the act mandated that the laws of Michigan Territory apply to Wisconsin Territory, and the laws of the former territory prohibited slavery. The executive branch, however, immediately sabotaged the ban on the institution in the latter by appointing slaveholders to forts there. One of the appointees was Dr. John Emerson.[43]

By the time of his army appointment to Wisconsin Territory, Emerson had already spent a few years upriver with his slave Sam Blow. They had been in Rock Island County, Illinois, in the early 1830s. Still, the Fort Snelling appointment complicated Emerson's enslavement of Sam for reasons relating to the circumstances of *Rachel v. Walker*. In both situations, the families of the slaves expanded in free territory. First, the slave met his wife, Harriet, in the Upper Mississippi, showing that African American family and community, while difficult for slaves to facilitate, were neither impossible nor impractical to develop. In 1835, Harriet's master, U.S. Army officer Major Taliaferro, took her with him to his new appointment at Fort Snelling. The following year he sold her to Emerson at the fort — one of the few slave transactions to take place in Wisconsin Territory. Second, Sam and Harriet became a couple in the free territory and lived as though husband and wife although, as slaves, not legally recognized as such. Finally, they began their family in free land. Their daughter, Eliza, was born to the north of the state of Missouri.[44]

The new family went forcibly to Missouri, and the state's subsequent treatment of them as slaves showed that Missouri suffered the same inconsistency among government branches concerning slavery as the federal government did. Although the state's judicial branch had established the freedom of any African American having lived upriver, the enslavement of Emerson's laborers in Missouri demonstrated that the state's executive branch neglected to enforce the decision. In 1838 Emerson and his workers eventually parted ways. He stayed in the northwest but sent the African American family south. After the physician relocated Sam, Harriet, and their daughter, Eliza, to the slave state, they remained there as slaves over the next two decades. In that time Emerson never emancipated them, and no one intervened to argue that the doctor was violating *Winny v. Whitesides* and *Rachel v. Walker*. As a result, Sam decided to take matters into his own hands and sue his master for the liberating of his family and himself. He argued that the Northwest Ordinance and the Missouri Compromise made him free upon arrival at Fort Snelling. The case grew in importance, and in 1856, it appeared on the docket of the Supreme Court.[45]

The new territory influenced not only political developments regarding slavery but also cultural ones. As with the Northwest Territory, slavery in Wisconsin Territory served as an inspiration for literature. George W. Featherstonhaugh, an English geologist, traveled through Wisconsin Territory in 1837 and recorded his adventures. In his book *A Canoe Voyage up the Minnay Sotor*, he mentioned having seen an African American, whom he assumed was a slave, at English Prairie, on Wisconsin River. The slave accompanied lead smelter Charles L. Stephenson, a future presidential appointee to the land office at Mineral Point. Featherstonhaugh recalled that Stephenson had directed him to a hut, but the African American positioned himself by the door of the hut and built a fire to prevent his master and guest from entering.[46]

Meanwhile, the Reverend Lowry became a government employee and experienced firsthand the government's tolerance of slavery at his mission. Having relocated to Iowa, he served as an Indian agent for the Ho-Chunk Tribe. His commanding officer was Wisconsin governor Henry Dodge. Appointed by President Jackson in 1836, the fellow slaveholder from Kentucky also owned slaves in Wisconsin Territory while serving in office. He had previously brought slaves to Michigan Territory while serving as colonel of the militia there as the decade began; the census of 1830 listed nine slaves in his ownership. As a veteran of both the War of 1812 and the Black Hawk War, he had the military experience to not only command Wisconsin's army but also to handle situations involving indigenous people. His holding of slaves, in contrast, clashed with the Reverend Lowry's staunch antislavery feelings.

In addition, Dodge received favorable coverage from the local press. Like much of Illinois at the time, Wisconsin Territory had a proslavery press. The *Miner's Free Press* of Mineral Point blamed abolitionists for ruining the pacing by proslavery forces for the gradual emancipation of slaves.

Fortunately for the missionary, his new boss had no intention on keeping his human property in Wisconsin forever. Still, the new governor did not want immediate emancipation. Upon hearing of his gubernatorial appointment, Dodge promised his slaves that he would free any of them who accompanied him to Wisconsin and worked for him for the next five years. His holding of African Americans there eventually became a political liability for him. He suffered criticism from the press. Journalists of Whig Party newspapers questioned the appropriateness "for the Governor to hold slaves."[47]

Henry Dodge, a slaveholding governor of Wisconsin Territory. Courtesy Library of Congress.

Bowing to media pressure, Dodge freed his slaves—a move which now made him more similar to his antislavery agent, the Reverend Lowry. In addition to emancipation, Dodge gave each of his slaves forty acres of land and a yoke of oxen in order to make a living. He held no hard feelings towards his former property. Moreover, his ex-slaves continued to visit him and his family for many years afterward.

Still, slavery persisted in Wisconsin into the 1840s, albeit on an extremely small scale. By that time Dodge had believed that a slave became free upon entering the territory. He mistakenly thought that the territory itself had no slaves in the new decade. His acquaintance Edward Mathews informed him that as of the 1840 census, eleven of the territory's 30,945 residents were slaves—a decrease from the seventeen held in Fort Crawford alone four years earlier. The governor then remarked that lawyers had told him that a slave in Wisconsin was not free until his freedom was legally recorded. The lawyers to whom Mathews had spoken, meanwhile, had said that anyone in the territory who held slaves did so in defiance of the law. The confusion of the executive officer over whether slavery legally existed in the territory under-scored the ambiguity of federal law towards the practice there. He could not effectively enforce a ban if he did not conclusively know whether a ban existed.[48]

By 1840 the culture of slavery in Wisconsin had dramatically shifted away from its military roots. No slaves appeared in that year's census for Crawford County, which meant that soldiers no longer kept bondservants there. Now Grant County was the undisputed center of slavery in the territory. As a result nearly all of the slaveholders possessed considerable wealth. The census recorded Edward Laffor, John Rountree, Jonathan Craig of Virginia, and Thomas Parish as the county's masters that year.

Iowa County had only one slaveholder in residence that year — a far cry from the sixteen that had lived there ten years earlier. On the other hand, Grant County formed from the western portion of the original Iowa County in the mid–1830s. Consequently Grant acquired nearly all of the slaveholders that had formerly belonged to Iowa. The one holdover was Philip W. Thomas, who held a male slave there. Whereas Grant welcomed enslaved miners and Crawford kept soldiers' servants, the institution in Iowa County did not pos-sess as distinct an identity and never developed one for the remainder of the antebellum period.

One of those slaveholders of the new decade served in the territorial government alongside Dodge. The Rev. James Mitchell, a minister of the Methodist Episcopal Church in Platteville, also served as chaplain of the ter-ritorial legislature and, therefore, as a government official. He kept two slave girls that he had brought from the South upon his appointment in 1841, how-ever. He did not claim to own them but merely to hold them in Wisconsin. He professed that his wife actually owned the slaves. In addition, she was fol-lowing family tradition, for her brother was a fellow slaveholding migrant — John Rountree.[49]

As with Dodge's case, an outcry soon rose over the Reverend Mitchell's practicing of slavery. The fury of Platteville's residents owed as much to his selling of his slaves as his ownership of them. When complaints arose about his holding of the slave girls in Wisconsin, he took them back to the South and sold them. Mathews confronted Mitchell and his wife in December 1841, reminding them, "It is a thousand dollars' penalty, madam, for any one to hold slaves in our Territory." The couple, however, was unmoved. Platteville's constable, Anthony Laughlin, advertised in print his fundraising efforts for the fee to send a lawyer to St. Louis to emancipate Mitchell's slave Alice, whom he had left there, but the constable's efforts were unsuccessful. Mean-while, the deacon of the town's Presbyterian Church found the captain of the steamboat that had taken Alice south, and he confirmed that the minister had ordered him to leave her in St. Louis.[50]

Mitchell soon learned that antislavery sentiment in Wisconsin Territory extended well beyond Platteville. An antislavery society begun in the city of Racine in 1840 grew territory-wide two years later. Then, the Methodist denomination transferred Mitchell out of Platteville in 1843. The following year the Territorial Anti-Slavery Society examined his case. He testified that he had lost at most $15,000 by relinquishing his own property in slaves upon leaving Missouri. His father-in-law, however, gave two slaves to his wife upon her departure with the clergyman, but she promised to return them to her father if she had to separate from them. Mitchell admitted to sending the slaves south individually, and he bragged, "I would do so again, to the tenth time." Moreover, he claimed that they had wanted to return there. The Rock River Conference of his denomination exonerated him from guilt in 1847, but by the end of the decade, he had returned to Missouri.[51]

In 1840, Rountree held two slaves in Grant County—a male between the ages of ten and twenty-four and a female between fifty-five and one hundred years old. The bonded young man was arguably the more monetarily valuable of the two slaves. He fit in the age bracket that most buyers of male slaves desired. The laborers at that point had the maturity to work but enough youth to serve the same master for at least one generation if not two. On the other hand, the female slave had considerably less monetary worth. She had passed the age of childbirth, which meant that she no longer had the capability of reproducing Rountree's workforce. Also, at her age, she had less stamina and strength than most slaves of her coworker's age bracket. Masters typically did not have old slaves—and certainly did not bring them to the Midwest—unless they had performed faithful service for the household or the family for many years. Rountree's female slave was, most likely, this kind of person, because the household called her Aunt Rachel. She was born in Missouri, instead of Kentucky like her master. Thus, he probably bought her at some point after he had migrated from the South to the Upper Mississippi.

Although Rountree owned slaves in an increasingly abolitionist territory, his political career ascended. The success had less to do with his slaving than with his military and entrepreneurial contributions to Wisconsin. After fighting in the Black Hawk War, he became chief justice of the Iowa County court. He then became the judge of probate in the county in 1836. Two years later he began serving on the territorial council. In 1844 he was a delegate for the Whig Party's national convention, where the party nominated its presidential candidate. Then in 1847 he won election to the Constitutional Convention but also started an unsuccessful campaign on the Whig ticket for lieutenant governor. He was elected to the Wisconsin Senate in 1849 and served two years.[52]

Rountree had become such a formidable presence in Platteville that he attracted fellow slaveholders to the town. Many of them were southerners like himself. Others came from Illinois. For example, Asa Edgerton Hough, a steamboat captain, kept five slaves—a woman and her two daughters and two sons from the late 1830s into the 1840s. In Wisconsin, his holdings of slaves had doubled from the number he had possessed in the South, for he had owned two women in Waterford, Loudoun County, Virginia, in 1830. America was the woman he held in Grant County, and Felix was one of her sons.[53]

As in the rest of the United States, Wisconsin settlers developed standards of beauty that depended to an extent upon skin color. Not everyone in Grant had come from the South. Therefore, whatever ideas that many European American locals had about African Americans did not come from any long-standing contact with them. Still, they were introduced to the concept— whether through literature, informed adults, uninformed adults, or initial contact with slaves—of dark skin as ugly. Hough's slave Felix, according to resident Elizabeth Lyons Davies, was "dark and homely, like his mother, America," but his brother was "not very dark and really handsome."[54]

A European American's acknowledgment of a slave's beauty, however, did not lessen the owner's claim to that person. Hough took America and her entire family out of Wisconsin and back down south. Their departure devastated many in the community. As a girl, Elizabeth Lyons Davies of British Hollow heard a mother and her sons crying one night as Hough rushed them from Potosi down the Mississippi River to the South. Many years later her memory of that night had not waned. She wrote as an adult, "That midnight cry is not yet forgotten; it helped make my father, mother, and myself abolitionists. The next morning we heard that poor 'Merica and her children had been taken South." Adding to the tragedy was the stifled potential for long-term social interaction of European Americans and African Americans there, for two of Hough's slaves were Davies' schoolmates.[55]

Contrary to the Reverend Lowry's wish against the existence of slavery in Prairie du Chien, the institution continued to survive there through the 1840s. Moreover, the slaveholder-slave relationships had grown more violent than in the previous decade, not unlike the physical dangers of slavery in the southern states. In 1845 a female slave was whipped to death at Fort Crawford, and her body was thrown into the Mississippi River. The mighty waterway, which had just begun to give life to previously isolated areas in Wisconsin Territory, now served as the final resting place for at least one of the slaves it had brought.[56]

Eventually, anti-slavery sentiment grew in Wisconsin to the extent that it influenced how owners treated their slaves. Allen Wolfolk brought a female slave from Missouri with him to the territory, and she labored as his servant for years. He attempted to bring her with him on the occasion of his return to Missouri. However, because of the protest of the locals, Wolfolk returned alone.[57]

Anti-slavery sentiment, however, did not mean an absence of discrimination by European Americans against African Americans, especially in relation to political concerns. For example, many of the people opposing the extension of voting rights to African Americans were neighbors of Wisconsin Territory's slaveholders if not the slaveholders themselves. In 1846 male European American residents, whom the territory permitted to vote, refused suffrage to African Americans in a vote by nearly a 2:1 margin. In favor were 7,564 people, but 14,615 were against it. The large negative vote resulted principally from the significant presence of southern migrants, masters and ex-masters in the southwestern corner of Wisconsin, especially in Grant, Iowa and Crawford counties.[58]

Southerners were not the only migrants in opposition to the measure. In areas of the territory with heavy German American concentrations, the residents killed the measure. The resistance of this ethnic group typified attempts by new European arrivals to become accepted by longtime residents as fellow U.S. citizens. Ethnic groups such as Irish Americans and German Americans intensely fought against the political and economic advancement of African Americans. Many immigrants rioted in New York, for instance, as a means of demonstrating opposition to abolition.[59]

The politicians deciding on the political fate of local African Americans offered viewpoints largely based on ignorance about the ethnic group they were discussing. Some supporters of African American suffrage saw the denial of the extension of the right to vote to African Americans as a means for abolitionists to gain traction towards the abolition of slavery. Legislator Warren Chase supported African American suffrage, despite his lack of involvement in the abolition movement and the absence of African Americans from the area he represented. He believed that if the local government excluded only African Americans, the abolition movement would quickly rise in Wisconsin.[60]

Similarly, opponents of African American suffrage operated out of ignorance about the ethnic group. Some of the naysayers, for example, cited negative ethnic stereotypes to support their positions. One legislator believed that suffrage would cause runaway slaves to leave the South in droves and overwhelm Wisconsin residents. He also worried that runaways en route to Canada would instead remain in Wisconsin because of suffrage. His desire to keep African Americans in the South came from his belief in the divine separation of Africans from Europeans, interpreting "that those whom God had joined together no man should put asunder" as a call to disenfranchise as well as to segregate. He referred to troubles in New York as his proof, noting that every African American there was a thief, and every African American woman committing worse acts. He preferred the colonization of African Americans elsewhere, instead of their equal treatment under the law with European Americans in the United States.[61]

Meanwhile, slavery persisted, and Grant County remained the dominant participant of the institution in the state. The number of slaves and slave-holders dwindled to less than half their numbers from one decade earlier. In contrast to the people who had owned slaves there in 1840, Rountree was the only Grant County slaveholder from that year's census to still keep an African American at home ten years later. In addition, he now held one African American instead of two. His slave's listing in the 1850 census revealed very little about her. Because she was in a free state and was consequently listed as a free person instead of a number on a slave schedule, the census revealed more information about her than a slave schedule from a slave state would have disclosed. She was listed as black, sixty-five years old, someone who had not attended school, and illiterate. However, her name was only Rachel. The Rountrees gave her no surname, showing that she still belonged to them and that she, as an African American, was fundamentally different from them.

Only one new master joined Rountree in the enslaving of African Americans in Grant during the 1840s, but he brought two slaves with him. Since Rountree had only Rachel for a servant, the new slaver became the primary slaveholder of the county. Nevertheless, Tyree Oldham had quite a bit in common with Rountree. They both came from the same southern state, for Oldham had moved with several members of his family from Kentucky to Wisconsin in the mid–1840s. When he had lived in Madison County, Kentucky, he owned two slaves. When he later moved to Falmouth in the 1810s, he owned twenty more. Also, like Rountree, Oldham belonged to a prominent Kentucky family. His relatives were acquainted with Henry Clay and Daniel Boone. In addition, Oldham and Rountree were wealthy.

In Grant he tried to recreate some aspects of his southern lifestyle. He built a house reminiscent of the Greco-Roman plantation homes of the South. More importantly, he and his wife, Mary, kept two slaves—Tom and Eliza—who shared their surname as well as their Kentucky roots. The Oldhams probably took Tom and Eliza with them from Kentucky to Wisconsin when they left home. As with Rountree, Oldham owned slaves of completely different monetary values in the slave market. Although Tom was at the very marketable age of seventeen in 1850, he suffered physical defects and received the diagnosis "idiotic" in that year's census. Eliza, on the other hand, was twelve and either near or at the beginning of her fertile period, able to bear children for at least the next twenty-five years. Thus, unlike Rountree's pair of servants, Oldham's female slave was worth more than the male one.

The presence of the Oldham slaves did not go unnoticed in the Grant community. Local citizens, however, remembered them more for their physical attributes than for their character. The people there referred to Tom primarily by his designated color—as "Black Tom." In addition to his deformity, he suffered paralysis, and his skin was dark. Eliza, on the other hand, was a "mulatto girl," but her color did not become part of her name. By bringing only two slaves to Wisconsin, Oldham was able only to maintain whatever domestic labor some of the twenty-two slaves had performed. Neither his girl nor his physically challenged man had the capability of performing strenuous field labor. Elizabeth Lyons Davies offered a brief remembrance of Tom's life as a slave in Grant: "I was often distressed at seeing Black Tom sitting on the ground, chopping wood with one hand; I think he was partially paralyzed."[62]

Oldham related to his servants in manners that typified the master-slave relationships of the South, despite their relocation to Wisconsin. Davies recalled the inferior treatment Tom had received, and she identified his skin color and enslavement as the sources of the discrimination. However, she recognized a certain degree of humanity the community had given to him despite his bondage. In a sense Oldham's relationship with Tom, as described by Davies, illustrated the dilemma slaveholders faced in discerning how to treat people as property and vice-versa. "But, though he had to work hard and was not treated like white folks," she began, "they were otherwise kind to him."[63]

Tyree's son Simpson and his nuclear family also included a slave in their household. Local resident J. W. Seaton recalled that Simpson had brought the slave with him from Missouri sometime in the 1840s and held him until his death. The junior Oldham, therefore, conducted slavery in a manner more like that of Rountree, whose local slave was Missouri-born, than Tyree's act of bringing slaves from Kentucky. In addition, by holding only one African American in the Upper Mississippi, as opposed to the multiple slaves of his relatives and neighbors, Simpson demonstrated that slavery was not crucial to his livelihood. Moreover, he apparently made a conscious decision not to be dependent on slave labor, because when he had lived in the South, he used a respectable amount of human chattel. Back in Pike County, Missouri, in 1830, Simpson had owned eleven slaves.[64]

In neighboring Iowa County, meanwhile, time had stood still throughout the 1840s. Slavery had remained unchanged there between 1840 and 1850. In the new decade, Philip W. Thomas was still the county's only slaveholder, and he still held only one slave. That person, identified in the 1850 census as George Smith, may have been the same person enslaved by Thomas in 1840. Smith and Thomas were born in the same state (Maryland), and very few people migrated from there to the Midwest.

In Trempealeau County very few African Americans resided, but some of the citizens witnessed them enter and leave the county as laborers on a regular basis. European American residents saw them working on riverboat that passed through the county up and down the Mississippi. A fugitive crew member from one of the steamers may have wandered into Trempealeau.[65]

The arrival of African Americans to La Crosse County in the 1850s demonstrated how well abolitionists had turned Wisconsin into an anti-slavery state. As a result the new residents started their lives there from a greater position of strength than previous newcomers to the state's riverside counties had enjoyed. La Crosse was among the first counties in the state to have developed an African American community whose members had not previously been enslaved there. Very few of them were born in the South. However, they came to the Upper Mississippi in freedom, which meant that the river increasingly served as a gateway for emancipation in addition to its usual transporting of slaves from owner to owner. In addition, several of the migrants traveled northwest as families— another unique aspect of the county's African Americans.

After having arrived in La Crosse, they started working. Their employment in specific positions received the approval of European American residents, and European Americans patronized the businesses. Several of the African American settlers found success as barbers. Others continued employment aboard the steamboats or performed field labor. All the jobs transcended region, which meant that both northern and southern African Americans found employment in each kind of job.

Wisconsin's slavery along the Mississippi consisted of a small, elite group of people. They did not gain a strong foothold upon the government of the state, as the slaveholders of Illinois had done. Nor did they tend to use slave labor for any locations outside of their homes, except for the mines. Wisconsin had neither land nor climate conducive for the maintenance of large plantations and certainly not for a plantation-based economy. As a result, the migrant masters attracted very few newcomers and in a short period of time. In addition, the fact that few Wisconsin slaves had started families in counties along the Upper Mississippi meant that they had not only little incentive to remain in those counties but also more agency to relocate if they desired to do so. Iowa, on the other hand, welcomed many slaveholders over two decades, although it had even more hostile policies towards African Americans than Wisconsin had enacted.

CHAPTER FOUR

Migrating Southerners: Slavery in Iowa

SLAVERY IN IOWA WAS DIFFERENT from its practice in earlier territories and states of the Upper Mississippi because the institution relied more upon nineteenth-century migrants for support than upon pre–Northwest Ordinance French settlers and presidential appointees. Hardly a European American had settled there before the 1830s. To be sure, Iowa eventually drew its share of slaveholding politicians, but they were few and far between. Rather, the territory attracted numerous southerners, many of whom were proslavery if not slaveholders themselves. Some of them practiced an informal version of popular sovereignty; when they comprised the majority of a town's or county's population, they allowed masters to bring slaves into those locations.

Iowa had the most in common with Illinois concerning the bonding of African Americans in the Midwest. Both places struggled with the slavery question for decades, especially because of their high numbers of proslavery residents. Iowa and Illinois also shared intense anti–African American feelings among their European American citizens. They manifested this animosity similarly, as well, by banning African Americans. Iowa did not have the detailed, formalized system of legal indentured servitude that the constitution of Illinois had outlined. Still, they both neglected enforcement of the Missouri Compromise by permitting slavery, and the federal government contributed to the institution in both places.

Iowa's early demographics were very similar to those of Illinois and Wisconsin. Among the first European migrants were Canadians involved in the fur trade. By the early nineteenth century, Kentuckians had also arrived. With both groups of people, slaveholding commonly took place. Following the examples of Illinois and Wisconsin, Iowa subsequently became the third *de facto* enslaving territory of the Upper Mississippi.[1]

Iowa, however, had an important fundamental difference from Illinois and Wisconsin. The latter two states were originally part of the Northwest Territory, which Congress had declared free in 1796. In contrast, Iowa was located on land in which Congress had legalized slavery. Therefore, the people who migrated there expected to be able to keep slaves not merely because of tradition but also because of legal precedent. Before the nineteenth century, the federal government had not organized Iowa as its own territory or state. Rather, it was known as part of the District of Louisiana, and a sizable proportion of its residents disagreed with how the federal government ruled it. They requested more of a say in the affairs of the district and wanted to own slaves. In response Congress changed the district into Louisiana Territory on July 4, 1805, and made no law for or against slavery, which prompted slaveholders to continue to migrate there with slaves without penalty — just as they had always done. Seven years later the lower portion of the territory became the state of Louisiana, and Congress created Missouri Territory from the upper portion.[2]

For nearly a decade, slavery remained a legal practice in Missouri Territory. Then in 1818 the people of the territory asked the federal government for Missouri's statehood. Three years later, after the passage of the Missouri Compromise, part of the territory became the slave state of Missouri. The portion of the former territory that lay above the 36° 30' parallel did not become part of the new state, because the compromise prohibited slavery in that area. Instead, the federal government disorganized that land, neither making it a new territory or a new state. Although this area was now in free land, the government's neglect of it resulted in more arrivals of masters and slaves.[3]

As part of Missouri Territory from 1812 to 1821, the future state of Iowa witnessed legal slavery by various classes of people. In addition to the settlers of poor, modest or wealthy means, federal officers of high social stature and political power brought the institution to Missouri. In addition, they did not tend to use their laborers for anything beyond domestic labor. The shift in work for the new slaves reflected how widespread European American settlement had become since the Lewis-Clark expedition. In 1812 President Madison appointed William Clark to serve as governor of the territory. In contrast to his dependence on his male slave, York, for survival in the Upper Mississippi one decade earlier, he now brought a female slave with him to Missouri Territory, and she labored for him as a house servant during his tenure. She had light skin color, and local people identified her as a mulatto. In addition, unlike York's return from Iowa to the South in slavery, the female slave eventually became free in Missouri Territory. However, she continued to live in the territory and resettled in the Upper Mississippi county of Clayton in Iowa. By doing so, she practically guaranteed a life free from recapture and re-enslavement in the South, but she no longer had access to a community of African Americans who shared her experience of bondage.[4]

Many southerners who came to live in the northern Missouri Territory stayed only temporarily. Some of them returned to the South and kept slaves there. Quite a few former residents of northern Missouri helped determine the evolution of slavery not only in the territory but also throughout the United States. Future Confederate general Robert E. Lee spent some time in the area in the 1830s. Lieutenants Simon B. Buckner, Abraham Buford and Alexander W. Reynolds also lived in the territory before defending the states that seceded from the Union. On the other hand, former Missourians captain J. J. Abercrombie from Tennessee and Lieutenant Alfred Pleasanton of Washington, D.C., later served in the Union Army. General Winfield Scott, who had served in the military in northern Missouri, later sided with the Union despite his residency in the Confederate state of Virginia. The split among former northern Missourians during the Civil War served as a lasting legacy of the neglect the federal government had given to the territory, especially in relation to the enforcement of antislavery laws after years of legal slavery there.[5]

The federal government demonstrated its apathy for the land by appointing people with proslavery beliefs to control the territory. Even after Iowa Territory finally formed in 1838, the practice continued. Like the aforementioned soldiers, many of the government appointees also lived here temporarily and returned to the South with their slaves. Robert Lucas, the first territorial governor, came from Virginia. His successor, John Chambers, although born in New Jersey in 1789, spent his life mainly in Kentucky from 1792 to his appointment in the 1840s. He brought slaves with him. When his tenure as governor ended, he returned to Kentucky with slaves and died there. Governor James Clark moved in the 1830s from his birthplace of Pennsylvania to Missouri before settling in Iowa. In addition, he was related to a slaveholding migrant, having married a daughter of another slaveholding governor — Henry Dodge of Wisconsin Territory.[6]

Individual counties followed the lead of territorial leaders in perpetuating slavery. Lee County, the county farthest southeast in Iowa, is also the southernmost county in Iowa to border the Mississippi River. Upon arriving in Lee, upriver travelers exited not only Missouri but also the South itself and crossed into the Midwest. Whenever the federal government enforced the Northwest Ordinance and the Missouri Compromise, the county became a gateway from the region of legal slavery to the land of emancipation. However, in its early years, Lee also suffered from poor enforcement of the antislavery legislation, and the institution survived for several years.

Indeed, some of the first settlers in Lee County were not only southerners but slaveholders. Richard Chaney of Maryland, for example, kept at least one slave. Most of the southern migrants, however, owned no African Americans. Still, some European Americans were heads of many households in which free

African Americans resided. General Joseph M. Street housed several free African Americans. Southerners helped start the local economy; Fort Madison's first merchant was a man from Baltimore by the name of Walsh. Southerners also embodied local law and order; in 1838, four of the five county representatives of the territory's legislature originally hailed from southern states — two from Kentucky, one from Virginia, and one from North Carolina. The near-total control of the southern transplants over the economy and politics of the county almost ensured that local enforcement of antislavery laws would not take place.[7]

Isaac R. Campbell differed from many of his fellow slaveholders in Lee County in that he had been born in the North before moving to the South and then the Upper Mississippi. He was born in New York on May 2, 1798. In his youth in the North, he went on sailing adventures, helped build the Erie Canal, performed agricultural labor, and worked as a cook. Upon relocating to Missouri Territory as a young adult, he continued agricultural work while making shoes, as well. By 1830 he and his wife had settled up the Mississippi River, and he found work at Galena's lead mines in Illinois. In addition, he owned African American slaves while in Galena, thus continuing a tradition that James Johnson had started nearly one decade earlier. Then in 1831, he relocated to the town of Keokuk in Lee County, Iowa, and he began trading with the indigenous peoples. His slaves went with him, and at least one slave remained with him at the time of his departure from Iowa six years later. As a result, African American slavery defined Campbell's life in the territory.[8]

Although living in Keokuk, Campbell was still able to socialize with southerners on a regular basis. Consequently, his slaves dealt with people who were accustomed to certain behaviors from African Americans — namely humility and submissiveness. In 1834, Campbell formed the St. Louis Land Company with J. and E. Walsh of St. Louis, Missouri, and J.H. Overhall, of St. Charles, Missouri, among others. They transformed their business into a lucrative enterprise. Campbell, for example, eventually managed one-thirteenth of 119,000 acres of land, and when he sold it in the late 1830s, its value was priced at $14,000.[9]

For all his wealth, however, Campbell had no control over the changing politics of the county. A growing number of antislavery migrants settled in the territory, including Lee County. Lee eventually became a well-traveled county by slaves escaping from the slave state of Missouri that bordered the county. Campbell decided not to resist the political climate. On the other hand, he did not free any slaves. Instead, he resettled in St. Francisville, Missouri, in 1837 and lived there well into his retirement years. As he left for his second migration to the South, he held a slave named John in Lee County. John was saving money to purchase his emancipation at the time. He eventually succeeded in doing so.[10]

Col. Stephen Watts Kearny owned a female slave at Fort Des Moines in Lee County. When he arrived there on September 25, 1834, an African American woman had accompanied him to work as the servant of his residence. She stayed with him for the duration of his assignment and left when he did. The locals identified her as a mulatto. Whether she had a light skin tone or Kearney informed his neighbors of her heritage, her European ancestry was no secret at the fort. Fort Des Moines was a new facility, with construction having begun earlier in the year. As a result, thanks in part to Kearny, slavery was part of the culture at the fort from the very beginning.[11]

Having to live in bondage in an uncompleted fort, Kearny's slave did not labor in the best of conditions. On September 26, her master voiced his own complaints, which indicated the harshness of the environment. He wrote, "The quarters for the officers and soldiers are not as far advanced as I had expected and not a log is yet laid for stables for our horses." He believed that by the end of October, his soldiers could complete the construction but lamentably predicted that the buildings "will be less comfortable and of meaner appearance, than those occupied by any other portion of the Army." After only one day on the job, one of his main concerns was his uncertainty about whether "we are to occupy this post, after the ensuing winter." He was responsible for prohibiting settlers from coming to the area, which meant that any possible abolitionist migrants could not set foot there. No potential existed, therefore, for any nearby residents to help Kearny's servant escape if she had wanted to do so. Consequently, because of the government's permissiveness towards soldiers' transporting of slaves upriver, Kearny's slave would be surrounded only by soldiers and fellow slaves.[12]

The slave was at the mercy of the soldiers. When Fort Des Moines first opened, no laws or courts or justices of the peace kept the surrounding area under control. Kearny, therefore, *was* the law, and his captains helped him enforce his orders. He eventually declared martial law there, and the few settlers who lived in Lee County received lessons from him on performing civilized behavior and respecting their fellow citizens' rights. Fellow resident Isaac Campbell remembered of the militant rule of Kearny and Captains Sumner, Boone and Browne, "Their bayonets taught us to respect the rights of others, and from martial law we learned the necessity of a civil code." The martial law under which Kearny's servant worked was a more militarized form of the physical intimidation — whippings, beatings, etc.— under which African American slaves commonly labored at the time.[13]

Van Buren County bordered Lee to the west but also bordered the state of Missouri to the north, and the county eventually gained a significant number of slaveholders and slaves because of its proximity to the river and the slave state. In its early years, however, Van Buren also welcomed slavers from outside the South. In the late 1830s, a man by the last name of McCrary traveled from Indiana to the county's town of Keosauqua. With him was a very loyal enslaved African American man. McCrary's slave served him until the master's death, at which point the servant returned to Indiana.[14]

Rarely during the 1830s did Iowa Territory's African Americans marry among themselves and start families while enslaved. Iowa, like the other upriver territories, did not have a sizable African American population — slave or free. Moreover, none developed through the 1830s. As a result, African Americans did not easily find other African Americans to marry, and even less often did relationships between two people of different ethnic groups exist. John Emerson's slave Sam Blow, who had accompanied his master to other locations across the Upper Mississippi, was a notable exception. During the period that Blow principally spent his enslavement at Fort Snelling, Wisconsin Territory, Emerson took him on assignment in Fort Armstrong, Iowa Territory. Meanwhile, Sam Blow renamed himself Dred Scott and married fellow slave Harriet.[15]

Emerson's working relationships with other local slaveholders contributed to the political and demographic development of the Upper Mississippi. Over the years the physician had become a prominent citizen of the former Northwest Territory, especially as a presidential appointee to military forts. In 1837, for example, he met with Governor Henry Dodge of Wisconsin Territory and two others in Fort Snelling to negotiate a treaty with the indigenous Chippewa tribe. To be sure, the slaves that Emerson and his colleagues brought to the region contributed little to the work the officers conducted with the Chippewas. On the other hand, the federal government overlooked the soldiers' ownership of African Americans in order to assign them to their work.[16]

More importantly, in the case of the Scotts' marriage, the executive branch's refusal to enforce the Missouri Compromise played a role in the coupling. If the government had not called the Scotts' respective masters to the Upper Mississippi and allowed the Scotts to join them, the couple would not have met there. The meetings of Iowa slave couples like Dred and Harriet happened not only because of federal intransigence regarding enforcement of antislavery laws but also because of military necessity — the government's prioritization of manning the forts with southerners. The slave communities of forts in the Midwest largely consisted of domestic servants, and by keeping house the domestics likely entertained slaveholding neighbors of the fort and their slaves.

Emerson's treatment of the Scotts soon became standard practice among slaveholding soldiers towards their slaves in Iowa Territory. Southerners eventually expected to be able to settle in the territory with their human chattel despite the Missouri Compromise, because earlier migrants had set precedents of Iowa-based slavery. In 1838, as the Scotts left the Upper Mississippi, Shapley

Prince Ross lived with two African American slaves—a man and a woman—he had brought from Missouri to Bentonsport, Iowa. After no more than two years, he sent his female slave back to the slave state. Such dealings were part of Ross's family for at least two generations, for his father and grandfather were large slaveholders in Kentucky. Born in that state in 1811, Ross himself lived on his father's enormous plantation there until the family relocated with the slaves to Missouri. He later traveled to Galena's lead mines as a teenager in the late 1820s, consequently witnessing slave labor in the Upper Mississippi. When he moved his own family and slaves upriver to Iowa

Dred Scott, a slave held in the Upper Mississippi. Courtesy Library of Congress.

Territory in 1834, he was continuing his ancestors' tradition of migrating with slaves as well as perpetuating the extralegal slavery he had seen other southern migrants do nearly a decade earlier.[17]

Ross, however, could not take for granted the compliance of both of his slaves towards their enslavement. His male slave escaped from him to Illinois in order to become liberated. The fugitive ultimately failed in his efforts, for Giles A. Sullivan helped Ross apprehend the runaway in Illinois. Ross, however, soon found himself in legal trouble. En route to Missouri, police arrested him and Sullivan in Carthage, Illinois, for kidnapping. Before he could leave town after his detainment, he struck in the face another lawyer seeking to arrest him on another charge. In an ironic turn of events, Ross then became the fugitive, fleeing south with his family beyond Missouri to Texas.[18]

Another female slave also escaped her bondage but in a different manner. Another aspect of the legacy of Ross' slaving in Iowa Territory lay in his distinction of owning a slave who met an untimely end there. He held a slave named Aunt Mournin in Iowa Territory until her death in 1839. Her body was found in the Mississippi River. Hers was the first death recorded in Van Buren County, thus breaking the pattern of African Americans leaving slavery in Iowa either through emancipation in the territory or a return to the South as property. The Mississippi River, which had previously given slaves hope for liberation upriver, now had delivered a slave to her doom.[19]

Ross did not appear to publicly mourn the loss of Mournin either in Iowa Territory or in Texas. Upon his arrival to the southern state, President Martin Van Buren appointed him to serve as an Indian agent. He later became a Texas Ranger. His sons also served the state, whether as rangers themselves or as governors. The biographies of the Rosses that eventually proliferated in Texas discussed Ross's time in Iowa in passing. The various reasons the books gave for his migration to Texas ranged from health concerns to attractive advertisements for the state, but they did not mention Mournin. Only books about Iowa's history memorialized her and, in doing so, cast Ross's Iowa years in a negative light.

By the end of the 1830s, public sentiment in Iowa Territory had soured against slavery. More recent immigrants from Europe outnumbered southerners in many parts of the state, and the new arrivals opposed slavery. Southern migrants increasingly felt pressured by their abolitionist neighbors to liberate their human chattel. Many local slaveholders indeed emancipated their slaves; but several kept theirs, and new masters and slaves continued to slowly trickle into Wisconsin.

Meanwhile, the judicial branch of Iowa Territory launched the beginning of the end of local slavery in 1839. In doing so, it was taking the firm stance against the institution that the federal government and its local appointees had failed to do. Five years earlier a man named Jordan Montgomery had brought his slave Ralph to the territory. The servant contracted with his master for manumission by working in the lead mines and earning five hundred dollars plus fifty for his hire. Montgomery claimed that Ralph did not honor his contract and sent him to Missouri as a consequence. The Iowa Supreme Court ruled, however, that Ralph's indebtedness to Montgomery did not entitle Montgomery to consider Ralph his property. In effect, the court declared slavery illegal in the territory. Appropriately enough, the court issued the verdict on Independence Day, linking the celebration of U.S. freedom from Britain with African American freedom in Iowa Territory. African American citizenship in the new territory seemed off to a promising start.

In contrast, the ban of legal slavery became the one bright spot in a prolonged period of territorial discrimination against African Americans. In 1839 Iowa Territory also prohibited African American immigration. The policy was more emotional than practical, however, for many owners of local mining companies depended on African American labor, especially slave labor. In the 1840s and 1850s, traders, soldiers, miners, and government officials brought slaves to Iowa, especially Des Moines, Keokuk, Dubuque, and Middle Fork. Still, the population of the territory was shifting. The early slaveholding migrants dwindled in number, and new migrants who were hostile not only to slave labor but to African Americans altogether moved into the territory.[20]

Nevertheless, the prohibition of African Americans from settlement affected how people outside of Iowa Territory viewed them. Proslavery residents were now able to advertise the land as a place where European Americans would not have to compete with free African Americans for employment. Abolitionists, on the other hand, could portray the migration ban as the unfortunate result of greedy proslavery officials unsatisfied with preserving slavery and needing to completely humiliate African Americans. For some the exclusionary measure gave Iowa Territory's residents the reputation of intolerance. The secretary of the Home Mission Society wrote, "So strong in that State is the popular hatred to God's colored children, that even in its Constitution there is a clause expressly prohibiting our colored brethren from settling within its precincts." Here, the anti–African American sentiment was not restricted to the government officials but broadened to Iowa itself.[21]

Some European Americans tried to subject other groups of people to the same kinds of work and service as the African American slaves had performed. After leaving Prairie du Chien, the Ho-Chunk and the Lowrys settled in Iowa. Before their arrival, only indigenous people had lived there. As in Wisconsin, the Reverend Lowry had the distinction of starting Iowa's first protestant church. He received plenty of help in building it with the local soldiers, army officers, government workers, and indigenous people. His helpers eventually became members of his new church. The school, meanwhile, measured $40' \times 50'$, stood two stories high, and housed forty students.[22]

The Reverend Lowry had the intention of converting the Ho-Chunk tribe members into Christians behaving like European Americans and serving like African Americans. He did not respect the Ho-Chunk and spent his missionary years criticizing their culture and trying to teach them European values. In addition, the Indians of the school performed labor at the Lowry residence, not unlike the duties of slaves. Ho-Chunk girls learned to cook at the mission school and served food to the Lowrys' guests. The boys of the tribe, meanwhile, were agricultural laborers on the missionary's farm.[23]

One major difference between slavery and the mission lay in the treatment by the missionaries of their most helpless wards. Instead of making the indigenous people responsible for the care of their own infants, the Lowrys volunteered to babysit them. "The cradle always stood there with its snowy pillows, and any Indian woman might leave the baby there and claim it again when she chose. It was seldom empty," one local resident remembered. "Twice had mothers left their little ones and never returned, and two little Indian girls outgrew the cradle and learned to call our agent and his wife 'Papa' and 'Mama' and were adopted and cared for by the Lowrys as their own."[24]

Another significant difference lay in Iowa Territory's permitting of the indigenous to remain in the territory. The federal government, in keeping the indigenous peoples in the territory, tacitly acknowledged that they were the original inhabitants of the land. In addition, the government played an active role in assimilating the indigenous peoples into Iowa, albeit in ways that did not reflect sensitivity to them. In contrast, the territory called for the expulsion of African Americans in 1839. This action represented the disposable treatment the ruling European Americans believed that African Americans deserved. After all, with slavery in the territory now declared illegal by the territorial judicial branch, African Americans were of little use to European Americans for the purpose of exploiting labor. And European Americans did not want to compete with ex-slaves for work. Now that European Americans were finished with their former slaves, they wanted their servants to go back to the lands from which their ex-masters had originally forced them to vacate. Also, the federal government left the fate of the relocated African Americans to whoever bought them. Unlike the various Indian agents appointed by presidents, no president appointed any African American agents to help the exiled ex-slaves' transition to life after Upper Mississippi slavery.

The Reverend Lowry failed to westernize the Ho-Chunk Indians, underestimating their social and economic problems and overestimating their receptiveness to European values. He sensed trouble immediately upon his family's arrival in Iowa. The Lowrys were dismayed to find the Indians naked, howling, and conducting an orgy during a funeral, according to the Reverend Lowry's account of his first ten years with the tribe. He noted that Indians bought whiskey with the annuity they received from the federal government and that they fought and stabbed one another. He counted thirty-nine Ho-Chunk murders in one year.[25]

Working with the tribe certainly appeared to pay more than working against it did. The American Fur Company controlled the Ho-Chunks by encouraging their indulgence in their weaknesses. Joseph Rolette was the local company agent, and he was the undisputed leader of the county as well as in nearby Prairie du Chien, Wisconsin. He convinced the tribe to catch animals and sell the furs to him in exchange for liquor. His relationship with the tribe represented a continuation of the exploitation he had inflicted upon other ethnic minorities for years because he had owned African American slaves when he first arrived in the area. In addition, he hated the mission school, fearing that it would discourage Indians from trapping for him. Lowry, in turn, had no love lost for Rolette because of how the liquor the trader gave the tribe complicated the missionary's work with them. Also, as a former slaveholder, he disagreed with Rolette's bondage of African Americans.[26]

The federal government tried to relocate Lowry and the tribe in order to salvage the mission. In 1840 the government moved the Ho-Chunk tribe and its mission school farther up the Mississippi River to Winneshiek County,

Iowa, along the Turkey River. The government built a new military outpost there — Fort Atkinson. The clergyman conducted religious services in a chapel that measured 22' × 34' and stood twelve feet high.[27]

None of these changes proved fruitful, however, and Lowry's days there were numbered. In 1844 the government dismissed the minister from the agent position and the school itself. He blamed his firing on local Catholic priests allegedly spreading rumors that defamed his work in Iowa. "Mr. Lowry informed me, while at his post, that he was fearful that all his labor was labor lost, or worse than useless," wrote acquaintance William Folsom. "He felt quite disheartened as to the prospect of accomplishing any good." The minister did not blame himself for the futility of his work but rather predictably continued to blame whiskey consumption for "neutralizing every effort for the moral and intellectual advancement of the Indian." He saw the Indian as suffering the "stereotyped curse" of "whisky and intercourse with the whites." Also, despite his opposition of Colonel Zachary Taylor's holding of slaves in the Upper Mississippi, he shared his fellow southerner's assessment of the fur trappers and agents as "the greatest scoundrels the world ever knew."[28]

Lowry's time in the Upper Mississippi did not reform him from interacting closely with slaveholders. After the Lowry family left Iowa, the Reverend Lowry served as the pastor of a Cumberland Presbyterian Church in Lebanon, Tennessee, for slightly longer than one year. The church was a perfect fit for him, because Cumberland Presbyterians of that state strongly opposed slavery, just as he did. The leading ministers not only held antislavery views but also produced literature that denounced the peculiar institution and its supportive legislation from southern states. On the other hand, some ministers of the denomination owned African Americans, and Lowry not only worked with them but became close friends with a few of them.[29]

The missionary moved his family from Midwestern military life to southern upper class life. Lebanon was in the state's middle or Cumberland section, which was a higher-income area than the Cumberland of Kentucky, from which the Lowrys had originated. The typical house in Lebanon was a square, brick building of Greek architectural style and stood two stories tall; the wings of the house only reached one story in height. Among the preacher's local colleagues in ministry was the Rev. Thomas Calhoun. The Calhouns of the Cumberland area were wealthy immigrants and, therefore, part of the local elite.[30]

After years of hardship in starting a school for the Ho-Chunk, the minister now had success in creating an institution. His labor in Iowa Territory may have given him training in establishing educational facilities from scratch. Indeed, the Reverend Lowry's greater legacy lay in his contributions to academic life in Lebanon. In the early 1840s, he helped establish a local branch of the denomination's institute of higher learning: Cumberland College. At the school he served as a trustee board member and president and later worked as a professor of moral philosophy. The European American locals of Middle Tennessee responded better to Cumberland than the indigenous people had responded to the Reverend Lowry's mission school. Then again, Cumberland did not train its students to abandon their lifestyles or educate them about irrelevant topics. Moreover, Lowry did not have people to distract the students as fur traders had attracted the indigenous peoples with liquor.[31]

Before returning to the Midwest in the 1850s, Lowry built his reputation in the South and established relationships that continued when he resumed his labor as a private citizen in the Upper Mississippi. Cumberland College became the center of life in Lebanon, and the town itself evolved into a prized cultural center in Tennessee during the antebellum era. As a result, the Reverend Lowry's work at the school gave him access to more socially and politically powerful people. One of his fellow cofounders was Robert Looney Caruthers. He had already built a significant career in public service by the time he helped start the college. He had served as a county chancery court clerk, Tennessee's attorney general, a state legislator, and a congressman by the time the Reverend Lowry had arrived at the school. Caruthers, in fact, had just ended his first (and only) congressional term in March 1843.[32]

During the Reverend Lowry's second tenure at Cumberland, Caruthers and his brother Abraham created the college's law school — one of the earliest law schools in the nation. Abraham had been a circuit court judge in Tennessee. Courts rarely reversed his decisions, and the Supreme Court occasionally incorporated his verdicts into theirs. In the mid–1840s, he left the legal system for academia, becoming the first dean of Cumberland's law school upon its formation. He wrote an influential book on the state's legal system, *History of a Lawsuit*, during his tenure and taught from it for his courses.[33]

By taking up residency in the South, the Reverend Lowry exposed himself and his family to African American slavery of a much greater degree than in the Upper Mississippi. Not only were there more slaves in Tennessee than in Iowa, but a greater percentage of Tennessee's residents were slaves than the percentage of Iowa's residents. According to the 1840 census, slaves comprised one-fourth of the population of Middle Tennessee. In addition, some of his colleagues at Cumberland College supported slavery. Abraham Caruthers, for example, was a slaveholder, possessing nine human beings — one of the larger holdings of slaves in Lebanon. And just as the church in Iowa did not isolate the Reverend Lowry from slaveholders, the antislavery ministers served the Lebanon community, which included several masters. Even some of the ministers themselves owned slaves.[34]

When the Reverend Lowry returned to the Upper Mississippi, he and his family were eventually joined by the children of the minister's slaveholding friends — many of whom became powerful politicians in the Midwest. As a result, his lack of success as a missionary in Iowa Territory indirectly contributed to the continuation of proslavery politics in the Midwest into the 1850s. Among the Calhoun and Caruthers families were children of similar ages to the Lowry children. Sylvanus was the oldest among them, but he established a lifelong friendship with Abraham's son William Caruthers. William, meanwhile, was approximately the same age as Sylvanus' sister Elizabeth and the Reverend Calhoun's son who shared his first name. Both William and the junior Thomas Calhoun — also known as T. P. Calhoun — attended college in Lebanon in the 1840s. They consolidated their power upon arriving in the Midwest in order to preserve their lifestyle as slaveholders in a free land.

Meanwhile, slavery remained strong in Iowa Territory in the 1840s. Just as presidents had called upon slaveholders to run military forts, the commanders in chief also chose masters for high political positions in territorial government. President William Henry Harrison did not serve long before dying a few months into his term of office, but his appointments for Iowa Territory legitimized Upper Mississippi slavery for years. He laid the foundation for slavery there, just as Andrew Jackson had done for Wisconsin Territory a decade earlier. Also, because Harrison had supported Jacksonian Democracy, his appointees for Iowa Territory continued in that vein.

Harrison's imprint upon the territory signified his distinction as the first president of the United States to have previously served in public office in the Midwest. His constant support of slavery throughout his political career led to his low popularity among abolitionists in the Northwest. Early in his public service, he had partnered with proslavery politicians. During his tenure as Indiana Territory's governor, he passed the Servants Act of 1803 and the indenture laws of 1805 and 1807. Whenever Congress addressed proposals to have the Northwest Ordinance's sixth article removed, he consistently declared his support of its extraction. As antislavery politicians grew in power in Iowa Territory, an increasing number of residents disliked his politics. Nevertheless, his embrace of Upper Mississippi slavery as governor contributed, however indirectly, to his rise to the presidency.[35]

In addition, because so many politicians in Iowa Territory were slaveholders, slavery displayed more of an elite quality there than among the soldiers and miners who owned humans in Illinois and Wisconsin. In the other areas, southerners brought their slaves to perform manual labor such as mining for lead or helping to guard forts. In contrast, the slaves of politicians in Iowa Territory functioned largely as domestic servants. Furthermore, these presidential appointees were usually people who had already achieved wealth and prominence in the South if not in the nation, and they could afford to temporarily relocate to perform the duty of public service.

Kentuckian John Chambers arrived in Iowa with his slaves in 1841, upon his appointment to governor of the territory by President Harrison. He held a body servant named Uncle Cassius and a female slave named Carey Bennett. His ownership of humans during his term of office continued the tradition that Henry Dodge had begun in Iowa Territory. Some members of his administration also openly practiced slavery in the territory, further demonstrating the federal government's sabotage of the enforcement of its own prohibition of slavery in the Upper Mississippi. No fewer than seven slaves resided with the officials at their headquarters in Burlington, Iowa Territory.[36]

Slavery under Chambers' administration was significantly different, however, than under Dodge's rule. More Iowans opposed slavery during Chambers' governance than when his predecessor had ruled. As a result, he defied the wishes of the majority of the people he led. Even worse, he gave the appearance of breaking the law of the Northwest Ordinance despite his responsibility as an executive officer to uphold the law. In addition, although Dodge emancipated his slaves in Iowa, Chambers never did. President Harrison's successor, John Tyler, reappointed Chambers in 1844, but the following year, Tyler's successor, James K. Polk, removed him from office. At that point, the governor simply returned to the South with his slaves. Moreover, his ability to have his slaves remain his property despite their presence in a free territory demonstrated that the Northwest Ordinance and the Missouri Compromise were dead letters.

Antislavery residents expressed financial concerns regarding the governor's slaveholding. They wanted his servants to pay a bond, reminding Chambers that Iowa Territory law required such payments. Chambers argued, however, that his servants were actually his slaves, they could not afford to pay the bond, they were not permanent residents of the territory, and he intended to return with them to the South at the end of his term. The county commissioners sided with the governor, decrying the abolitionists' request as an insult to Chambers, and the slaves remained with him while he led the territory.[37]

Maryland resident O. H. W. Stull arrived in Iowa with his slaves in 1841, upon his appointment by President Harrison to become secretary of Iowa Territory. Stull had requested his own servants upon discovering those belonging to Governor Chambers. In April 1841 the secretary had just emancipated his slave Margaret Dorsey for $200 and had sold his slave Mary and her two children for $600 before joining the Chambers administration in July. Upon arriving in Iowa Territory, he bought a slave from a fellow former southerner — one of the few occurrences of the purchase of an African American in antebellum Iowa. A man with the last name of Chaney from the state of Virginia sold him a mulatto boy for $250. The transaction took place in the National Hotel, run by Chauncey Swan. A witness, S. C. Trowbridge, claimed to have been in the hotel at the time and overheard Stull and Chaney bargaining over the servant. Trowbridge also said that he saw Stull pay the money and saw Chaney deliver the slave. This sale also angered the local antislavery citizens, but they retreated from pursuing the issue out of respect for his political service, as with Chambers.[38]

Chambers was not the first governor of an upriver territory to allow sales of bonded African Americans in his territory. He stood out from others, however, in permitting it to take place within his administration. Moreover, Stull's exchanges of money for slaves did not stop with his dealings with Chaney. Upon John Tyler's inauguration as president, he removed Stull from office. The former officer then relocated with his enslaved boy to Burlington in the upriver county of Des Moines. While there Stull sold the boy to his son-in-law named Cassell, who then brought the child to Alleghany County, Maryland. Cassell remained the boy's master for an extended time there. In both of these violations of the Missouri Compromise, two of President Harrison's men — Chambers and Stull — were complicit if not involved. The defiance by Iowa Territory's settlers of federal anti-slavery laws, as modeled by the two appointees, became a legacy of Harrison's presidency; it was his final contribution to the development of the Upper Mississippi.[39]

Stull's history of slave ownership in Iowa did not prevent him from gaining political power as the population grew increasingly anti-slavery. Nearly a year after becoming secretary, he temporarily served as acting governor in May 1842. Four years later, after having left the executive branch, he was elected probate court judge of Dubuque County. His victory showed that either people were willing to overlook his slaveholding past or that Iowa still had a sufficiently sizable proslavery population to elect him.[40]

By the time Chaney had sold the slave, he had lived in the Upper Mississippi with his servant for a decade — a relatively long time for a southern migrant to the region. Upon arriving in the early 1830s, Chaney first lived in Lee County. He claimed land by the river, built his cabin there, and began raising corn in 1834. He eventually became a prominent local citizen. He built a mill there, and the creek by which he lived was later renamed Chaney Creek.[41]

According to a local free African American, the slavery that the politicians practiced largely resembled the servitude that Illinois had legalized in its constitution. Frank Reno, an acquaintance of at least two slaves belonging to Chambers, noted that Chaney and Stull had made an agreement by which Stull would pay for his servant's board and clothing. After the servant reached a certain age, Stull was then to pay him $250 and help him — if the slave desired — to return to Virginia. Reno recalled that the servant had considered himself under great care by both Chaney and Stull but preferred the indoor labor that Stull assigned to him.[42]

As for Chambers' work force, Reno relayed a servant's compliments regarding his employer. The slave — a man who had served the governor during his earlier days as a congressman — told Reno that Chambers paid well and offered him an "easy time." In addition, the governor promised his property that after coming to Iowa, the servant had the option of returning home to Kentucky if displeased with Midwestern life. The servant expressed fondness for life in Iowa, except for the indigenous people, the snow, and the whiskey. He considered Chambers a southern gentleman and, for that reason, remained loyal to him.[43]

The selling of slaves in the free territory was not restricted to the governor's administration. In the 1840s recent arrival Joseph Smart worked two jobs; he was a blacksmith, and he was an interpreter of indigenous languages. He had brought an African American woman with him to the county. After keeping her as a slave there for no more than two years, he sold her to a man named James Jordan. Not unlike the case of Stull's human chattel, Jordan took his new purchase to Missouri and sold her to someone else there.[44]

These financial transactions vividly demonstrated the weakness of governmental checks and balances where upriver slavery was concerned. Now the president's neglect of Congress' anti-slavery laws infected state-level politics in the South. Nearly one decade had passed since Missouri's court decisions of *Winny v. Whitesides* and *Rachel v. Walker*— both of which had clearly prohibited the enslavement and sale of any African American resident of the Upper Mississippi in the slave state. Missouri's executive branch, however, refused to enforce those verdicts and allowed Jordan to enslave and sell an African American from Iowa without a conviction or a punishment.

Slavery was not the only means European Americans used to oppress African Americans in Iowa Territory. By 1840 the citizens had begun to practice segregation according to skin color. That year the state made illegal any marriages between European Americans and African Americans, whether the territory considered the African Americans "negro" or "mulatto." Such marriages had rarely taken place in the territory at the time of the law's passage, largely because few African Americans— enslaved or not — resided there. This law was not widespread throughout the Upper Mississippi region; Wisconsin Territory did not enact such a law, and upon the creation of Minnesota Territory in 1849, no similar law ever appeared in its books. In addition, many of the masters who took slaves to the territory were already married. The law, therefore, more likely applied to free African Americans unaccountable to anyone of European descent than to slaves restricted through intense European American authority.

Despite the restrictions the territory placed against African Americans since 1839, they continued to migrate upriver. Fugitive slaves especially flocked to Iowa, believing that they became free when they stepped foot out of the South. Some slaves indeed enjoyed their freedom and developed sizable African American communities like that of Muscatine County. Others benefited from helpful abolitionist neighbors who helped the fugitives secure their free status. Still others were isolated in counties and towns of nearly completely European American populations.

On the other hand, European American residents further strengthened their authority over African Americans on the occasion of Iowa Territory's entrance into statehood in 1846. As African Americans maintained their presence in the territory, European Americans debated over how to legally regard the minority group's rights and privileges. The majority ultimately concluded that, in conjunction with limiting the physical presence of African Americans, the political presence needed restricting. Therefore, upon Iowa's becoming a state, only European Americans received the right to vote.

Over the next five years, the state perpetuated the second-class citizenship of African Americans by denying them access to education. In 1846 state law mandated that only European Americans be permitted to attend Iowa's schools. Two years later the state recognized only European Americans in the school list. Three years afterward, Iowa exempted all the property of African Americans from taxation for school purposes. These restrictions merely formalized similar prohibitions that southern states had devised against their slaves. To be sure, Iowa did not forbid African Americans from learning to read or write, as some slaveholding states did. On the other hand, Iowa's laws meant that only in private homes would African Americans be able to learn. Iowa significantly resembled the South in that the anti-literacy and anti-education laws in both locations guaranteed that European Americans would have more access to education and, as a result, more education and of better quality than African Americans would.

Slaveholders and proslavery politicians in power in Iowa's government significantly influenced these hindering outcomes for African Americans. In Iowa's constitutional conventions of 1844, 1846 and 1857, men from southern states overwhelmingly outnumbered those from New England. In the first convention, eleven Virginians, six North Carolinians, eight Kentuckians, and one man from Tennessee participated—collectively more than twice the number of the ten from the Northeast. The next convention hosted fifteen participants from the South, eight from New England, four from the Midwest and five from the Southwest. In the third convention, ten southerners attended, as opposed to only six New Englanders. As long as slaveholding migrants and proslavery Democrats voted as a block, laws sympathetic to African Americans stood no chance of passing.

By the 1840s Dubuque County was the most likely place for a slaveholder in Iowa to have a successful political career. Named after Julien Dubuque, the first European American settler, the county had become a haven for Upper Mississippi slaveholders six years after it was founded in 1834. As in Jo Daviess County, Illinois, a mining boom brought southern migrants to Dubuque

County. Most of them brought only one or two slaves with them to work in the mines if not to work in their homes.

Aside from slaveholders, proslavery southerners also lived in the county and helped foster the climate that led to Dubuque's replacing of Jo Daviess as the most popular attraction for migrant slaveholding miners. The people who came to Dubuque from Jo Daviess throughout the 1830s mining region were of the French-Canadian, Scotch, and Irish ethnic groups as well as Yankees and southerners. Powerful southerners included William Carter, Iowa's first manufacturer of shot, and General John G. Shields, both of Kentucky. In 1836 John King of Virginia founded and edited the periodical the Dubuque *Visitor*, the first newspaper printed in Iowa. His associate, Andrew Keersecker, also came from Virginia.[45]

The federal government helped facilitate the county's development as a slaveholder sanctuary. Regardless of whether President Martin Van Buren supported Dubuque's proslavery sentiment or was ignorant of the human ownership of his appointees, he appointed Thomas McKnight the county's receiver of public moneys in 1838. McKnight held two slaves in Dubuque County in 1840. Van Buren's appointments perpetuated slavery in Iowa Territory, just as those of Andrew Jackson had done in Wisconsin Territory. As Jackson's vice president, Van Buren had supported the proslavery policies of the Jackson presidency. He then retained nearly all of Jackson's cabinet members upon assuming the presidency. As a result, the new president's shaping of Iowa Territory into a proslavery area merely exemplified his deliberate continuation of his predecessor's style of government.

McKnight's exceptionally long tenure in his federal office in Dubuque demonstrated not only the strong willingness of the local Upper Mississippians to comply with the president's sabotage of federal law but also the longevity of the policies of Jacksonian Democracy. McKnight remained in office when reappointed by Van Buren's successors William Henry Harrison and John Tyler. When President James Polk finally removed him from office in 1845, he was one of the few slaveholders of the region to have worked for three successive presidential administrations.

The citizens of Dubuque eventually began choosing slaveholders for public office after having been primed by the federal government's appointments of masters to state and county positions for nearly a decade. Governor Chambers and Receiver McKnight still held their offices in 1844 when Francis Kelly O'Ferrall began his tenure as the mayor of the city of Dubuque. Although O'Ferrall was one of the few citizens to document on a federal census that he held slaves in Iowa, the city's electorate still voted for him. In addition, the federal government did not enforce the prohibition against slavery by requiring him to emancipate his slaves. He served as the mayor from 1844 to 1846. Moreover, he was the first mayor of the town to be reelected to the office.

By the late 1840s, slavery in Iowa had spread to several counties along the Mississippi River. Dubuque County was no longer a haven for slaveholders due to the influx of antislavery migrants, the exodus of many of the slavers, and the emancipating of most of the county's slaves. In addition, slavery in Dubuque was temporary in character because of the owners' limited time there as presidential appointees. When terms of service ended, the politicians left the county if not the territory.

Politics was not the only vocation in which slaveholding migrants prospered in Iowa. As Gov. Chambers departed the state, a minister from Tennessee brought his family and his African American property to the state. The Rev. John C. Ewing of the Presbyterian Church and his company arrived in Van Buren County in 1845, eleven years after his ordination in Tennessee. His sixteen-year-old slave woman, Ellen, also born in Tennessee, was given his surname. In the 1850 federal census, John, his family, and Ellen were the only Ewings from that state to be recorded as residents of Iowa.

By the time that the census was taken, however, the Reverend Ewing had rid himself of his servant. Fellow Van Buren resident John Elbert now housed not only Ellen but three-year-old African American girl Catharine Ewing. Ellen was, most likely, Catharine's mother. They shared the same surname and household. The only other African American resident of the county, Kate McMananey, had at age sixty-one in 1850 well surpassed her childbearing years. On the other hand, Ellen was twenty-one years old that year and had given birth to Catharine only three years earlier. Many slaves and servants gave birth to children between their teenage years and their twenties. Therefore, Catharine's birth to an eighteen-year-old was not unusual in the context of slavery.

Like the Reverend Ewing, Elbert hailed from the South but from Kentucky. He did not live there as long as Ewing had, however. Elbert, a doctor, had received a fine education. Like other well-to-do southern migrants before him, he moved to the Upper Mississippi after having professionally established himself and started a family. Before coming to Iowa, he had already worked for years as a physician in Ohio, and he had married and had begun raising five children. Still, in that time he also learned of stories about beautiful prairies in the West and wanted to see them for himself. His daughter Annie said, "In the heavy timbered lands of Ohio the physician's life was a hard one. The only way of getting about over bad roads was on horseback. This entailed great fatigue and he conceived the mistaken notion that farm life in that wonderful far off West would be the most restful and happy that he could lead." Annie concluded that her father never did as well with farming as with his career in medicine. Regardless, after leaving for Iowa in 1840, he remained there for the remainder of his life.[46]

Elbert had much better fortune in politics than in farming in his new home. In July 1841 he became president of the territorial council of Iowa, thus joining Chambers and Stull as members of the territorial government who also employed African American servants. Moreover, he was now a member of a lawmaking body despite having broken the territorial law against the migration of African Americans. If his servants were also his slaves, then he also violated the Missouri Compromise.[47]

When the Elberts and their servants arrived in Iowa, slavery had already been a family practice for at least one previous generation. Annie recalled memories of having witnessed her grandparents' relationships with their slaves after they had relocated from Kentucky to Ohio. Her grandfather read the Bible to his servants and chastised those who did not pay close attention. "No sleepy headed African should indulge in a nap," she advised in retrospect before adding, "Woe to the darkie who was caught nodding. One cannot but smile at the thought of pounding piety into wooly heads." Her grandmother, meanwhile, took on the role of household manager, which was a significant challenge. Her husband was often absent from home because of his work, and she had to take charge of her children and the slaves by herself.[48]

The Elberts made an abortive attempt to foster a seamless transition for their slaves as they traveled west. Annie stated that the family took two girls to Iowa to serve as the cooks of the household. While in transit their wagon became entrenched in mud. One of the servants went outside of the wagon and sank to her waist in mud. The Elberts reasoned that the large size of the girl prohibited her retrieval from the mud. Annie did not say whether the family abandoned the servant. If she were still a slave, her abandonment would have resulted in a financial loss to the family. If she were officially free but performing the same labor as during slavery, her freedom would have eliminated her monetary value and, as a result, would have made abandonment more likely.[49]

Elbert was one of many southern doctors to settle in Iowa but one of few slaveholders. At least two others came from his birth state, while one was from Virginia and another hailed from Tennessee. Like Elbert, several doctors from slaveholding states served in the state government. One of them chaired Iowa's constitutional convention in Iowa City in 1846. In addition, the two doctors who served in Iowa's first territorial legislature were southerners. These physicians who served in politics collectively made a formidable southern-interest power in Iowa if not a slave power. But among all of them, only Elbert held African Americans in his household for an extended period of time in a county bordering the Mississippi River in Iowa.[50]

The Elbert family spoke very highly of the service Ellen rendered to them. John Elbert's daughter Annie called Ellen "a Southern cook of the old type" and made note of the servant's tenure of fourteen years in the kitchen. As with the praises of G. W. Girdon for Barney Norris in Illinois, Annie limited her compliments about Ellen to the context of only her labor to the Elberts. "Ellen, black as night, shrewd, industrious and faithful to the interests of the family," Annie began, "how she loved us all, and what grand dinners she cooked." The daughter slightly hinted at a personal relationship between the servant and the employer by boasting, "She always spoke of the Elberts as 'our folks.'"[51]

On the other hand, Annie also occasionally illustrated Ellen with a degree of emotional complexity. Although she still restricted the context of her remarks to her servant's labor, Annie described Ellen as someone who deeply cared for her employers. Annie's brother Samuel left Van Buren County for West Point Military Academy sometime in the 1850s. His relationship with Ellen was informal to the point that he "loved to tease" her, according to a descendant. The playfulness likely came from their closeness in age, because Samuel was only four years younger than Ellen. Before he departed, his sister had watched Ellen prepare the clothes he was to take with him. As the servant gathered the garments, she was crying—her face "bathed in tears," as Annie put it.[52]

Catharine Ewing was born in Iowa in either 1846 or 1847. No male African American servant lived with either the Ewings or the Elberts in the state at that time, and censuses list her as mulatto. As a result, a European American resident of the state was most likely Catharine's father. The inconsistencies in the identification of Catharine among federal and state censuses symbolized the lack of a cohesive government policy on slavery in Iowa. Although carrying the surname Ewing in 1850, she acquired the name Townsend six years later. It changed again—to Wood—by the 1860 census. Her mother's last name similarly changed, but from Ewing to Woods, by that year.

Almost unique to slavery in this county, the slaveholders came from antislavery backgrounds. The Elberts opposed slavery but, through the wealth of John Elbert as a doctor, had the financial means to employ servants. In addition, the employees may have lived in their own housing. Annie recalled that Ellen and other servants had resided in a house near the Elberts. Servants occasionally ran away while working and dined at the servant quarters with their family members. Annie noted that for the employees, life in a separate house did not diminish the servitude, although the masters did not deserve Ellen's hard work. Rather, they "were proud to wait on us and with what consideration they flattered our childish vanities." Annie concluded, "With that abundance of love and trust we repaid the kind and faithful creatures. Did it rain? The smiling black face would appear at the door, and bowing low, she would say, 'Missie, I'se come to tote the little folks to school.'"[53]

By 1846 the Elberts had gained company in housing southern African Americans in Van Buren County. The aforementioned Kate McMananey, an elderly African American woman born in Virginia, arrived from that state to

Iowa Territory with her master John McMananey — also Virginia-born — and his family. In his new home, he labored as a farmer. Kate, meanwhile, was most likely able to perform little more than domestic service because of her advanced age. The family did little to hide her status as a slave, for in the 1850 census, they gave her no surname. Six years later, when Iowa took its own census, it listed her under her owner's surname. More remarkable, however, was that she had remained a servant in the McMananey household for a decade by then. At the time, very few slaveholders in Iowa had lived with their human property for that long a period. In addition, Kate was, in fact, the only African American documented as part of the McMananey household during that time. Her durable tenure there reflected the weak enforcement of antislavery laws in Van Buren County.

Another person of antislavery heritage soon joined the Elberts and McMananeys in employing servants in Iowa. In 1853 John Selby Townsend, another southerner, married Elbert's daughter Annie. He was born at Morgansfield, Kentucky, on August 21, 1824. His father, James Townsend, owned thirty slaves until John was six years old, at which point the elder Townsend emancipated them all. James' grandson later recalled his grandfather's "strong religious convictions, becoming convinced of the evils of slavery." James then relocated the family to Indiana, where he labored as a merchant until ruined by the Panic of 1837.[54]

His son John rose from the economic disaster to become a prominent citizen in the Midwest. He received an education at Asbury University. He married in 1848 to Mary Brooks, and they eventually settled in Albia, Monroe County, Iowa, in 1850. Within a year he changed professions—from farming to practicing law — and won the 1851 election for prosecuting attorney for Monroe County.[55]

His professional success was marred by personal tragedy when his wife died in 1852. He did not, however, remain widowed long. Returning home from Iowa City, after the end of the session of the Fourth General Assembly, in January 1853, he stopped at Elbert's home in The Oaks in Van Buren County, Iowa. There he met Elbert's daughter, Annie Catherine, whom he married before year's end.[56]

The Elberts allowed Catharine Ewing to live with the newly married couple. She became their "domestic servant," as the 1860 federal census put it. Her servitude was similar to the practice of slavery not only in other parts of the Upper Mississippi but also in the South. In laboring for the Elbert and Townsend families while still a child, Catharine's enslavement resembled the institution in Illinois, where the state constitution only allowed African American children to work as indentured servants. Concerning the South, the transfer of Catharine's service from master to master in Iowa was not uncommon for southern slaves; owners often rented their servants to needier plantations and other businesses, sold them, or offered them as wedding presents for newlyweds. Catharine's move to her new employers, moreover, marked Townsend's return to experiencing slave ownership since his father's emancipating of all of his slaves during John's childhood in the South.

While separating an African American daughter from her mother and enslaving her, Townsend had come to represent law and order in southeastern Iowa in the 1850s. Every day that Townsend held Catharine in servitude in Iowa, he violated not only the Northwest Ordinance's sixth article (against slavery) but also the state's ban of African American residents. Regardless, he garnered enough support from his constituents to rise in local politics. In December 1852 he represented Monroe and Lucas counties in the Fourth General Assembly in Iowa City. Although a relatively young assemblyman, at twenty-eight years old, he became chairman of the committee on agriculture and chairman of a special committee that received all bills to change or repeal any sections of the code. He actively participated in the proceedings of that session. He effectively showed his talent as a lawyer there, and in April 1853, he was elected judge of Iowa's Ninth Judicial District, which consisted of twelve counties.[57]

By the 1850s several European American migrants from the South had brought their slaves to counties in Iowa. Some counties were more tolerant than others concerning the practice of the institution. Earlier traveling slaveholders who had acquired social, economic and political dominance of their communities helped foster environments of tolerance. Elbert's tenure as president of Iowa's legislative council exemplified this dominance.

European Americans were unable to totally stop the arrival of African American slaves, fugitives, and free people. In response to the continued migration, the state legally reinforced its ethnic apartheid. In 1851, for example, Iowa revised its anti-immigration policies. The new law put the onus on town and county officials to tell African Americans who were not emancipated to vacate Iowa in three days. After notification, if they remained, the officials could arrest them and fine them two dollars for each day they stayed past the three-day warning. The law required officials to incarcerate the offenders until their payment of their fines, at which point the authorities released them to leave the state. The new rules did not apply to free African Americans, whom the state had permitted to remain.

The state restrictions soon were replicated on the county level. Henry County bordered Lee County to the north and did not experience as much of a migration of African Americans as Lee had over the years. Then again, Lee directly bordered a slave state, but Henry did not. Nevertheless, the latter county became more sympathetic to slaveholders than the former did. In 1850, for example, a jury in the county awarded a man $290 in damages and approximately one thousand dollars in legal fees from the state's residents who helped his slaves escape from him. In so doing the county decidedly declined to support the Underground Railroad to which its southern neighbor belonged.[58]

The court case exemplified not only Henry County's sympathy toward slaveholders but also its permissiveness towards the practice of slavery itself there. Virginian Elijah Richards settled with his family and slave in the county around this time. He had married and started his family in Virginia. They relocated to the Iowa town of New London, where he began work as a merchant. The fifteen-year-old African American girl who came with them was born in Alabama instead of Virginia. In addition, in the 1850 census, she possessed no surname. As with other Upper Mississippi slaves like the Rountrees' Rachel in Wisconsin, the census simply identified Richards' servant by her first name — Kate.

As in Van Buren County, the juvenile servitude that characterized Illinois slavery extended to Henry County. In 1854 Kate gave birth to Rose Madison. The newborn was identified by state and federal censuses as mulatto. They stayed under the same roof for at least four years. Before the end of the decade, Kate no longer lived in the Richards household. On the other hand, Rose stayed and became the domestic servant for Elijah and his family before her eighth birthday. Although living in a different county, Rose had much in common with Catharine Townsend. Both were Iowa-born mulattoes with no African American men in the households where they resided, and both girls became the only domestic servants of otherwise European American households.

Meanwhile, in Des Moines County, a family of recent southern migrants had taken an adult slave, instead of a child, with them. Virginian Jacob Miller and his Kentucky-born wife, Nancy, added baby daughter Emaly to their family in Iowa in 1849. The following year's census showed that their household also included 42-year-old African American woman Arabla Haws from Jacob's home state. She labored for the Millers for only a short time. The subsequent state and federal censuses did not list her as part of the Miller household after 1850, but they did not indicate whether Haws had married, escaped, become emancipated, or died.

The interest of some settlers in the preservation of slavery was threatened by shifts in state politics throughout the 1850s. On April 8, 1854, James W. Grimes, Iowa's gubernatorial candidate from the Whig Party, wrote of his concern over the state's vulnerability to slavery, especially in the context of the Kansas-Nebraska Act. The Senate had just passed the bill, which allowed Kansas and Nebraska popular sovereignty to decide whether the two territories would enter the Union as slave or free states. Some of the frenzy politicians tried to incite pitted minority groups against one another. "In the boastfulness of anticipated triumph, the citizens of Iowa have been told by a Southern

Senator how much better would be the condition of our State with negro slaves than with our foreign population," he warned. Others tried to scare people with dramatic predictions. As Grimes put it, "A distinguished Representative from Georgia has announced that in fifteen years Iowa will be a slave State." Then, however, the gubernatorial candidate added his own dire foretelling: "I sincerely believe that, should the Missouri Compromise be repealed, there will soon be a contest for the mastery between freedom and slavery on the soil of Iowa." Oblivious to a growing cry among U.S. citizens for popular sovereignty, he did not understand why people were pushing for the repeal of the Missouri Compromise if Nebraska had no possibility of becoming a slave state. As someone detached from the South, he had no way of relating to the increasing anti-federalism from the southern migrants of the very state he wanted to lead.[59]

More importantly, he considered Iowa's survival contingent upon the confinement of slavery to the states where it currently existed. "If there is one State in the Union more interested than another, in the maintenance of the Missouri Compromise, it is the State of Iowa," he declared. "With a free, enterprising population on the west, our State will be vastly benefited by an early organization of Nebraska. With a slave State on our western border, I see nothing but trouble and darkness in the future." He predicted only trouble for Iowa if bordered not only by the slave state of Missouri but also a potential slave state of Nebraska. He worried that traffic from multiple new underground railroads and from southerners searching for fugitive slaves would increase. In addition Nebraskans would not align with Iowans against slavery but would quarrel with them because of their contrasting politics and interests. "The energies of our people will be paralyzed, our works of internal improvement will languish, and the bright anticipations of the future greatness of Iowa forever blasted," he predicted.[60]

The gubernatorial candidate then stated that the federal government would wash its hands of the issue of slavery if states were left to decide on their own whether to allow the institution. "The principle of non-intervention so strenuously contended for by the South will soon be extended to the free States of the Northwest," he said. In some places, he remarked, people believed that slaves were just part of a person's belongings and that the master could transfer them to a free state in a manner similar to transferring cattle and horses. To him, the repeal of the compromise threatened to bring the issue directly into the hands of Iowans. Whereas Iowans previously could take for granted that no public officials would directly address slavery, they were unable to do so with Grimes. "Citizens of Iowa," he called, "are you ready to meet this issue?"[61]

He elaborated about the readiness of the state's residents, because he foresaw only intense and prolonged discord as the result of the start of a discussion about slavery. "Are you prepared for the conflict that must assuredly come?" he inquired. "Whatever may be your opinions of the abstract question of slavery, or whatever might be your opinions of the Missouri Compromise, were it a new question, are you ready and willing to disturb it?" He reminded his fellow Iowans that southern legislators and their "southern votes" had already seemingly settled the question thirty-four years earlier. Pulling no punches regarding his judging of proslavery politicians, he accused supporters of the Kansas-Nebraska Bill of "sanction[ing] palpable violation of the public faith, merely for the sake of nationalizing slavery." To him the institution was not worth risking the citizens' trust in their government.[62]

Grimes, however, was not concerned simply for Iowa's welfare but for that of Nebraska, too. He reasoned that Nebraskans would harm their economy from the start if they allowed slave labor to fuel it. "Shall populous, thriving villages and cities spring up all over the face of Nebraska, or shall unthrift and sparseness, stand-still and decay, ever characterize that State?" he asked. He predicted that with Nebraska as a slave state, "unpaid, unwilling toil, inspired by no hope and impelled by no affection, [would] drag its weary, indolent limbs over that State, hurrying the soil to barrenness and leaving the wilderness a wilderness still." As a free state, however, Nebraska would "be thrown open to the hardy and adventurous freemen of our own country, and to the constantly-increasing tide of foreign exiles." Thus, he saw economic promise in the state's increasing ethnic diversity.[63]

He concluded by clarifying that he concerned himself merely with the expansion of slavery to the Upper Mississippi and further west. He had no quarrel with the South and did not intend to start one. He remarked, "I do not attempt or desire to interfere with slavery in the slaveholding States. I do not seek to violate any of the compromises of the Constitution." While implying disagreement with the South, he noted that he was no abolitionist. "I am content that the slaveholders of the South may possess their slaves, and be responsible for their control over them to their own laws and to their consciences," he stated. "I will not even presume to judge them." Concerning slavery's expansion, however, he threatened, "But, with the blessing of God, I will *war and war continually* against the abandonment to slavery of a single foot of soil now consecrated to freedom. Whether elected or defeated — whether in office or out of office — the Nebraska outrage shall receive no 'aid or comfort' from me." Advising that haste in expanding the United States itself makes waste, he promised, "And I here declare that, while I am as anxious as any man for the speedy organization of the new Territories, yet I will not only everywhere and at all times oppose their organization under a bill allowing the introduction of slavery, but, should the present bill pass, I will advocate its repeal and oppose the admission of Nebraska and Kansas into the Union as slave States." His remarks constituted the strongest antislavery rhetoric from an Upper Mississippi officeholder since the creation of the Northwest Territory. And it was unlikely to have emerged from Iowa earlier in its history, especially under slaveholding governors like Chambers. Through Grimes's words, Iowa showed that it had come a long way since then.[64]

In addition, the occupancy of Grimes in Iowa's governorship symbolized the state's political metamorphosis. The turmoil and violence in Kansas after the Kansas-Nebraska Bill's passage raised concerns among Iowa residents as to whether the unrest would spread north to Nebraskans and then east to themselves. Previous slaveholding governors and federal neglect of antislavery laws contributed to the confusion of the state's citizens as to where Iowa exactly stood on the issue of slavery. Grimes, on the other hand, was no southern migrant but rather a New Hampshire native who offered an uncompromising, clear articulation of his antislavery stance, and the voting populace rewarded him for it. Eight months after his aforementioned speech, Grimes assumed the state's highest office, ending the Democratic Party's long proslavery control over the governorship.[65]

While fewer in number than in other states of the Upper Mississippi Valley, enough abolitionists existed in Iowa to develop a system to help fugitive slaves to freedom. To be sure, some people supported the Fugitive Slave Law of 1850, but other residents demonstrated their opposition of it by expanding the Underground Railroad. In Iowa every county along the Mississippi River belonged to the railroad. On the other hand, some counties were more helpful than others. Lee County was one of the most active stops on the route, because it was the nearest free county to border the slave state of Missouri. Many fugitives continued upriver past Lee to the country of Canada, but some decided to stop in upriver Iowa and restart their lives as ex-slaves.[66]

Because of their involvement in the railroad, residents of the upriver counties occasionally courted conflict in relation to civil disobedience of the Fugitive Slave Law. In June 1855, one such event happened in Des Moines County in the town of Burlington. On June 23, 1855, a doctor named James was traveling with an African American before a mob encountered them and violently beat them. Authorities then arrested the two and incarcerated the African American, whom law enforcement believed was a runaway slave. "There is great excitement in town, and several collisions have grown out of it. How it will end no one knows," Grimes reported in a letter. The governor decided to not involve himself in the case, leaving it in the hands of the judicial branch. "I will furnish no aid to the man-stealer," he promised. "It has been determined the negro shall have able counsel and a resort to all legal means for his release before any other is resorted to." He hinted, however, that if not a public citizen, he would have sided with James. "I am sorry I am governor of the state," he lamented, "for, although I can and shall prevent the state authorities and officers from interfering in aid of the marshal, yet, if not in office, I am inclined to think I would be a law-breaker."[67]

The evolution of the case demonstrated the dangers of the Fugitive Slave Law. The son-in-law of the slave's owner declared by affidavit that the prisoner, whom he named Dick, was an enslaved laborer of his who stole one of his horses and fled north. After the filing of the affidavit, a United States marshal arrested Dick and placed him in jail. The case attracted an enormous crowd when it finally went to trial. The first witness—the son of the owner—admitted that the defendant was not Dick. The revelation caused a loud commotion inside and outside of the court. The judge closed the case, and the African American that people assumed was Dick went free. This kind of resolution to a fugitive slave case, however, was rare and even more so in southern states. If the master's son had misidentified the African American as Dick in the courtroom, the defendant would have stood a greater chance of being enslaved and returned to the South with the plaintiffs. Incidents of mistaken identity in cases involving runaway slaves happened often and usually to the detriment of the falsely accused.[68]

The celebration of Iowa citizens regarding the outcome of the trial proved that the state's political climate regarding slavery had changed. Spectators filled the courtroom to its capacity, and guards appeared at the door to keep any further interested people from going inside. The guards also controlled the crowd around the courthouse. Upon the announcement of the verdict, a loud shout erupted in the courtroom, and then the crowd outside of the building corresponded with a similar jubilant outcry. According to one spectator, the loud cheer went beyond the courthouse throughout the entire town of Burlington. Grimes recalled that about one thousand men then went with Dr. James to the Mississippi River and cheered once again as James set sail as a free man.[69]

As far as Grimes was concerned, no one would steal African Americans from Iowa for enslavement in the South on his watch as governor. "I am satisfied that the negro could never have been taken into slavery from Burlington," he bragged. The people who had beaten Doctor James and the man called Dick escaped before any legal official could hand them their writs for their mob violence. Nevertheless, no one had attempted to capture a fugitive slave in Des Moines County before this case, and no one else tried afterward. The case, which started as a possible example to antislavery activists to stop their abolitionism, instead encouraged them and signaled a further end to Iowa's slave power. Grimes, on the other hand, was overconfident in his prediction, because people not only continued to occasionally smuggled African Americans out as slaves but also kept enslaving people within the state during his administration.[70]

Still, African Americans continued to experience some social progress.

In the late 1850s, the foundation of segregation in Iowa had begun to crack. In 1857 the state mandated that the board of education provide public schools for the education of African American children as well as European American children. In effect, Iowa outlawed the denial of the access to education on the basis of skin color. In addition, the state eliminated its requirement for segregated transportation. These events collectively marked a significant change from the previous decade of the state's attempt to separate African Americans from European Americans as much as possible by law.

Politics that year, however, was another matter entirely. Iowa's new constitution restricted voting to European American men. All of the advancements African Americans had recently made in Iowa with public accommodations did not translate into political capital. European Americans no longer felt as threatened as they had one decade earlier about African American access to quality education or public travel. Neither of those aspects of socialization gave African Americans any control over the lives of European Americans, who still had the power to relegate African Americans to specific, less lucrative avenues for income. Suffrage, on the other hand, meant that African American votes could potentially influence the outcomes of elections. European Americans did not want the ethnic group to have the power to help determine who would govern the state, a county, or a town.

By this time Iowa had already embodied the history of slavery in the Upper Mississippi up to that point. The state's development consisted of events concerning slavery that paralleled those in the other upriver states. In the space of twenty years, Iowa's residents transformed the state from a proslavery area full of southern culture to a haven for abolitionists and fugitive slaves. In this regard the state was similar to Wisconsin. On the other hand, enough Iowans possessed an intense resistance to African Americans, slave or free, that Black Codes were the law. Illinois had already beaten Iowa in restricting African American migration and movement, and that state did so more systematically than Iowa, which — unlike Illinois — did not have a numerically significant African American population to restrict.

Iowa was the last upriver state to have the masses significantly determine the stances of counties on the slavery issue. With Iowa's entry into statehood, the only remaining territory of the Upper Mississippi was Minnesota. Although the territory became a state long after Iowa and the others had, Minnesota still followed the patterns of preceding upriver territories in having the federal government send officials to ignore federal antislavery laws. Its most powerful proslavery figure, however, was someone who had acquired power and prestige in the Upper Mississippi for all of his adult life.

CHAPTER FIVE

Hoteliers and Local Slaveholders: Slavery in Minnesota

THE RISE OF SLAVERY IN MINNESOTA happened when the institution had nationally begun to inspire harsh debate and had regionally declined in both popularity and practice. Congress passed bills that fueled the conflict. The growing migration of antislavery citizens to the Upper Mississippi resulted in the abandonment of slavery by all the other territories and states that had originally comprised the Northwest Territory, except for a few sporadic cases of slaveholding in the 1850s. Minnesota itself did not host many slaveholding presidential appointees in political offices or at military forts. In addition, most of the southern migrants who came to permanently reside in Minnesota did not own slaves.

Still, slavery survived Minnesota's period as a territory from 1849 to 1858. Many of the residents, despite lacking slaves, supported the Democratic Party, which promoted the existence of slavery without further federal restrictions. Although most of Minnesota's Democrats opposed the institution, they did not deny others the enjoyment of it. A few politicians and entrepreneurs capitalized upon the indifference of the local party towards the extension of slavery in areas of the territory that the party ruled. Publishers launched proslavery newspapers. Hoteliers built lodgings for proslavery vacationers and their non-vacationing slaves. Local Democrats preached on the good of slavery and the inferiority of African Americans, and some brought slaves to the territory when they found residents receptive to the presence of the institution.

Slavery emerged in Minnesota so late in the development of the Upper Mississippi partly because so few European Americans migrated from the South before the late 1840s. They were largely unable to do so in an efficient manner before upriver steamboat travel advanced. The first steamboat company of the Upper Mississippi — the Galena and Minnesota Packet — was formed in 1847 in Galena, Illinois, by Orrin Smith, H. L. Dousman, and B. W. Brisbois. The *Argo* was their first vessel.[1]

By the 1840s entrepreneurs in St. Louis had developed strong business ties to the Upper Mississippi. They conducted business in Alton and Galena, Illinois; Davenport, Dubuque and Keokuk, Iowa; and St. Paul, Minnesota. The steamboats that facilitated their transactions consisted of enslaved and free crew members. On the *Die Vernon*, the workforce was nearly evenly split — eleven slaves and thirteen freedmen. In contrast, vessels such as the *Kansas* and the *Iowa* carried more slaves than freedmen.[2]

The federal government organized Minnesota Territory while seeking to expand the South through war with Mexico. Unlike the new territories and states formed in the southwest region, Minnesota Territory did not result from military conflict with Mexico. On the other hand, the new northern territory and the lands acquired from Mexico had in common their roots in Jacksonian policy. President Jackson, who had led the country in the Black Hawk War and made slaveholders into Midwestern governors, had designs on Texas for statehood near the end of his presidency. He failed to accomplish his goal of Texas statehood, but he made some gains toward it. He sent an agent to Texas to draft propagandistic bulletins about the advantages of the country because he wanted to rally U.S. citizens to militarily conquer it. On December 22, 1836, the Jackson administration, relying on the content of the reports, asked Congress to recognize the independence of Texas. Such a move, the president's office argued, would lay the groundwork for Texas, Coahuila, Tamaulipas, and New Mexico to eventually become part of the United States. Congress agreed to acknowledge Texas as an independent country.[3]

The recognition did not immediately come to pass due, in large part, to differing views among citizens nationwide concerning slavery. Many residents of the northern states opposed Jackson's idea. As a population mostly of anti-slavery citizens, the northerners did not want to acquire more land for the purpose of creating more slave territory. Southerners and President Jackson's supporters, therefore, had to make Texas attractive to northerners by minimizing references to any possible expansion of slavery. The president decided, however, not to recognize Texas. He considered Mexico's acknowledgment of Texas more important and chose to have the United States wait "till the lapse of time or the course of events shall have proved beyond all cavil or dispute the ability of the people of that country to maintain their separate sovereignty, and to uphold the government established by them."[4]

Still, President John Tyler and his successor, James K. Polk, brought Jackson's vision to pass years later — an unsurprising development because both presidents had supported Jackson's candidacies for the office. They both governed like their predecessor, as well. Like Jackson in the Black Hawk War, President Polk waged war with indigenous people to acquire a significant amount of land. As a result, Texas became a new slave state, and, with Polk continuing Jackson's tradition of not enforcing antislavery legislation, the Southwest was poised to become another extralegal haven of slavery — just like the Upper Mississippi.

Southwestern slavery and Upper Mississippi slavery had another link in the person of Zachary Taylor. Over one decade earlier, he was a general and oversaw Fort Crawford at the upriver town of Prairie du Chien, Wisconsin Territory, and he had brought slaves to the fort during his tenure there. He still owned slaves at the time that war with Mexico began. Just as he had dealt with the indigenous peoples in the Midwest, he now fought other indigenous peoples for Texas in the 1840s.

The legacy of Taylor's involvement in upriver slavery soon affected the development of the United States itself. In May 1848, Wisconsin Territory entered statehood — an accomplishment owing markedly to Taylor's work two decades earlier while stationed there with his slaves. In the autumn of the same year, he had successfully exploited his leadership of the war against Mexico to his political advantage. The voting populace elected him to the presidency of the United States. He was the first former soldier of an Upper Mississippi territory to rise to the nation's highest office.[5]

Thus, his violation of federal law — holding slaves in a free land — did not hinder his ascension. Moreover, his opponents did not make his upriver slaveholding an issue in any of their campaigns against him. In essence they took his defiance of the Northwest Ordinance and the Missouri Compromise for granted. In addition, slavery transcended political party affiliation at the time. Because many southerners of various political beliefs took their slaves to forts nationwide, any attention that a politician gave to Taylor's enslaving would have ultimately drawn attention to the members of his own party who had done the same while in the military.

African American slavery in the Upper Mississippi had started several decades before Jackson's designs on opening the Southwest to the institution. In 1849 the creation of Minnesota Territory caused an influx of immigrants, which meant that more people from the South — including slaveholders— were on their way upriver to start their new lives. The increase in travelers consequently required more steamboat travel. The number of upriver arrivals by steamboat increased from forty-one in 1844 to forty-eight the following year. By the end of the decade, the number of arrivals had nearly doubled to eighty-five. Three years later, in 1852, the number doubled from its 1849 total to one hundred seventy-one migrants by steamboat.[6]

R. S. Harris was one of the earliest steamboat travelers to come to the Upper Mississippi, and slavery contributed to his experiences. He was born in New York in 1810 and spent some of his childhood in Ohio. Then at age fourteen, he and his family sailed upriver by flatboat to Galena. Thus, they

Five. Hoteliers and Local Slaveholders: Slavery in Minnesota

117

lived in the city when its mining industry had reached its peak, and they were exposed to southern migrants who had brought their slaves to the mines. In 1826, the Harrises themselves struck a significant amount of ore.[7]

At age seventeen, R. S. Harris left Galena for the steamboat-sailing profession and labored in it for the next seventeen years. Here, slavery impacted not only his job performance but also his life. He performed engineering, constructing, and commanding duties, many of which contributed to milestones in upriver transportation. In 1833, he constructed the *Jo Daviess*, the first boat erected on the Mississippi to the north of St. Louis, and he later commanded the *Otter* to St. Paul, the first vessel to regularly travel there. As a steamboat laborer on the Mississippi, he worked with southern crew members, which at times included slaves. In 1841, while sailing, he became ill with cholera at Vicksburg. He lay in bed for several days, and his mind was in a fog. Fellow passengers assumed that he was near death, but his African American servant nursed him back to health. Thanks in part to this servant, Harris lived to quit the steamboats four years later and work with his brother in trading boat supplies. By starting stores in Galena, Dubuque, St. Louis and St. Paul, they were dependent on southern customers as well as northern ones—just like when Harris was on the riverboats.[8]

When the federal government requested that the Reverend Lowry return to service in 1846, he obliged and took his family back to the Midwest. He resumed his work with the Ho-Chunk in Iowa. The family readjusted to life in a community without slavery. They also faced the new adjustment of living among impoverished indigenous people after having lived in a town populated by high-income European Americans.

Upon the return of the Lowrys to the Upper Mississippi in 1846, Sylvanus emerged as a politically powerful figure in his own right. That year the federal government called upon him for the first time to travel to Washington, D.C., to serve as interpreter of the Ho-Chunk language during treaty negotiations. He witnessed the signing of the government's treaty with the tribe on October 13. Congress agreed to pay him $305 for his brief service at the nation's capital. He was only twenty-three years old.

Sylvanus and his father resumed their collaborative working relationship at the mission. The minister remained dependent upon his son to preserve the status quo there as much as possible. In 1848 the federal government ordered the tribe to relocate from Winneshiek County to Long Prairie, but the Ho-Chunk refused to move at first. The Reverend Lowry moved his family to Fort Snelling before the tribe had left Winneshiek, fearing that the indigenous people would not comply with a treaty forcing another removal. He called upon Sylvanus, now twenty-five years old, to come to Iowa to mediate between the Indians and dragoons, so that the Indians would move. Over the next few years, father and son interposed to prevent violence among the Ho-Chunk.[9]

Sylvanus soon surpassed his father in wealth and prestige. Born on July 24, 1823, his namesake was the Roman god of forests, fields, and herds. His nickname, "Sam," came from Samuel, the biblical figure who avoided the destructive behavior of his elders. As he grew into adulthood, he embodied the traits of those names. He became a rich fur trader while at Blue Earth in the late 1840s. As a result of his joining the fur trade, he became what his father had abhorred during earlier missions with the Ho-Chunk. Still, substantial income and social power were attractive qualities to the trade, and his father as an unsuccessful missionary had neither quality. Consequently, Sylvanus went into the trading business with Henry M. Rice and joined the American Fur Company, which established offices in Watab (where Lowry lived) and Winnebago Prairie.[10]

His business success only grew from then onward. Lowry, Rice, and Henry Hastings Sibley united in the summer of 1848 as the Northern Outfit, combining Dakota, Ho-Chunk, and Ojibwe trading. Lowry worked with the Ho-Chunk at Rice's direction, and Rice dealt with the Ojibwe. Sibley left the organization by 1850.[11]

Sylvanus, however, could not stop his father's self-sabotage of the mission. After fifteen years the Reverend Lowry still had not mastered the Ho-Chunk language. He remained frustrated at the resistance of the tribe towards his efforts. In addition, the minister at times initiated violence against members of the tribe. He forcefully struck drunken tribal members with a club as punishment for their inebriation, to "club them into good behavior," as *Todd County Histories* put it.[12]

The Reverend Lowry retired from missionary life in 1850. He, Mary Ann, and Elizabeth removed themselves to Lebanon once again. The minister remained active in the Cumberland Presbyterian denomination. He served as co-editor and co-proprietor of the church's periodical *Banner of Peace*. By this time his missionary work had spanned seventeen years and six presidents. Ironically, the last president under whom he served as Ho-Chunk missionary was Zachary Taylor, who as a colonel had directly supervised his work at Prairie du Chien and in Iowa in the 1830s.[13]

Regardless of whatever stance the Reverend Lowry took about slavery, that year his family renewed its participation in the institution. Elizabeth married a local clergyman, the Rev. Thomas P. Calhoun, who shared his father-in-law's profession of Cumberland Presbyterian minister. The two clergymen also had in common the holding of slaves. The Reverend Lowry had held one slave twenty years earlier in Kentucky, but no censuses of his previous seventeen years in the Upper Mississippi listed him with any human chattel. Calhoun's father, on the other hand, was a lifelong slaveholder. He owned fourteen slaves in 1840 and seventeen in 1850. The senior Calhoun, moreover, possessed a relatively high number of slaves among his neighbors in Wilson County, Tennessee. Most slaveholders of the county — and of the Cumberland area of the state, in general — owned no more than two or three enslaved African Americans.

Thomas P. Calhoun became ordained as a Cumberland Presbyterian minister, starting in 1852. The local branch of the denomination regarded African Americans as part of the religious community but as second-class members. At the time slaves often worshipped at the churches their owners attended. The seating was segregated, with the slaves sitting in the back pews. On the other hand, the Cumberland Presbyterians allowed slaves some agency regarding their worship experiences, however limited. The denomination's elders at Lebanon bought an old

Sylvanus Lowry, a slaveholding mayor in Minnesota. **Courtesy Stearns History Museum Archives.**

church building for African Americans to use for their own services. Despite this gift, the elders did not leave the slaves completely alone to worship as they pleased. A European American minister of the denomination supervised each African American church service. In addition, if a slave elder wanted to preach a sermon, he required the approval of a European American minister before doing so. Still, the denomination tended to supervise slave worship services in a casual manner.[14]

When Calhoun's father died in 1855, he inherited three slaves from his father. They were an African American woman named Cherry, her daughter named Lucinda, and an African American man named Pa. The new master's collective inheritance reflected some aspects of his lifestyle. Censuses listed him as either a student or a minister, but people rarely identified him as a farmer or someone engaged in some kind of agricultural work. Thus, his mostly female inheritance signaled that his father had not envisioned his son as a future planter and that his new slaves were to be domestics. Then again, by giving his son women to enslave, the elder Calhoun also gave his son an opportunity to obtain a male workforce by impregnating his new female possessions with sons. Still, any newborn sons would take years to grow into the physical traits needed for plantation labor. If Calhoun's father considered farming a possibility for him, it was still a deferred dream.

Calhoun had a tight bond with the Lowry family. He and the Reverend Lowry not only practiced ministry in the same denomination but also officiated services together. The Reverend Lowry was close in age to Calhoun's father, and Calhoun and General Lowry were also peers in age. Calhoun, therefore, was like the religious son that the Reverend Lowry never had, because Sylvanus did not follow in his father's path. Further showing his closeness to the family, Calhoun named two of his children after his parents-in-law. Most importantly, just as the Reverend Lowry had done in his youth, Calhoun was a small slaveholder.

Through Elizabeth's uniting of her family with the Calhouns, the Lowrys indirectly witnessed wealth and prestige that had completely eluded them in both Kentucky and the Upper Mississippi. In addition to holding a large number of slaves, Thomas P. Calhoun's parents could afford educational opportunities for him. Not only was he a college student — a privilege that Sylvanus and Elizabeth had missed while ministering to the Ho-Chunk — but also an out-of-state student. In addition, he studied at expensive private academies; he attended both Princeton and the Andover Theological Seminary. He did not, however, fully complete his studies.

By marrying into a slaveholding family, Elizabeth broke from her father's antislavery feelings. Both of the Reverend Lowry's children, however, were establishing ideological independence from him at around the same time. One major factor contributing to Sylvanus' decision not to move to Lebanon with his family was his newfound power and prestige in Minnesota. He involved himself in the fur trade that his father had both despised and blamed for the unruliness of the Ho-Chunk. In addition, he no longer participated in ministerial labor, which Elizabeth still performed but as a clergyman's wife as well as a missionary's daughter.

As the Lowrys resettled in the South, few of their fellow southerners ventured to the West, especially the Northwest. European American southern migrants had comprised the majority of settlers there before 1850. They found slavery less suitable in the new region than back home, which led the migration from the South to slow to nearly a halt. Meanwhile, more northerners than southerners journeyed westward. Migrants from Ohio, New York, and Illinois also helped give the region more of a northern than a southern character, although Illinois welcomed slaveholding migrants, too.[15]

By 1850, therefore, Sylvanus stood out from other Midwesterners by staying in the Upper Mississippi and supporting slavery despite the influx of northerners. He had established his own reputation in Minnesota Territory. He had crafted it by working on his father's mission, although the Reverend Lowry did not give his son the specific training by which he established his own identity. Sylvanus earned the trust and respect of the indigenous people through communication, which the elder Lowry had failed to do. He had impressed the federal government by learning the indigenous language that his father never grasped. Breaking further from his parentage, Sylvanus began the new decade by adding to his power and prestige through business. Ironically, by the end of the decade, he had acquired stature in the same way that his father had done — through appointments by proslavery, slaveholding politicians. In the process he became a proslavery, slaveholding politician himself.

In 1849 the antislavery provision of the Northwest Ordinance extended to Minnesota Territory. When organizing the new territory, the federal government extended the ordinance's provisions to the land. The government had already done so when organizing the territories of Wisconsin and Iowa. Minnesota Territory, in fact, received its ordinance provisions indirectly, because the federal government had extended Wisconsin Territory's privileges to its new territorial neighbor. Now, both the federal antislavery laws in the ordinance and compromise were officially Minnesota law.[16]

Meanwhile, upon his inauguration, President Taylor quickly became the victim of the legacy of slavery expansion that had catapulted him to the presidency. Some supporters of slavery, for example, were not satisfied with the potential for slavery in the southwest and the *de facto* slavery in the Upper Mississippi. Some of them now wanted to conquer Cuba and make it another potential area of legal slavery, just as Taylor had accomplished with Texas. Californians wanted statehood, but abolitionists and anti-expansionists did not want it to enter the Union as a slave state. Congress quarreled over the issue for months. The controversies unnerved the new president, and his mental health rapidly deteriorated as he assumed these and other national responsibilities.[17]

In the end the arguments about slavery, among other problems, proved too much for President Taylor to bear. After only one year, he caught a cold, and after suffering it for over five days, he died on July 9, 1850. His last words were, "I am not afraid to die. I am ready. I have endeavored to do my duty." He either felt that he had done all that he could regarding the issues he faced despite his health, or he was simply ready to leave behind the stresses of the job that had impaired his health in the first place. Regardless, with his passing, his long era of extending slavery to new lands, especially in the Midwest, came to an end. His successor, Millard Fillmore, had not helped Taylor bring slavery to the Upper Mississippi but did serve in the Mexican War.[18]

By the mid–1850s southern migration to Minnesota Territory by steamboat had reached a peak level. Some travelers went there simply to enjoy the experience of upriver sailing. They were in no rush to arrive at their destination. Minnesota resident Isaac Atwater wrote, "The first boats were small stern-wheelers, not noted for speed, but they were models of ease and comfort, and the trip through the lovely scenery of the Mississippi highlands was delightful." He appreciated the friendliness and helpfulness of the vessel's crew, and he marveled at their professionalism and the high quality of their work. "They presided at the table with old-time punctilious courtesy," he began, "and the meals were taken leisurely and agreeably as if in one's own home. As the table was furnished generously with the best products of the St. Louis market, the guests found themselves in such good case that no murmur of complaint arose even when the trip from Galena consumed five days."[19]

African Americans played a central role in the passengers' enjoyment of the voyages. Because so many southerners came to Minnesota Territory by boat, the captains tended to try to approximate the kind of service and entertainment the southerners would have received if they had never left their homes. In some cases the approximation involved the African American crew members' willingness to play to old ethnic stereotypes. "The negro servants were charming with their kindly ways," Atwater noted, "and willing service, as if given for love rather than money — the old-fashioned, jolly, care-free sort who worked all day, and played the banjo and sang and danced all night." With blackface minstrel shows beginning to appear all over the country at the time, captains tried to keep up with the times by having African Americans perform songs on board. "There were some very sweet voices among them," Atwater reminisced, "and their songs came floating to our ears from the lower deck, softened by distance and mingled with the gentle swish of the water with the most charming effect. These simple, impromptu concerts added much to the pleasures of the trip."[20]

Atwater's experiences with African Americans on the boat were not unusual at the time of his trip. In the 1850s, nearly every riverboat on the Mississippi River operated through slave labor. Bonded African Americans served as deck attendants, cabin attendants, cooks, and stevedores, among other positions. As long as the boats remained in the Mississippi River south of Iowa and Illinois, they were just another means by which slaveholders exploited slave labor in the South. On the other hand, when the steamboats were between Iowa and Illinois or between Minnesota and Wisconsin, they violated the Northwest Ordinance and the Missouri Compromise. Steamboat captains, therefore, continued a tradition that the Galena miners had begun thirty years earlier in the 1820s — the extralegal use of southern African American slaves to start and perpetuate an industry in the Midwest. Federal policing of riverboat transportation for slave contraband was nonexistent, not unlike the government's permissiveness towards James Johnson and his mining slaves.[21]

Slaveholders came to Minnesota Territory for various reasons. Southerners stayed during the summer months for the cooler climate not simply for enjoyment but also to escape malarial fever. The territory was very Democratic; in Congress territorial representatives and southern Democrats were friends. Some Minnesota legislators tried to capitalize on these demographics and pass proslavery legislation. They attempted to push through a law allowing southerners to bring slaves to the territory for six months per year. The Mississippi River also connected the territory with the South, which provided those below the Mason-Dixon Line with easy access to the Midwest.[22]

Many entrepreneurs came to Minnesota Territory to build businesses from the territory's popularity with southerners. Some of them were not even from the South, nor had they lived there for any considerable length of time. Nevertheless, they knew that some of their southern patrons were sensitive to how northerners would receive them if slaves were to accompany them. The entrepreneurs, therefore, promised to preserve their potential customers' southern lifestyles as much as possible. One such businessman, James Winslow, was born in Vermont and came to Minnesota in 1852 to make money from slaveholders.[23]

Winslow's vision took four years and a considerable amount of money to bring to fruition. He hired Robert Alden to design the Winslow House hotel. It was a five-story, $110,000 hotel of Nicollet Island limestone. Inside were two hundred guest rooms, a lavish ballroom, and $60,000 in settings. The waterfall was audible from inside. By 1856 construction was completed, and the hotel opened.[24]

James Winslow built the hotel partly, if not solely, to cater to the southerners and their African American slaves. Even when advertising to a particular region, however, he prioritized a particular economic class. The hotel housed vacationing wealthy and fashionable southerners during the summers, which meant that yeomen farmers with few to no slaves could not afford to stay there. By and large, planters were the southern clientele. As one settler remembered, "Ladies, old and young, plainly dressed and accompanied by their colored servants and nurses, each with goblet or drinking-cup of some description in hand, wending their way to the springs."[25]

The wealthy planters became prized patrons of the hoteliers. When they brought their slaves with them, they expected their African Americans to perform such duties as valets, maids, and nurses. People whose incomes depended on the slaveholding clientele made no fuss to the presence of the slaves. Some innkeepers did not want to risk offending their rich customers. Others considered the matter a southern issue for the South to handle and did not, therefore, want to bring the debate about the institution to the Midwest. In addition, the presence of the slaves in the hotels was only temporary; by the fall season, they would return with their masters to the South and not become an awkward issue again for another eight or nine months, when the summer season once again arrived.[26]

Some travelers concerned themselves with how well the territorial government enforced the ordinance and the compromise. Some of them believed that a slave remained a slave in Minnesota Territory as long as the owner had control over the slave; as soon as a slave escaped from the slaveholder in the territory, the African American became emancipated. Although some people refused to travel upriver with their slaves at the risk of their escape in free land, others decided to take the gamble. An annual Winslow guest named Col. Slaybeck, for example, resigned himself to the possibility of his slaves taking advantage of their legal emancipation upon setting foot in the Midwest. He always brought his family and his slaves to the hotel. Each year he reminded his slaves upon arrival, "Now you are in the north where they do not own slaves, and if you wish to escape, this is your chance to run away."[27]

None of Slaybeck's slaves ever took advantage of Minnesota Territory's free status, however. Instead, they returned to the South with him as his slaves at the end of each annual vacation. Thus, they did not see the territory as their promised land. They would not have had a significant population of African Americans with whom to socialize. They would have had to start new lives as their own people in an area in which European Americans restricted African Americans to the lowest-paying positions of employment. They also risked returning to enslavement anyway after 1850 because of the Fugitive Slave Law. Anyone could have captured them and sold them to a different master than Colonel Slaybeck.[28]

According to St. Anthony resident Cyrus Brooks, the locals generally assumed that all visiting slaves received legal counseling similar to what Slaybeck annually told his property. Brooks did not say whether the townspeople believed that slaves had learned about Minnesota's free status from their owners or from other sources. He remembered that the residents had taken for granted the territory's antislavery reputation and, therefore, had thought that slaves had only themselves to blame for remaining enslaved in Minnesota. "The feeling of the citizens seemed to be," William Fletcher King recalled of his conversation with Brooks, "that if slaves were so stupid that they did not desire liberty, it would not do much good if they had it." King himself expressed shock that, despite the freedom he believed was legally given to slaves upon setting foot in the territory, "still they appeared to choose to remain with [their masters], and to go back into slavery."[29]

Although Minnesota Territory was unique in its dependence on nonslaveholding migrants for maintaining slavery, more traditional means in the region such as proslavery presidential appointments still took place. In 1853 newly inaugurated President Franklin Pierce, a Democrat, appointed Willis A. Gorman to govern Minnesota because of his support of slavery. When Gorman had served as a congressman, he voted for the Fugitive Slave Bill. Gorman, in turn, followed Pierce's lead and appointed Sylvanus

Five. Hoteliers and Local Slaveholders: Slavery in Minnesota

125

Lowry to the territorial government office of adjutant general on May 15, 1853.[30]

By the time of his gubernatorial appointment, Lowry had already won territorial elections, thus demonstrating support from the local masses despite (or perhaps because of) his proslavery stance. He was elected a Minnesota Territory legislator, representing the fifth district in the session that lasted from January 7 to March 6, 1852. Lowry now had political power in Minnesota for the first time. He won reelection for a second consecutive term and returned to the legislature on January 5, 1853. When Gorman appointed Lowry adjutant general, he accepted and abruptly resigned from the territorial legislature. Meanwhile, he worked well with other masses besides European American ones. He lived in Watab on a farm among the 500 members of the Ho-Chunk tribe — a development that validated how well he had related to them over the years.[31]

Governor Gorman initially took Lowry personally and professionally under his wing. He gave the general other responsibilities that extended beyond his new political appointment. The governor took him to interpret for the Ho-Chunk on the occasion of another treaty-signing on August 6, 1853. The trip was mutually beneficial. Gorman was able to show President Pierce that he could effectively manage the indigenous affairs of his territory as governor. Meanwhile, Lowry gained more experience and time among influential federal politicians in the nation's capital.[32]

Lowry's experience in the office, however brief, changed the course of his life. His relationship with Gorman soured soon after the treaty-signing trip. Lowry quarreled with the governor, who then dismissed him from the position of adjutant general. However, he had served so effectively there that for the remainder of his life, no matter what new positions he acquired, the locals continued to refer to him as General Lowry. In addition, upon his firing he had attained significant sociopolitical influence in Minnesota Territory and was now poised to parlay it into a political career without Gorman's help. In fact, in the year after his dismissal, he became the district attorney for Benton County, Minnesota. Having begun his practice of bringing slaves upriver from the South to live with him, he now practiced law on a local governmental level while breaking laws (the ordinance and the compromise) on a federal level.

The rise in power of sympathizers with slavery in Minnesota Territory took place as the federal government began devising new federal laws to weaken the old federal prohibitions of slavery in the Midwest. Congress passed the Fugitive Slave Bill in 1850, which mandated that all Americans, whether in free or slave land, return any fugitive slaves to their owners. African Americans, whether free or slaves, now ran the risk of apprehension by people who claimed to own them. Living in the North now offered no protection for them from that risk.

The Midwest offered a mixed reaction to the legislation — a symbol of the inconsistent policies among the territories and states there concerning slavery over the past nearly seven decades. A couple of Upper Mississippi congressmen supported the bill. From Burlington, Iowa, in Des Moines County, Rep. Shepherd Leffler voted for its passage. Rep. William A. Richardson — another aye vote — represented Quincy, Illinois, a city in a county (Adams) that almost bordered Iowa. Wisconsin, however, was notable in that none of its congressmen voted in favor of the bill; rather, the three representatives of that state rejected the legislation. Meanwhile, eight of Iowa's congressmen did not vote on the measure at all.

The federal government delivered a second, even more devastating blow to freedom in the Upper Mississippi only four years later. Congress passed the Kansas-Nebraska Bill in 1854. By invalidating the Missouri Compromise, the law now made possible the addition of slave states in any region of the country, including the Upper Mississippi. Popular sovereignty, which served as the way of life in the Northwest Territory, was now part of the West.

One of the leading supporters of the bill was a product of slavery in the Upper Mississippi — Henry Dodge's son Augustus, now a senator from Iowa. When Congress assembled in December 1853, Senator Dodge became chairman of the Committee on Public Lands. Almost immediately he introduced a bill to organize the Territory of Nebraska. The proposal called for the inclusion of lands now comprising the states of Nebraska, North Dakota, South Dakota, Kansas, Montana and portions of Colorado and Wyoming. Barely one thousand people lived in that large area. He did not mention slavery at all.

The institution became an issue one month later, when Senator Stephen Douglas offered a substitute for Dodge's proposal. Known as the Kansas-Nebraska Bill, it called for the repeal of the 36° 30' boundary of slavery from the Compromise of 1820. It also permitted slavery into the proposed territories as long as the residents of the territories decided to have it. In a sense Douglas's proposal was already a reality in much of the Upper Mississippi. Slavery existed in several communities there, because the local residents permitted it; and among those residents, some of them facilitated it. Thus, the Missouri Compromise had long been an ignored letter by the federal government. Passage of the Kansas-Nebraska Bill made the compromise a dead letter by officially repealing it.

Governor Gorman soon became unwittingly involved in Kansas's conflict over slavery. He received a letter from Free Soil Party member Jim Lane, in which he asked the governor for help against armed "Border Ruffians." The governor, however, warned Minnesota Territory politicians to stay out of the discord in Kansas. As part of his policy of non-intervention, he refused to recognize Lane and fellow Free Soil Party member Charles Robinson as Kansas officers. Gorman supported popular sovereignty there without interference from outside that territory.

Shortly after the Kansas-Nebraska bill became law in May 1854, more masters became emboldened to resettle in Minnesota Territory now that the new law invalidated the Missouri Compromise. For example, a new slave-holding family moved from Boone County, Kentucky, to settle in Hennepin County, Minnesota. According to the 1850 census, John Kirtley had owned three slaves before moving northwest. One of them, a woman in her fifties named Silvia, had served the Kirtleys for decades. After John Kirtley's grand-father Jeremiah died in 1806, Boone County listed "1 Negro girl named Silvey" among the property of the deceased, and she was worth $300. Fifty years later, she was the only slave in the Kirtley household in Minnesota. In her first census as a Minnesota slave, the Kirtleys did not even bother to give Silvia a surname.[33]

John Kirtley was a rarity among Upper Mississippi masters at this time. He traveled at his own volition instead of migrating because of a federal appointment. In addition, he deviated from most of the other southern migrants by staying permanently in the Midwest in the 1850s. As one of the wealthier slaveholders in Minnesota, he could certainly afford to do so. In 1850, he owned $7,000 worth of real estate. When he moved to Hennepin County, he settled on land worth $3,000 but held a personal estate worth $5,000. He continued the profession of farming in Minnesota that he had practiced in Kentucky.

Still, for all his uniqueness, the kind of slavery that Kirtley practiced in Minnesota reflected the aristocratic proslavery culture that some of the migrant politicians and hoteliers had fostered. He followed the lead of Upper Mississippi slaveholders of the previous decade by bringing a domestic slave from the South. Even when he had lived in Kentucky, however, he did not rely entirely on a labor force of slaves for his farming. Besides Silvia, the only slaves on Kirtley's farm were a woman in her seventies and a man in his thir-ties. Unsurprisingly, he employed European American free laborers to farm his land in both Boone County and Hennepin County.

In Minnesota Territory Sylvanus Lowry finally separated from the family to chart his own course in life. When the Reverend Lowry took the family back down South in 1850 upon retirement from mission work, the young Ho-Chunk translator refused to go. He decided, instead, to work in Watab (now Brockway), Minnesota, for the same fur-trade company as Rolette had, which could not have pleased the minister. He became the first European American to settle in central Minnesota for an extended period. According to the Still-water, Minnesota, Land Office, he bought 72.4 acres of land in Benton County on August 7, 1853. Later that year he claimed land in northern Stearns County and built the town's first white-owned dwelling there the following spring.[34]

Upper Saint Cloud, Minnesota, 1858. The community consisted of slaveholders and supporters of slavery. Courtesy Stearns History Museum Archives.

He was one of three people who platted land in the 1850s in what later became St Cloud. George Brott's section of Lower Town and John Wilson's Middle Town had populations mostly of recent European immigrants. Meanwhile, Lowry's Upper Town, which he called Acadia, eventually consisted of at least five wealthy, educated, pro-slavery southern families, including his own.[35]

St. Cloud had an ideal location. It was less than one hundred miles northwest of the Twin Cities. It sat along the western side of the Upper Mississippi River, making the city accessible by water. European immigrants leaving the East Coast by land could then take the river to the central Minnesota city. Several southerners also took advantage of its proximity to the river by either migrating or vacationing there. Thus, when Lowry called for others from the South to settle in Acadia, he found several takers.

Gen. Lowry lived slightly above St. Cloud's boundary, in Acadia, and owned a 300-acre farm of very fertile land. The farm was bordered with a durable fence, and cattle heavily populated the land. He brought slaves there, too. He lived in a house of Southern-style splendor with columns in St. Cloud;

Five. Hoteliers and Local Slaveholders: Slavery in Minnesota

129

the house overlooked the Mississippi River. He constructed his house by dismantling his fur trading post at Watab and rebuilding it in St. Cloud. Beautiful flower gardens stretched to a prairie full of wild strawberries. As someone who had grown up alongside the Yellow River and the Turkey River, his building of his home by the Mississippi River was par for the course.[36]

Visiting Acadia in October 1856, his close friend, C. C. Andrews, described Lowry's lavish, Southern-style house: "The residence of my friend is a little above the limits of St. Cloud, midway on the gradual rise from the river to the prairie. It is a neat white two-story cottage, with a piazza in front. The yard extends to the water's edge, and it is in a grove of handsome shade trees." Because he saw Acadia in the fall, he could "sit on the piazza and have a full view of the river through the branches of the trees." He depicted the farm as "splendid land, which is well stocked with cattle and durably fenced. A better barn, or a neater farm-yard than he has, cannot be found between Boston and Worcester."[37]

Lowry's home served as a microcosm of St. Cloud's social and political imbalance of power. In 1856 Lowry, his parents, Uncle Leonard Jones, and European immigrant farm laborers lived in the General's Acadia home. In this household the southerners ruled the estate and exploited the immigrants. After having received care and service from slaves and Winnebagoes all of his life, Lowry apparently still needed people to cater to him and manage the household labor, even if the laborers were white. Similarly, Upper Town was the most commercially successful of the city's three sections. Southerners owned the businesses there and served in the political offices of the city. Immigrants had little economic or political voice.

Gen. Lowry's power in St. Cloud expanded geographically as well as politically. As of February 13, 1856, he had legal permission to possess and maintain a ferry across the Mississippi River on or close to Ferry Street in town. Two months later on April 2, the town of St. Cloud officially organized. The residents then formed a town council and elected Gen. Lowry to serve as its president. He had, in effect, become St. Cloud's first mayor. He served in that capacity for one year.[38]

He possessed a great talent in mesmerizing people, and they respected his wealth and his opening of much of Minnesota's Indian land to European Americans. Moreover, they seemed to endorse his pro-slavery position. The immigrant population consisted mostly of Democrats. They demonstrated considerable loyalty to their party by electing their southern migrant fellow party-members, despite their differences of opinion on slavery.

That same spring, the Reverend Lowry made one more attempt at missionary work but not for the federal government or with the indigenous peoples. Coming out of a six-year retirement, he returned to Minnesota Territory to organize a Cumberland Presbyterian Church among European Americans.

The Biggerstaff, Lamb and Ketcham families were among his parishioners in the city of St. Cloud. Whereas he had experienced difficulty in keeping slavery out of Prairie du Chien in Wisconsin Territory, he now worked in a community that largely disapproved of slavery. In another point to his advantage, he did not have detractors like the old fur traders of years past to deliberately hinder his ministerial efforts.[39]

As news accounts of slavery in Minnesota Territory spread across the country, a migrant from Connecticut significantly contributed to the survival of the peculiar institution in the territory. Alpheus Fuller built the Fuller House in 1856. He had come to Minnesota Territory in 1850. His hotel was five stories high and 120 square feet. He paid $110,000 in order to build a hotel to eclipse other local hotels like the Winslow, although coincidentally both he and Winslow paid exactly the same amount of money to establish their hotels.[40]

Slaveholders and other southerners spent vacations at the hotel. Christopher C. Andrews stayed there for three days in October 1856, shortly after it had first opened. He saw the southern clientele and sampled the high-class amenities for himself. "There were a number of guests from the South," he remarked. "At the Sunday dinner, many of the guests had champagne." His stay there and his visit to General Lowry exemplified how deeply southern culture and slaveholding culture had saturated central Minnesota Territory.[41]

Another northern migrant — Orrin Day — bought the Hyperborean Hotel of Sauk Rapids on August 5, 1857. It was famous as a lodge on the stage routes between St. Paul and Fort Ripley and between St. Paul and Breckenridge. He, like James Winslow and Alpheus Fuller before him, was an unlikely facilitator of African American upriver slavery. At the time of his purchase of the hotel, Day was the county coroner and the town postmaster. He was born in New York. Several members of central Minnesota's slaveocracy lived in the Hyperborean. The Caruthers brothers and the Hays men stayed there simultaneously in the fall of 1857.[42]

Minnesota Territory generated income from the presence of slaves, just as Wisconsin Territory had done over three decades earlier. The lodging of slaveholders and their slaves in Minnesota Territory gave the hotel-owners steady income, not unlike the wealth accumulated by mine owners in Wisconsin Territory through their mining slaves. When James Winslow's large investment paid off in a grand manner, for example, he tried to enrich himself throughout Minnesota and bring in tourism to each new location. By the following year, the Winslow House was at its peak in business. He decided to try his luck by making a chain out of the hotel. Winslow constructed St. Paul and St. Peter, Minnesota, branches of the Winslow House. That summer the hotel receipts averaged at $6,000 per month.[43]

The hotels of Minnesota Territory and the old mines of Galena had in common the exploitation of slave labor as the foundation of free-territory industries. But many more major differences existed between the two kinds of businesses. In the mines the slaves had produced the lead that enriched the mine owners. In the hotels, however, the hotel owners worked for their money by quartering the slaveholders and slaves. The chattel produced nothing to increase the wealth of the hoteliers. In addition, the owners of the mining slaves had run the mines, meaning that the slaves generated wealth for their owners. The owners of the hotels, however, were not slaveholders. Therefore, the slaveholders made the hoteliers richer, not themselves. Also, the mining slaves had lived in Wisconsin Territory on a permanent basis in order to work, and they founded some African American communities there after being emancipated by their owners. In contrast, the slaves in hotels stayed in Minnesota Territory only temporarily and did not permanently become part of the area's population; they returned to the South enslaved.

Not every southern migrant chose to stay in hotels. Rather, some developed their own towns and counties after enough of them had settled in those areas in the territory. Migrants named both a town and county after Kentucky's proslavery senator John C. Breckinridge. Another community christened its county after Senator Robert Toombs of Georgia, who also supported enslaving African Americans. Monongalia's namesake was a county in Virginia. Still, none of these communities supported and practiced slavery as intensely as Stearns and Benton counties did.

The federal government, meanwhile, prepared to reinforce slavery even further in central Minnesota. Upon his inauguration in 1857, President James Buchanan appointed southerners William Allen Caruthers and Samuel Lewis Hays to the Sauk Rapids Land Office. Both officers lived in slaveholding households and brought their proslavery views to central Minnesota Territory. They dominated the politics of that part of the territory for the next two years. As a result, Buchanan indirectly helped perpetuate slavery there. His predecessors Martin Van Buren and William Henry Harrison had strengthened the institution in Iowa Territory through their appointments, as had Andrew Jackson in Wisconsin Territory.

Born and raised in Tennessee, Caruthers was from a prominent family in both law and public service. His uncle Robert L. Caruthers served the state in both federal and state governmental capacities. He was a congressman from 1841 to 1843, and he also served as a state legislator and the attorney general. Robert also held the position of judge. On the bench he developed a reputation for discouraging vigilantism. He spoke out against the lynching of slaves. He declared, "There is neither valor nor patriotism in deeds like these." He added that "courts and juries, public officers and citizens, should set their faces like flint against popular outbreaks and mobs, in all their forms."[44]

The judge also held progressive views about the rights of slaves in relation to work contracts. He was disgusted "to see to what an extent some men will go against the rights of the weak, in eager pursuit of gain." A slave named Isaac contracted to work for eight years for a man named Michael George, who agreed to pay $300 to Isaac's owner to emancipate him. The owner, however, sold him after seven of those eight years to another person, and George reluctantly relinquished his title and Isaac. The slave sued, and Judge Caruthers ruled in his favor. Isaac "was allowed by his mistress to become a party to this contract and arrangement for his benefit, and is entitled to the advantages of it, subject alone to the legal condition, that the judicial authorities acting for the State shall sanction it," Caruthers stated. The case hit a particular nerve for the judge, because he also was a slaveholder who had agreed to sell one of his slaves for manumission if the slave desired emancipation. If he indeed believed that slaves held rights enforceable against masters who contracted with other people for the slave's benefit, then he was swimming against the tide of southern judicial thought.[45]

Samuel L. Hays, a Minnesota slaveholder and an appointee of President James Buchanan. Courtesy Virginia Military Institute Archives.

The Caruthers family produced a significant legacy for their various law careers on a local level by starting an institution. Robert cofounded Cumberland School of Law with William's father, Abraham, another slaveholder. The law school opened on October 1, 1847, when Abraham met with seven students in Robert's law office in Lebanon. Abraham's son attended Cumberland University and benefited from his family connections on at least one occasion. Although a literary student, he was prone to impulsively act to his detriment. For example, he refused to obey a faculty member's directive and insulted him while doing so. The institution expelled him, but his father promised better behavior out of his son. Only then was young William readmitted. The incident did not further hinder him from advancing through school and into law.[46]

President James Buchanan, the last appointer of slaveholders to Upper Mississippi offices. Courtesy Library of Congress.

The extent to which William's family assisted him contributed to his entry into the law profession. After receiving his legal training at his father's and uncle's school, he became a lawyer in Tennessee in the early 1850s. He moved his practice to central Minnesota Territory upon his appointment by President Buchanan to serve as the register of public moneys at the Sauk Rapids branch of the U.S. Land Office in Benton County as of March 19, 1857. Even this appointment may have had familial influence, because Buchanan had served in Congress years earlier at the same time that Robert Caruthers had. The following year, when the office moved to St. Cloud on April 8, 1858, Buchanan appointed him there, too.

Even before the appointment, Caruthers had become Gen. Lowry's closest associate and traveling companion in Minnesota. By October 6, 1856, he had stayed as a guest in Lowry's home. At the time Christopher C. Andrews, another acquaintance of Lowry's, stayed overnight in Acadia. Andrews mentioned Caruthers only in passing, devoting more space in his writing to Lowry, his home, and his relatives.

The benefits of the nepotism that William enjoyed extended to other members of his family. Samuel G. Caruthers, William's brother, lived a similar lifestyle. He, too, was a student of the law. He accompanied his brother to central Minnesota but did not serve in any federal government office. On the other hand, he practiced law with William in the city of St. Cloud from 1857 onward.

Whereas the Caruthers brothers were Gen. Lowry's peers, Samuel Hays was closer in age to the Reverend Lowry than to the General. Born on October 20, 1794, and raised in Western Virginia, he came from a community of very few slaveholders. The county where he lived — Lewis County — was in a district containing a meager 3-percent African American population. Petersburg resident John T. Brown said of the western part of the state in 1832, "A few slaves there may be, in the west, to fill the menial, domestic offices." He did not consider them "the labourers of that region." Similarly, William O. Goode of Mecklenburg County noted that western Virginians were primarily farmers or herders. They consequently needed laborers not throughout the year but rather only on a seasonal basis, "confined for the most part to seed time, and harvest," as he put it. "They can procure labor on occasion, in quantities suited to their demand. Hence, their demand for slave labor will not be effectual. It cannot compete with the greater demand, which will exist in the planting country." Because planters needed laborers more than the people of western Virginia, planters would pay more money for slaves than the farmers and herders would. Hays himself owned only one slave at the time.[47]

Meanwhile, in the 1830s Hays began a long career in politics. It was certainly in his blood, because his father was Virginia congressman George Jackson, who had had an illicit relationship with a woman named Roanna Hays. At age thirty-six, Samuel Hays became a Virginia assemblyman in 1831 and remained in office until 1836. In 1833 he also served as a court justice in Lewis County. He then followed in his father's footsteps by winning an election to the House of Representatives in 1840.[48]

While in Congress, Hays did not stand out among his peers, some of whom had more stellar careers in government than he enjoyed. He served in the same congressional session as future president James Buchanan and Robert Looney Caruthers, the uncle of his future colleague in St. Cloud's Land Office. Hays made arguably his most significant contribution to the country as a representative when he appointed his young relative Thomas Jackson to West Point Military Academy in 1842. Even with this act of nepotism, however, Hays' own kin overshadowed him as "Stonewall" Jackson grew into a soldier of high esteem after leaving West Point and became a Confederate general during the Civil War. Nevertheless, upon appointing Jackson, a lifelong friendship between the two resulted, and "Stonewall" never forgot the favor that his benefactor had granted to him. Years later Jackson called Hays "my best friend" and told one of the congressman's sons, "I am indebted to your father more than to any other man for the deep interest he has taken in my success." One successful military appointment, however, could not save Hays' political career. He lost his bid for reelection and left Congress in 1843. Long after his service in Congress had ended, Hays continued to act as a resource for military affairs. He was on the Board of Trustees of Northwestern Military Academy and later served on the Board of Visitors of Virginia Military Institute from 1852 to 1854.[49]

Upon retreating to his home state after leaving Congress, he started a new life. Concerning his political career, he ran for his old job in the Virginia

Assembly and successfully returned to local office for a year in 1844 and 1845. He ended his service there with one more term between 1850 and 1851. Concerning his household, over the years his family had expanded, and he now had time to spend with his children, but his wife died in childbirth to son Calhoun while Hays was away in Washington, D.C., in Congress. He also increased his holdings of slaves—from only one in 1830 to five in 1840 and then to eleven in 1850.

President James Buchanan, Hays' former colleague in Congress, appointed the southern slaveholder to the Upper Mississippi for the position of receiver of public moneys of Sauk Rapids in 1857. Hays relocated to Sauk Rapids with his son John by August. Two months later, on October 7, he left for Virginia to bring his wife, niece, and two slaves to Minnesota. At sixty-three years old in 1857, he had become the oldest member of Minnesota Territory's slave power. He was also one of the wealthiest members.[50]

Hays is said to have become close friends with Gen. Lowry. The ex-congressman was similar in age to Lowry's father. However, Gen. Lowry's politics resembled those of Hays more than those of his own father. Whereas the Reverend Lowry opposed slavery and held no slaves in the Upper Mississippi, Hays supported the institution, as demonstrated by his partaking of it. Both the General and Hays brought the institution to the Upper Mississippi. The two also had in common enormous wealth. Just before the Civil War began, Lowry had a real estate value of $10,000, and Hays owned $23,000 in real estate.

Unlike Lowry, who gradually gained sociopolitical power in Minnesota Territory, Hays acquired significant local power shortly upon his arrival. The influence of the slave power of central Minnesota spread beyond Stearns County into its neighboring county to the north soon after Hays settled there. The Benton County Democratic Club formed on August 12, 1857. The organization elected Hays its president and hotelier Orrin Day vice president. Also in attendance were George W. Sweet and William A. Caruthers.[51]

Hays' son John Elliot Hays resembled and differed from his father. Born on April 15, 1821, John shared his father's distinction of having a Virginia congressman for a father. The junior Hays also studied law. He became a lawyer in Wirt County, Virginia, on April 4, 1848, and practiced for the remainder of his life. Unlike his father, John had no attraction to politics but remained steadfastly focused on his law practice. Still, by extension of his father's wealth and power, John enjoyed a substantial amount of sociopolitical power. For example, he was an influential friend to his military relative, Thomas "Stonewall" Jackson. In January 1857 Jackson asked him to support second cousin W. L. Jackson for 19th Circuit Court judge. Jackson lost the election.[52]

John came to central Minnesota with his father. John set up a law practice in Sauk Rapids, Minnesota, in 1857. He promised in the *Frontiersman* that he "will attend punctually, and he hopes satisfactorily, to all business pertaining to his profession," which included "contested claims before the Land Office" and the drafting of preemption proofs. In the same issue, the periodical called him a "competent lawyer and able to give satisfaction to those who may desire his services." He set up his office in the same building as his father's land register office.[53]

His business and his time in central Minnesota Territory both ultimately turned out to be brief. The following year, he discontinued his law practice. He left his father and brothers in the Upper Mississippi and returned to Virginia, where another brother named Peregrine lived. John resumed practicing law there.

During his time in Sauk Rapids, however, the Minnesota town bore the unique distinction of having a slaveholder practice law in a free territory. John also followed in his father's footsteps by holding slaves. John had owned one slave in 1850. Neither he nor his father brought African Americans upriver in the summer of 1857, but Samuel did soon afterward. Similarly, John's time in Minnesota Territory did not alter his proslavery views, and he doubled his holdings upon returning to Virginia.

While Caruthers and Hays politically ascended, General Lowry began his long sociopolitical decline. A sabbatical he took at the peak of his political career cost him some governmental control but did improve his health. On March 20, 1857, he received his passport. Accompanied by local doctor Benjamin Palmer, Lowry left for Europe because of health problems. They both returned to St. Cloud at the end of the year. His influence over the city had not waned, for proslavery Democrats still held offices. On the other hand, Lowry was no longer mayor, and he never regained a political position as high or influential as he had achieved before leaving the country.

While he was away, someone had to manage the Lowry estate. He called upon his brother-in-law, the Rev. Thomas P. Calhoun, and the Tennessee-based minister agreed to do it. His life experiences of a well-to-do childhood and several years of higher learning did not reveal much by way of experience in running an Upper Mississippi farm. His parents-in-law, however, made the trip upriver as well and lived next to the Calhoun family, and the Reverend Lowry had considerable farming experience from which the Reverend Calhoun could benefit.

St. Cloud now had a new church denomination facilitated completely by former and current slaveholders—another rare accomplishment in the Upper Mississippi by 1857. Calhoun and Lowry worked together professionally in their new home, just as they had done in Tennessee. In so doing, they brought the Cumberland Presbyterian denomination to St. Cloud together, starting with the pair's arrival in 1857. They essentially served as each other's co-pastors

Five. Hoteliers and Local Slaveholders: Slavery in Minnesota

137

at the mission. Finding little initial success in attracting worshipers, they were slow to building a membership. In order to keep working, Calhoun filled in for absent ministers at other churches.

Slavery, meanwhile, influenced how Calhoun ran Lowry's household. The minister brought cattle to St. Cloud, just as his father-in-law had done three years earlier. He wanted to raise cattle in Minnesota Territory. According to one story, he brought an African American slave along to drive the cattle. Upon arrival in the territory, the slave had the opportunity to claim freedom but decided instead to return as a slave to Tennessee to be with his wife. Nevertheless, the slave's labor was crucial in the local establishing of cattle ranches.[54]

When Calhoun brought his wife and children upriver with him to settle in the General's mansion, the minister took along two slaves to Minnesota Territory — a pregnant mother and her toddler child. Among all the African Americans he owned in Tennessee, those two were perhaps the most practical choices for upriver relocation. Calhoun's wife, Elizabeth, had young children, and the pregnant slave would have been able to nurse them. Also, the inability for a plantation economy to thrive in the territory meant that Calhoun needed domestic help more than he needed field labor. By keeping his male slaves in Tennessee, he did not have to put himself in potential financial jeopardy by risking their deaths during their interstate travel during the winter. The female slave was in her thirties and, as a result, less valuable on the slave market than bonded male field workers.

The conditions of slavery in middle Tennessee had some similarities to those of central Minnesota. Both areas consisted of slaveholders of very few slaves. European Americans of both communities referred to slaves as servants. By doing so they focused with their vocabulary on the nature of the labor instead of the status of the people as property. On the other hand, slaves of both locations also had in common the absence of agency over any part of their lives.[55]

St. Cloud and Lebanon differed in their applications of slave labor, however. Lebanon's slaves did not have personal relations with their masters, nor did masters respect slaves. The town needed slave labor because it grew cotton and tobacco. Slaves were too important to cotton production for slaveholders to even think of emancipating them. Aside from agricultural work, they also labored as miners, colliers, and molders at iron furnaces. St. Cloud, in contrast, did not require slave labor for its businesses. Moreover, the slaveholders there did not even need their slaves to farm the land. Rather, the owners adopted the practice of the northern migrants in employing recent European immigrants to agricultural labor. The slaves were largely domestic servants or personal drivers.[56]

In the 1850s slaveholders in Tennessee further tightened controls over their human property in the aftermath of slave rebellions across the country. The fear had begun to set in among slaveholders when Nat Turner's revolt happened in Virginia in 1831. Two decades later in Tennessee, slaves were executed for allegedly having conspired to capture the town of Clarksville. Multiple towns in middle Tennessee started curfew systems and civilian patrols to keep track of the whereabouts of the slaves. In addition, slaves lost control of their labor and needed the permission of their owners before making financial transactions. Thomas Calhoun's relocation to an area where pro–Democratic European Americans vastly outnumbered slaves almost ensured the complete absence of opportunity the slaves had for rebellion. Whereas slaves comprised 25 percent of Wilson County, Tennessee, they barely made 1 percent of Stearns County, Minnesota.[57]

In 1857 new resident and well-known abolitionist Jane Grey Swisshelm learned about central Minnesota's proslavery reputation even before her arrival there. While traveling there she received warning from a local citizen that her antislavery rhetoric would fall on deaf ears in Lowry-dominated northern Minnesota. The support of slavery she encountered was unique in the Midwest. To be sure all the other territories had reputations of being proslavery in certain counties if not all over each territory. However, masses of slaveholding migrants had reinforced the reputations of the other territories. In contrast people tended to associate support of slavery in central Minnesota Territory with support of General Lowry's politics. In the absence of an influx of slaveholding migrants to the land, he alone personified the institution in Minnesota.[58]

Calhoun's slave Mary, thirty-two years old in 1857, was pregnant during her first year in St. Cloud. In the *Democrat* reporter Jane Grey Swisshelm documented the disintegration of Mary's Tennessee slave community at the hands of her master earlier that year. The reporter claimed that Calhoun had sold Mary's slave husband and her two oldest sons before leaving Tennessee. If these transactions actually occurred, they were unusual for the town of Lebanon, because masters there rarely sold their slaves. In addition, the newspaper claimed that Calhoun had spared her two-year-old son from the auction block; at that age, the boy had little monetary value to people wanting to purchase laborers. Mary's husband may not have been the father of her children, and Swisshelm did not identify him specifically in that manner; rather, she used the phrase "[Mary's] husband and two oldest children." Descendants of the minister have mentioned the probability that Calhoun himself fathered Mary's children, including the two-year-old and the child she carried in her womb in the Upper Mississippi. If true, the child in the womb became the latest example, like Rose Madison and Catherine Ewing before him, of children born in the Midwest to slave mothers and slaveholder fathers. According to the descendants, Calhoun most likely felt guilty about betraying his wife with his sexual indiscretions. As a result, he allowed the two-year-old to die in the elements.[59]

If Calhoun's wife, Elizabeth, approved of the treatment her slaves experienced, her approval demonstrated more than her hurt over any possible betrayal on the part of her husband. Her neglect of Mary and child also reflected her life in both the Upper Mississippi as a child and her adult years as a southern plantation mistress. She had grown up seeing Indians performing chores like serving guests, cooking and farming at her mission home in Iowa. For the past seven years, she had been married into her husband's family and, as a result, possessed some authority over his slaves. As the mistress of the plantation, she likely exerted control over her female slaves like Mary, instead of the male ones like Mary's husband. Still, she jeopardized her own property by informing Mary that the boat on which they traveled had no

Jane Grey Swisshelm, Minnesota-based abolitionist. Courtesy Stearns History Museum Archives.

room inside for Mary and her toddler son. By confining the enslaved mother and child to the harsh rain that fell as they sailed and risking their deaths, Elizabeth ironically almost lost the very lifestyle she sought to preserve.[60]

If Calhoun and his wife subjected Mary to the rigors of the trip, as Swisshelm alleged, they demonstrated their desperation to maintain their lifestyle in St. Cloud. A pregnant slave had enormous value to owners and traders, because her fertility meant that she could produce a new generation of bonded laborers. She had already begun reproducing Calhoun's workforce in Tennessee by birthing three children. At thirty-two years of age, she still had more childbearing years ahead. Her accidental death on the excursion would have robbed the Calhouns of their most prized slave. For whatever value the couple saw in Mary to take her with them, their mistreatment of Mary and child — whether reflecting superior feelings to slaves, superior feelings to African Americans, or personal animosity — meant that emotionality took precedence over practicality with them.[61]

Mary did not die on the boat trip, but she lost yet another family member while traveling to St. Cloud, according to Swisshelm. The journalist revealed in 1861 that Mary's toddler son had spent the last moments of his life battling severe illness. While on the road, he contracted the measles. When traveling by boat but outside in the cold weather and rain, Mary cradled him as she sat out on the vessel's guards. Lacking a blanket, she had to turn up the bottom of her dress and roll him in it as she shivered in the elements. Still, the long, cruel exposure to those elements killed the boy. One person observing Mary shortly after her arrival later described her to Swisshelm as "the most heart-broken looking creature I ever saw." The only bright moment of the slave's time in St. Cloud was the birth of her son John in either late July or early August 1857.[62]

Although the Reverend Lowry's missionary work at St. Cloud did not involve the indigenous, he still had difficulty performing it with success—just as in his work with the Ho-Chunk tribe. He struggled to start a Cumberland Presbyterian Church in central Minnesota. Throughout the years of his ministry there, he held services in other people's buildings. A largely southern denomination, the Cumberland Presbyterians gained little traction in the Midwest. The people who attended Lowry's services were of the Presbyterian faith and disinterested in adding Cumberland to it. Lowry also had too few attendees to help him support and maintain a new church. Finally, as an antislavery people, the local residents may have resisted Lowry because of his history of owning and exploiting slave labor.

The Reverend Lowry engaged in other pursuits besides clerical ones. One of his activities significantly and permanently altered the agriculture of central Minnesota. He introduced cattle and, by extension, cattle-ranching to St. Cloud; two African Americans assisted Lowry in driving the cattle from Tennessee in 1854, two years before the founding of St. Cloud. The pair did not stay in town, however, but returned to Tennessee. Swisshelm later reported that their families had awaited their return and that the pair of slaves did not want to split their families by settling in the Upper Mississippi as free people.

Swisshelm did not begin her journalistic career in St. Cloud as an antagonist of the local slaveholder. Rather, she and the Lowry family dealt cordially with each other. She often depicted the Reverend Lowry favorably in St. Cloud. She reported his ministerial activities. She complimented him on his sermons. Meanwhile, General Lowry offered his assistance to her as she started her own newspaper at the end of the year.

As with all the previous Upper Mississippi territories, Minnesota Territory carved its own niche in the development of slavery in the former Northwest Territory. Minnesota's proslavery faction consisted of people who had either spent very little of their lives as southerners or were never southerners

Five. Hoteliers and Local Slaveholders: Slavery in Minnesota

141

at all. In addition, the territory's leading proslavery public official was not a presidential appointee but instead a Minnesota resident who rose to prominence through local work. The entrenchment of the territory's slavery in numerous local political and financial investments made the institution extremely difficult for local abolitionists to eradicate.

CHAPTER SIX

Dred Scott and the Boom
in Upper Mississippi Slavery

ON MARCH 6, 1857, THE U.S. Supreme Court announced its decision in *Dred Scott v. Sanford*. The case irreversibly altered slavery and ethnic relations as U.S. citizens had known them for years. The court ruled that the Upper Mississippi's most famous slave legally remained a slave; Scott's presence in the region's free territories did not make him emancipated. By extension, therefore, the court nullified the Missouri Compromise, providing a judicial complement to Congress' invalidating of its own law with the Kansas-Nebraska Act of three years earlier. Moreover, due to President Buchanan's support of slavery and his facilitation of its expansion through his appointments, all three branches of the federal government collectively adopted a definitive stance against the citizenship of African Americans. Chief Justice Roger Taney expressed this position when he declared that a black man had no rights "which the white man was bound to respect."[1]

Scott v. Sanford also had important ramifications for the Upper Mississippi communities. The decision validated all of the previous attempts by territories and states to implement slavery. More importantly, the advantage of legal argumentation shifted from abolitionists to slaveholders. For generations the local opponents of slavery were able to cite the sixth article of the Northwest Ordinance and the Missouri Compromise when calling for the prohibition of slavery in the Midwest. In response, the local advocates of slavery could only try to find loopholes that allowed some semblance of the practice to exist. Masters now, however, had the law on their side via *Scott*, and the opponents of slavery had merely the option of arguing why the Supreme Court did not possess the right to terminate the laws that had been the centerpiece of the antislavery position. Minnesota, in particular, was still a territory, and *Scott* made even more possible the land's entrance into the union as a slave state.

For Taney, part of the reason for Scott's rightful status as a slave lay in the timing of the Northwest Ordinance. He noted that the law had predated the implementation of the Constitution, having been enacted when the Articles of Confederation guided the new country. He argued that "when the present United States came into existence under the new Government, it was a new political body, a new nation, then for the first time taking its place in the family of nations. It took nothing by succession from the Confederation." The new nation had no claim to "any property or rights of property which it had acquired, and was not liable for any of its obligations." In addition, Taney reasoned that the new territories that had been part of the former Northwest Territory did not fall under antislavery protection from any pre–Constitution laws. To him, laws like the ordinance applied only to the Northwest Territory as it had existed in 1787. The legislation, he declared, "cannot, by any just rule of interpretation, be extended to territory which the new Government might afterwards obtain from a foreign nation." He added, "Consequently, the power which Congress may have lawfully exercised in this Territory, while it remained under a Territorial Government, and which may have been sanctioned by judicial decision, can furnish no justification and no argument to support a similar exercise of power over territory afterwards acquired by the Federal Government." He dismissively concluded, "We put aside, therefore, any argument, drawn from precedents, showing the extent of the power which the General Government exercised over slavery in this Territory, as altogether inapplicable to the case before us."[2]

Fellow Supreme Court justice John McLean, in his dissenting opinion, delivered a plea for non-slavery states to remain free from slavery. Ironically, in contrast to proslavery officials citing state sovereignty to allow Kansas to decide its own fate, McLean referred to states' rights as a means of restricting slavery. "Each State rests upon the basis of *its* own sovereignty, protected by the Constitution," he wrote. "Our Union has been the foundation of our prosperity and national glory. Shall we not cherish and maintain it? This can only be done by respecting the legal rights of each State." He noted that Illinois had a right to be free and that Missouri had a right to be a slave state, and he worried that the *Dred Scott* decision voided each state's power to declare African Americans free.[3]

The verdict similarly enraged many abolitionists, who had already become angry about the potential extension of slavery into Kansas. Among the leaders of Upper Mississippi states, Governor Grimes of Iowa was especially openly livid about the *Dred Scott* decision. He cited federal law to show how the court's decision contradicted it. He said that one of the Supreme Court justices was incorrect in asserting that "the only *private property* which the Constitution has *specifically recognized,* and has imposed it as a direct obligation both on the States and the Federal Government to protect and *enforce,* is the *property* of the master in the slave" and that "no other right of *property* is placed by the Constitution upon the same high ground or shielded by a similar guarantee." In addition, Grimes acknowledged the humanity of African American slaves and noted that the Constitution did, as well. He observed, "The Constitution nowhere regards slaves as property. They are uniformly spoken of as '*persons.*' As '*persons*' they are enumerated and entitled to representation. As '*persons*' they are subject to rendition as fugitives from 'service or labor,' as are apprentices and minors. As '*persons*' their 'immigration or importation' could not be prohibited prior to 1808."[4]

Grimes then accused the federal government of making an unlawful decision. Using stronger language than Justice McLean, the governor called the court's decision "unwarranted by the facts," "subversive," and "extra-judicial." Also, he ironically used patriotic terminology to encourage the challenging of the verdict. He concluded his message by calling for all "freedom-loving citizens of Iowa" to dissent from the *Dred Scott* verdict and keep Iowa from transforming into "an integral part of a great slave republic."[5]

What happened instead was a rash of southerners traveling upriver with slaves. Slaveholders became emboldened by the *Scott* decision and tested it by bringing their human chattel with them to the Upper Mississippi for business trips and personal vacations. The influx happened just as most of the region had effectively rid itself of slavery. Only a few small communities in the region supported slavery. After *Scott* the communities grew as travelers settled in areas with people who shared held similar views on slavery, and some new proslavery communities started to form.

Towards the end of the 1850s, fewer steamboats employed African American slaves. They were too pricey to be part of a northbound riverboat crew. Their value would decrease if bad weather damaged their bodies. In addition, slaves escaping in the Upper Mississippi were more likely to find antislavery communities to assist in their flights from bondage. Such communities increased as the decade concluded, for the decision had made them as vigilant in fighting slavery as others were to extend it beyond its current borders.[6]

Still, riverboat travel continued, and slaves kept working on the steamboats. As fewer slaveholders brought slaves to the Midwest, the boats provided the rare opportunities for residents of the region to witness a sizable community of African Americans. Citizens of states like Illinois and Iowa, both of which outlawed the immigration of African Americans, could see the ethnic group aboard the boats for however long they sailed through their states.

On the steamboats African Americans worked as the firemen or as the cabin crew. Composed of southerners, the workforce tended to sing spirituals as they labored. European Americans aboard the boats immensely enjoyed the performances. Residents of states that prohibited African American settlement had virtually no exposure to such musicianship beyond the steamboat arrivals. They marveled at the singing of "real slave music." One worker considered such singing better than the blackface minstrel songs of the day. His opinion notwithstanding, crewmembers occasionally engaged in the self-deprecating humor that constituted blackface performance. One laborer remarked that his coworker's mouth was larger than that of any person "'cept a alligator."[7]

African Americans highly prized steamboat labor. The captains allowed them to physically and aggressively compete for work. Hundreds of them fought each other for only a small number of tickets offered for employment aboard the vessels. A person became part of the crew after having acquired a ticket and escaped the other fighters up the vessel's gangplank. The more intense competitions came in the spring, after African Americans had starved through the winter. A few of them brought weapons such as razors in order to increase their likelihood of successfully claiming a ticket.[8]

The ticket brawl served other purposes. It kept a captain from conducting a lengthier although more humane process of seeking potential crewmembers himself. It also served as entertainment for onlookers. A tourist asked why the hiring process was not more "business-like and Christian-like." The mate of the ship noted the efficiency of the fights, concluding that the "best" crewmen were the victors of the brawls. He added that the brawlers jeopardized their lives for riverboat labor; many of the ticketless ones went from the fight to the hospital, and others died from injuries sustained in the competition.[9]

The workforce concerts and ticket melees demonstrated the rigid ethnic hierarchy of the steamboats. Aboard the ships, as in the homes of their masters, African Americans behaved according to European Americans' expectations in order to stay aboard and work. One mate remarked that he had little concern for crewmen bringing razors aboard, because they did not use the weapons on the European Americans of the boat. Expressing a common antebellum refrain, he paternalistically claimed, "We look out for them," before noting that due to their lack of life insurance, they "don't want to fool with the white folks much." He neglected, however, to reveal the means by which he was able to keep his crew from attacking the upper echelons.[10]

African Americans in bondage in the Upper Mississippi generally did not have much incentive to attempt to escape to freedom. The *Dred Scott* decision of 1857 only strengthened the premise of the Fugitive Slave Law — that a slave remained an owner's property, no matter where the slave relocated. Slaves not only had left their communities to come north but also had moved to a territory where their development of new kin networks was nearly impossible. Too few African Americans lived in Minnesota Territory, and owners did not bring enough slaves for the kin networks to survive relocation.

One of Minnesota Territory's first tests of the *Dred Scott* decision took place within months of the verdict. Newspapers outside of the territory reported the incident — a development that showed how the territory was fostering a national reputation for tolerance of African American slavery. In late spring a Tennessean and his slave stopped for lodging at the Stearns House in St. Cloud. Someone made an attempt to help the slave escape from the slaveholder. However, according to the Chicago *Daily Tribune*, "the 'law and order' people turned out in great numbers and prevented the outrage upon our laws from being consummated." Local opponents of slavery, despite their commitments to civil disobedience, were not numerous enough to keep the institution from taking place. No underground railroad existed in central Minnesota.[11]

St. Cloud law enforcement protected the rights of the slaveholder in a supposedly free territory. The people embodying "law and order" in town were supporters of Gen. Lowry. The charter of St. Cloud authorized the mayor to "call upon any male inhabitant of the town over eighteen years of age to aid in enforcing the laws or carrying into effect any law or ordinance." Gen. Lowry's immediate successor as mayor was John L. Wilson, who shared the General's support for the Democratic Party and, therefore, publicly supported many of his political positions— even those that strengthened slavery. In addition, Prussian immigrant Joseph Edelbrock, who had come to town by Lowry's invitation to become the postmaster in 1855, now served as the sheriff of Stearns County, too.[12]

The St. Paul *Times* was especially vigilant about reporting the rash of legal claims to Minnesota Territory slavery. According to the paper, the presence of African Americans in bondage there now amounted to "a considerable number." An article told of a local man who "holds his gangs of slaves over on the Minnesota River, which he works upon his farm." He challenged the "open hostility" from the locals because of the *Scott* decision. Although not given a name, he was identified as "a man of means ... who has once received the vote of his fellow Democrats for the legislature." Like Gen. Lowry, this slaveholder was a longstanding resident instead of a visitor. His use of slaves was atypical for the territory in that it involved agricultural labor instead of domestic service.[13]

The article noted that the wave of reports on slavery in the summer represented a continuation of similar and ongoing incidents from before that season. Just before the summer travel season began, a southerner paid for the use of more than one room at a first-class hotel in St. Paul. The other rooms went to his five slaves. He had signed the guest register with his name "and servants." Even before then men traveled through St. Paul with their slaves many times in the winter season.[14]

Travel by boat up the Mississippi River also made St. Paul a likely place to witness slavery. The city's *Times* mentioned that boats from St. Louis, Missouri, were almost daily anchored at St. Paul's levee. Several of the vessels from the southern city consisted of slave crews.[15]

Another story about Upper Mississippi slavery reached the East Coast that same month. The *Hartford Daily Courant* noted a report in St. Anthony, Minnesota's periodical *Minnesota Republican* about men "now held as slaves, as property in Minnesota." The article told of men traveling from the South, bringing their "body servants" with them to the territory's hotels, and returning to the South with their slaves. The report also announced that one southern migrant with a permanent residence in Stillwater, Minnesota, kept a slave. The paper lamented that his permanence in the territory would "render slavery a permanent institution." Moreover, the Supreme Court's decision gave the slaveholder his legal justification for his actions. "Under the Dred Scott decision," said the *Republican*, "he defies the authorities to intervene."[16]

Minnesota Territory was not alone in the Upper Mississippi in experiencing slavery in the aftermath of the *Scott* decision. In November 1857 a slaveholder from Missouri relocated to Warren County, Iowa, with five or six of his slaves, according to the county's newspaper, *Fairfield Ledger*. As with the Minnesota slavers, the Missourian in Iowa claimed that *Scott* authorized him to do so. The periodical's editor feared that every free state would eventually become a de facto slave state by that rationale. "Iowa owes it to herself," the *Ledger* declared, "to strike the manacles from every slave brought within her limits, by an explicit and peremptory statute."[17]

The federal government granted Minnesota Territory statehood in 1858. The state's constitution banned slavery within its borders. Abolitionists now argued more vehemently for Minnesota's cities and towns to stop permitting the presence of African American slaves. They not only professed the immorality of the practice but now also its illegality. Statehood, however, did not bring immediate change to the permissiveness of residents towards the slaveholding migrants and their human property. The travelers continued to patronize the hotels of central and southeastern Minnesota, and hoteliers and other vacationer-dependent merchants welcomed the influx of money from them each summer.

In addition, local slaveholders still held several legal advantages over the abolitionists. The *Dred Scott* decision rendered Minnesota's ban of slavery somewhat irrelevant, because travelers still had the right to bring slaves to free states as well as slave states. Also, statehood did not keep most proslavery federal appointees from the Buchanan presidency from retaining their positions of power. Samuel Hays and William Caruthers remained in the Land Office, for example. As a result, even if the local prohibition of slavery had taken precedence over the *Dred Scott* case, the proslavery domination of some Minnesota communities ensured that local enforcement of the prohibition would be nonexistent.

After Minnesota became a state, its hotels became targets of protest by abolitionists. Now that the state constitution prohibited slavery, the protesters did not want slaveholders to bring their slaves to Minnesota hotels. That November, the Rev. Henry M. Nichols gave the speech "Glimpses of Duty for Anti-Slavery Men" to an antislavery audience in St. Anthony. "Slave Masters have brought their chattels here, & held them as such, before our faces & when they get ready, have taken them away again," he reported. Calling for more local abolitionism, he lamented that "there has not been enough of the noble blood of Liberty in Minnesota to protest this outrage in the name of God & injured Human Rights." Of greater concern to him was the potential for local tolerance of slavery in hotels to lead to expansion of slavery. "This is the demand they make," he began, "that all our free States shall be a free tramping ground for them & their slaves, that if they please they may call their roll of slaves on Bunker's Hill, & we must stand by them, and support them in their right."[18]

In the absence of cohesive antislavery laws and their enforcement, residents quarreled among themselves—verbally and physically—in several parts of the former Northwest Territory. Vigilante justice significantly increased from people on both sides of the slavery debate after *Dred Scott*. Just as some Upper Mississippi communities had proslavery law enforcement, local antislavery citizens increasingly deputized themselves to police the state in relation to slavery. Slaveholding hotel guests faced increased harassment from state residents. Adding to the confusion surrounding the protests were the name-changes of the hotels themselves. The Fuller became the International after Alpheus Fuller had left the state. He relocated to Sioux Falls—South Dakota's first white settlement. The Winslow renamed itself the Wheeler and then the Ewing.[19]

Abolitionists opposed how the new president of the United States dealt with the volatile issue. Inaugurated in 1857, President James Buchanan continued to enable slavery, especially in the Midwest. He perplexed some critics by supporting the expansion of slavery despite his having come from a free state. He appointed proslavery people to govern the free Upper Mississippi territories. He publicly declared his agreement with the Supreme Court's verdict in the *Dred Scott* case. He also angered slavery's opponents by openly advocating the entrance of Kansas into the Union as a slave state. On February 2, 1858, near the end of his first year in office, he declared that the Lecompton Constitution, drafted by proslavery legislators in Kansas Territory to permit ownership of African Americans, should be the law of Kansas upon statehood. He considered the debate over slavery closed and cited *Dred Scott* as the reason why. "It has been solemnly adjudged by the highest judicial tribunal known to our laws that slavery exists in Kansas by virtue of the Constitution of the United States," President Buchanan wrote. "Kansas is at this moment as much a slave State as Georgia or South Carolina." Despite his endorsement, Congress did not allow Kansas into the Union under the Lecompton Constitution, and the debate in that territory continued.[20]

After the *Dred Scott* decision, new types of slaveholders came to settle in Minnesota Territory. No longer were the migrants either prominent politicians from the Upper South or yeoman farmers of one or two slaves from nearby Missouri or Kentucky. Now, wealthy planters from all over the South went to Minnesota. Theobald Forstall of New Orleans, Louisiana, typified the new kind of upriver master. He was born on October 31, 1836, into a powerful family of the Deep South. His father, Alfred Edmond Forstall, had graduated from Yale University. Alfred, in turn, was the only son of Felix Edmond Forstall, who once was connected to the U.S. Mint. Both Felix and Alfred held slaves.

Theobald, on the other hand, benefited less from his pedigree as time progressed. He was orphaned by the start of his teenage years. He and his brothers Numa and Robert lived with their grandmother Fidelite Polk and her children. She had no slaves when the Forstalls first arrived. Even when the Forstalls and Polks had decided to relocate together to Minnesota, slavery had yet not become part of their family culture again. A relative named Morgan May had started working in the territory at a warehouse provisions business on a levee in 1856, vacationing in the city of Stillwater in the summer months. In 1857, May and his wife brought the Forstall brothers and his grandmother to Minnesota.[21]

The family did not stay together long after they arrived. In his new environment, Theobald eventually began to experience some of the kind of respectability that his ancestors had enjoyed. He started by working for Morgan but then branched out into journalism. He served as column editor of the Stillwater *Democrat*—a newspaper that reached out to slaveholders to convince them to continue vacationing in Minnesota. The staff published the first issue on December 11, 1858, and kept the periodical in operation for two years. As a result he became an influential proslavery figure in Washington County. Robert, on the other hand, left for Louisiana not long after having settled in Stillwater to work as a clerk. He and Theobald had been rooming together in a hotel. Meanwhile, brother Numa lived in a house with his uncle Morgan, and aunt, and his grandmother.

Theobald stood out further from his relatives by contributing significantly to local education. In 1859, Senator Henry Rice designated Stillwater as one of only six cities in Minnesota to receive congressional publications. Forstall was one of six people chosen to attend to the books. He and the five others placed the volumes in various rooms, whether in law offices, city government rooms, or the city jail. Their collective work served as the foundation of the Stillwater Library Association, which then evolved into the city's public library.[22]

Theobald Forstall's family distinguished itself even more from others in Stillwater by practicing African American slavery. When he married Anne Walton in Louisiana in 1859, he returned to Stillwater with not only her but also her mother, who in turn brought her two slaves. The oldest, Rosina, was an elderly woman born in Virginia. In Rosina the Forstalls had an especially valuable slave because of her Virginia roots. Slave traders frequently advertised specializing in African Americans from that state. Slaves from other states did not generate as much advertisement because of their relative undesirability. William, the other slave, was a young adult born in Mississippi. Both slaves labored as domestic servants when they relocated to Minnesota. Also, the Forstall household neglected to give the servants any surnames in the 1860 census, lending proof as to their status as slaves.[23]

By bringing slaves to Stillwater, the Forstalls perpetuated the urban slavery that characterized New Orleans. They came from a city that openly sold human beings. Consequently, they carried that openness about slavery with them to Minnesota. In New Orleans slave auctions took place in large hotels. Slaves appeared on display in slave depots, showrooms, business windows, verandas, and neighborhoods. The slave trade had a glamorous quality in that city, because it hosted the most numerous markets and purchasers and generated the largest profits in the transactions. The slaves themselves were diverse in nationality, skin tone, and vocation.[24]

The Forstalls were not unlike the Lowrys and Hayses in coming to Minnesota to permanently hold slaves inside the state, but the Forstalls did not create a powerful proslavery political base. They were not politicians, nor did they have or develop strong ties to any on either the state or national level. They had merely come to Minnesota to seek their fortune and to exercise the slaveholding right that the *Dred Scott* case appeared to have given them. With their slaveholding, however, they made more enemies than friends. And because no powerful supporter of slavery ran Stillwater the way that Lowry controlled St. Cloud, the Forstalls were swimming against a strong tide and doing so nearly alone.

Abolitionists, for example, struck establishments in nearby Stillwater just as hard as the hotels in Minneapolis and St. Paul in the late 1850s. They tried to discourage southerners from bringing their slaves with them and keeping them enslaved while in Minnesota. Despite the local unrest over slavery, Theobald Forstall's newspaper attempted to convince slaveholding vacationers that the hotels still provided restful holidays. Other sympathetic journalists decried the antics of the protesters.

After only one year in St. Cloud, local slaveholder Samuel Hays had become a popular public speaker. By 1858 he had become more outspoken in his support of slavery, especially on religious grounds. He generated not only a large audience but also local media support. The newspaper Sauk Rapids

Frontiersman eagerly anticipated his next speech. The periodical predicted large attendance for his March 30 speech, "Southern Institutions," because of his "happy manner of speaking." In his address, however, he tried to prove through the Bible that God had designed African Americans specifically for slavery. He argued that African Americans possessed bodies of inferior quality to those of other groups of people. He predicted that because African Americans were "in the scale of being, too low to make much advancement in political knowledge," the ethnic group "would never be any thing else but slaves as a race, as long as they existed."[25]

The fallout from the speech was immediate and negative, and it prompted one of the few public debates about slavery that took place in central Minnesota in person from among the supporters of slavery. The local, pro–Hays press was among the first to publicly take issue with the ex-congressman's remarks. The *Frontiersman* "beg[ged] to dissent" with his speech. Swisshelm apparently did not have to write about him in order for people to speak out against his beliefs. In addition, the *Frontiersman*'s rebuke demonstrated that supporters of local slavery did not necessarily consider African Americans inferior. They simply respected that the federal government granted one person's legal right to own and purchase another, and they believed that Hays was within his rights to engage in such ownership, even if they themselves did not own African Americans or think of them as inferior.[26]

From that point onward, Hays became a publicly polarizing figure, almost to the same degree as Gen. Lowry. The former congressman continued to draw audiences, however, and did not deviate from his message. In a speech from March 16 of the following year, he cited the book of Romans and Philippians 2 to justify African American slavery. That address drew the ire of one of the abolitionists in attendance. Republican politician Stephen Miller proclaimed from among the audience, "When I reflect upon [slavery] and remember that God is just, I tremble for my country."[27]

As Hays rose to local prominence, he became a more vulnerable target of criticism from Swisshelm. She described him as a "Moccasin Democrat" in 1858. She also depicted him as a ruler of St. Cloud as part of the land office. On the occasion of reporting one of Hays' proslavery speeches, Swisshelm addressed his slaveholding. He had stated in his public lecture "African Slavery and American-Isms" that his slaves deliberately chose to remain his property but had the option to choose freedom. In doing so he divorced himself from any responsibility for owning slaves in St. Cloud by blaming them for remaining owned — a problematic argument because of the inherent lack of agency in slavery. By denying responsibility for enslaving and by portraying himself as someone willing to emancipate, he tried to appeal to the abolitionists of the city. However, emancipation was not his decision to make, for the Northwest Ordinance and Minnesota state law legally made Hays' local slaves free.

Swisshelm, moreover, mentioned that he had neglected to disclose that local slave Chloe's children, except for Ellen, "are held as hostages on his Virginia plantation." Therefore, all of Hays' slaves did not possess the opportunity to free themselves.[28]

Hays further showed contempt for African Americans by giving his slaves the ethnic slur Darkey for their surnames. To be sure, he had no obligation to assign surnames to Chloe and Ellen, and most slaves indeed had no last names. Nevertheless, the word darkey had already begun to appear in blackface minstrel shows to identify comical characters on stage. The characters were African Americans too ignorant to speak intelligibly or intelligently and too dependent on massa to survive without his care. The assignation of an ethnic word with humorous connotations implied a sense that Hays found the giving of that much humanity to his slaves nothing more than an amusing exercise.

More importantly, by bringing their slaves to a land where no other slaves lived, Hays and Calhoun made their respective servants socially and economically dependent on them. That dependence through isolation meant that Chloe and Ellen had no other recourse for survival than to choose to remain Hays' slaves. Similarly, by 1858, Mary Butler, Calhoun's slave, had lost every one of her family members except for her newborn son because of either sales or death. In addition, as the only slave in Lowry's home at the time, she lacked a slave community to comfort her during her time of bereavement. In St. Cloud she was the only adult slave and African American woman. Moreover, she worked while grieving; she still belonged to the Calhouns and had to keep working at their home.[29]

Swisshelm alleged in her newspaper that the Lowry family had intimidated Calhoun into delaying the emancipation of the Butlers. Indeed, he did not need Mary's services as much as his wife, Elizabeth, did. European immigrants performed all the farm labor at the Lowry estate, thus restricting Mary to the domestic chores. Moreover, as a new mother, she had breast milk to nurse not only her infant son but also Elizabeth's two-year-old daughter. The following year the mistress became pregnant and consequently needed Mary's child-rearing services even more than before. Elizabeth would have had very little reason to rid herself of such a valuable slave.[30]

Suddenly, however, the Reverend Calhoun took the Butlers back to Tennessee. Two conflicting reports exist as to what happened next. Andrews claimed that Calhoun freed Mary and John there. This emancipation was not a practical business transaction, because Mary was so financially valuable as a fertile slave. Moreover, such an act broke the law, for Tennessee had outlawed the freeing of slaves by this time. A more likely report came from Swisshelm, who claimed that Calhoun took them "to a Tennessee auction block." He badly needed the money, complaining once of his inability to pay a five-dollar bill. He sold his human property for $1400. With some if not all of the money from the transaction, he bought an ornate carriage, a harness, and a horse. The transaction demonstrated the effects of the Supreme Court's 1857 decision in *Dred Scott v. Sanford*. The court ruled that Scott and his family were still the property of their southern master, despite having lived in free Minnesota Territory. Therefore, Mary's birthing of her son John in Minnesota did not make him free.[31]

Swisshelm's account also fit the common progression of breakups of plantations and slave communities in the South, although the Calhouns and Butlers were in the Midwest. Many slaveholders who fathered children with their female slaves sold the offspring and the slave women, because the presence of the slaves involved in the owners' indiscretions angered the mistresses. According to Calhoun's descendants, the minister most likely returned Mary and John to Tennessee because of his feelings of guilt in betraying Elizabeth with Mary. John's birth in Minnesota would not have helped Elizabeth heal from any emotional wounds but would rather have exacerbated them.[32]

Swisshelm vehemently protested the sale despite its legality. Moreover, her repeated references to the incident over the next few years comprised a portion of her tactics in speaking out against slavery. She lost no opportunity to decry Gen. Lowry's support and practice of the institution. As a Christian, she could not reconcile Calhoun's preaching of the Word of God with his enslaving of the Butlers. For her trouble she suffered the destruction of her first printing press in St. Cloud and verbal attacks from Lowry and his friends. However, she held her ground, started another newspaper, and used it to hasten Lowry's decline in power in the city as St. Cloud grew increasingly antislavery.

No local slaves received more coverage in Swisshelm's newspapers than Mary and John. The abolitionist and the slave mother had several experiences in common. Both women, for example, arrived in St. Cloud as mothers of young children. An abolitionist journalist in Pittsburgh, Pennsylvania, Swisshelm's public activism conflicted with her husband's desire for a wife confined to the home. She left him in 1857 and relocated with her infant daughter to Lower Town to live with brother-in-law Henry Swisshelm. Also, Mary's life as Calhoun's servant slightly mirrored famous literary passages, to which the editor constructed allusions. She likened Calhoun's ownership of slaves to European American character St. Clair's possession of African American slaves Uncle Tom and Topsy in Harriet Beecher Stowe's abolitionist novel *Uncle Tom's Cabin*.

Members of Gen. Lowry's family made efforts to protect his reputation against the journalist's diatribes. Their drive to do so suggested that the reporter's comments had started to register among her readers and that central Minnesotans had begun to oppose the General's practice of slavery. To be sure, Lowry was a politician, and any rise in antislavery thought in the community threatened to undermine his power and that of his supporters. His uncle, Leonard Jones, "very eccentric," according to Swisshelm, gave her another ominous warning about her abolitionism in St. Cloud. She perceived him as "greatly distressed" about her feud with his nephew. "He begged me to desist for Lowrie's sake," she recalled, "that I might not drive him to cover himself with shame, and bring lasting regret. He insisted that I knew nothing of the dangers which environed me; I would be secretly murdered, with personal indignities; would be tied to a log and set afloat on the Mississippi." While she wished no danger upon herself, "if I let this man escape," she reasoned, "his power, now tottering, would be re-established; slavery triumphant in the great Northwest."[33]

Other issues plagued Lowry besides slavery in 1858. Shortly thereafter a dispute regarding Lowry's claim to Upper Town irrevocably ruined its business community. The citizens of St. Cloud no longer trusted in the General or in the legality of his power over the city. Consequently, they stripped it away from him. The residents of Middle Town and Lower Town started their own businesses in their own respective sections. Even the businessmen of Upper Town grew nervous about the questions concerning Lowry's claim. They deserted him, transferring their stores and offices to Middle Town. By the end of the year, Acadia was slowly becoming a ghost town.[34]

Nevertheless, thanks to the Calhoun question, the journalist was able to continue to use a local context to push for abolition. Through her newspaper Swisshelm tried unsuccessfully to engage with Calhoun about the controversy of the disappearance of his slaves. She publicly accused him of selling his slaves to another slaveholder in Tennessee. She alleged that he had received a horse and carriage from the transaction. Calhoun, however, never responded to her in print. He neither confirmed nor denied her allegations. His acquaintances and supporters, meanwhile, defended him in sympathetic newspapers printed in other towns. Calhoun was depicted by friend Christopher C. Andrews as sympathetic to his slave's difficulty with her new life as the only adult slave of the family. As Andrews put it, Mary "became disoriented away from her acquaintances and desired to return." The minister then allegedly gave her the agency to choose wherever she wanted to relocate from St. Cloud, and she supposedly chose to return to Tennessee.[35]

More interesting, however, was how Andrews referred to the African Americans living with Calhoun. Andrews identified them explicitly as the minister's property and then admitted that the clergyman had brought one of his slaves northwest. The writer's article was one of the few written records from either a slaveholder or a political ally of a slaveholder confirming slave ownership in St. Cloud, as opposed to Swisshelm's frequent printed accusations of illegal enslavement. Andrews wrote, "He [Calhoun] had three or four slaves in Tennessee, and at their request, they were left there retaining what they earned and living in comfort. One accompanied his family to Minnesota."[36]

The Lowrys and Calhouns suffered more grief when, on February 20, 1859, the horse pulling the carriage of the Reverend Calhoun and Elizabeth fell into a ravine. Two days later the minister died. Swisshelm used the occasion of Calhoun's passing to decry his bringing of the institution of slavery to St. Cloud. She noted the irony of his death via the same horse that he had acquired from trading the Butlers. By continuing to do so long after Calhoun's demise, she enabled him to haunt Lowry from beyond the grave for the rest of his political career. As for the slaves the minister left behind in Tennessee, the journalist asked about their fates. She referred to a "noble, faithful fellow" who "drove his master's herd of cattle all the way from Tennessee to Northern Minnesota" and who decided not to be emancipated while his wife remained in Tennessee "alone in slavery." She lamented that, due to his sacrifice, "this noble fellow is to-day a slave, part of the assets of Mr. Calhoun's estate."[37]

His survivors soldiered on without him. His widow, Elizabeth, remained in St. Cloud with her children. Carrying on her late husband's work to an extent, she worked with her father on his Cumberland Presbyterian missionary work. By this time Sylvanus and Josephine lived in a separate dwelling house not far from their first home, where Elizabeth and her children now lived. When Calhoun died, his widow's participation in slavery died, too. She never replaced Mary and John with other bonded African Americans.

The turmoil in Lowry's family did not inspire Swisshelm to soften her criticism of the General. Rather, she began using a variety of antislavery slurs when identifying him in print. In reference to his proslavery influence and political power in central Minnesota, she called him "the boss." That year, a few of Lowry's supporters ran for state office, and the editor worried that the former mayor would acquire greater political control of the state if they won. She derisively hypothesized that if those candidates won, "when General Lowry of the St. Cloud Land Office takes snuff, they are all to sneeze." Her designation of "woman whipper" for Lowry was no less flattering.[38]

Of all the epithets, the journalist used the nickname "moccasin" for him and his cronies for the longest period — at least one year. She introduced the term when she reported a trip Lowry and Caruthers had taken to Fort Abercrombie on the morning following the Democrat District Convention, in which people voted for the party's candidates for state offices. She warned that the two southerners would come back to St. Cloud with the voting returns in their pockets and that they would use the returns at their discretion. "Look out for the moccasin tracks," she advised.[39]

Swisshelm accused Gen. Lowry of destroying her newspaper in 1858. She did not know exactly who dumped the *Visiter* press into the water after less than a year of the periodical's existence. She suspected her political nemesis, however, because of his anger towards her for her abolitionism. If he himself did not ruin her press, then she surmised that someone from the local slave power — a member of Lowry's inner circle — was guilty.

As with the moccasin reference, the accusations lasted well into the following year. In March 1859 she reported that someone had tried to break into her office at night. Identifying Caruthers as the culprit, she goaded him while blaming him for the attack from the previous year. "Come, little donkey," she teased, likening him to the Democrat Party mascot, "don't stand outside to bray; but get a crowbar, come in, and pay your respects to the type as you did last spring."[40]

Caruthers and his fellow supporters of Lowry had few opportunities to respond through the local press. In 1858 he received positive press from the *Frontiersman*, as Lowry and Hays had. On the occasion of his imminent return from a trip to Washington, D.C., "his friends will be glad to see him home again." The next year, however, the newspaper shut down, leaving the proslavery Democrats with the *St. Paul Pioneer and Democrat* as their geographically closest sympathetic periodical. From there, Caruthers responded to Swisshelm, calling her paper a "dirty sheet."[41]

As with her denunciations of Lowry, Swisshelm's slurs for Caruthers grew increasingly bitter over the course of the year. He shared Lowry's title of "Moccasin Democrat." Most of her epithets, however, related to her depiction of him as Lowry's lackey. She declared that Caruthers became the "boss" of central Minnesota whenever the General temporarily left the area. More often, she referred to Caruthers as "Jeemes," likening him to a butler for Lowry. The nickname had significance, because Lowry actually employed a butler — William, a sixteen-year-old African American male slave from the District of Columbia. Like Mary and John Butler before him, this new slave also received the surname Butler in the Lowry household. As a result, Swisshelm's usage of "Jeemes" inferred a subservience that Caruthers and his fellow supporters of slavery tended to consider beneath them as European Americans.[42]

The editor also used more direct ethnic language when insulting Caruthers. In one article from April 1859, she called him not only a "moccasin," "boss," and "Jeemes," but also "Governor Lowry's pet darkey." The phrase "pet darkey" referred to a humble, submissive African American slave. Darkey, moreover, had just become a pejorative word used by blackface minstrel shows to identify African Americans. As a result, the abolitionist used condescending language about them when depicting Caruthers as a figure treated as a subordinate by Lowry.[43]

Moreover, the pet darkey comment demonstrated the complexity of the image of African Americans that Swisshelm presented in her newspaper. The content of some issues of the *Democrat* revealed her condescension of the very people she fought to liberate. By discussing the travails of actual slaves like the Butlers, she portrayed them as figures deserving the sympathy of the public and emancipation by the federal government. On the other hand, the word darkey associated slaves with comical burlesque characters incapable of rational thought. In addition, the editor sometimes used that kind of humor to entertain her readers. One issue featured the following joke:

> Pious Darkey—"Sam, why don't you talk to your Massa and tell him to lay up a treasure in Heaven?"
> Practical Sam—"What's the use of his laying his treasure dare, where he neber see 'um again?"[44]

Swisshelm soon found another target of antislavery-fueled scorn. Local Democrat Ulysses S. Willey made a name for himself through law in Minnesota Territory, not unlike other upriver slaveholders like Hays and Caruthers. He first practiced law in Minneapolis in 1857. Then, the following year the Willeys migrated to Meeker County in the territory. He worked in the county's 1st District Court upon its opening in October 1859. As his legal career ascended, he did not gain a wealthier class of clientele. For example, a client mortgaged his yoke to Willie to help with legal fees. Still, he also had in common with Hays and Caruthers a high pedigree, because his lineage was prestigious in western Virginia.

Unlike most of the other upriver slaveholding migrants, Willey did not spend his younger years in an environment of slavery. His parents, for instance, did not own slaves. On the other hand, after becoming an adult, he increasingly surrounded himself with slaveholders. Not unlike Elizabeth Lowry, Willey married into a family of owners. He wed Ann Haymond, daughter of slaveholder William C. Haymond, on May 22, 1855, in Marion County, Virginia. His new father-in-law owned seven slaves in 1850. Then, by associating himself with Gen. Lowry's Democratic Party in central Minnesota, he became politically connected with local masters. Moreover, according to Swisshelm, Willey himself kept a slave in Minnesota in 1858. She did not specify whether the slave belonged to him or to his wife. But she may have considered actual possession irrelevant; what mattered more was that a politician running for office in a free state actively enslaved an African American in his household.

Willey was a Minnesota representative in 1859 and 1860. By the time he began his term, the state had increasingly become antislavery. In addition, Swisshelm now associated him in print with Lowry's other Democrats as a fellow moccasin. However, her teasing of him gave no hint as to the political shift developing in the state. Willey was one of the last of the state's new slaveholders to ascend to public office. Therefore, instead of riding a proslavery wave of popular support, his political victory was a fluke.[45]

St. Cloud's proslavery faction, in particular, received a sharp rebuke from within its own party statewide. In August 1859 Caruthers met with fellow Democrats as delegates of the party's state convention in St. Paul. He caused a stir by wanting delegates banned if they did not live in the counties they represented. This demand reflected his concern that too many federal appointees not residing in Minnesota would have power over the party. Indeed, in the latter half of his presidency, Buchanan began to distance himself from earlier proslavery positions. Unfortunately for Caruthers, the convention tabled his resolution.[46]

Meanwhile, General Lowry hesitantly navigated these new, more challenging political waters after having taken a two-year hiatus from serving in public office. He ran as a candidate for lieutenant governor of Minnesota in 1859. The St. Paul *Democrat* described the circumstances surrounding his return to politics: "For Lieutenant Governor, Sylvanus B. Lowry was nominated by acclamation. An old pioneer — a gentleman of culture and fine ability — a thorough and uncompromising Democrat." It concluded, "Gen. L. will add great strength to the ticket in the North." Another account in a later issue portrayed Lowry as a reluctant but selfless candidate. He "did not want the nomination for Lieutenant Governor," began a letter to the editor, "but as a good Democrat he could not disobey the will of his party." The letter complimented him constantly with such phrases as "a high-toned gentleman," "warm zeal," and "more than ordinary intellect and well educated." The letter assured that Minnesotans would proudly support him.[47]

A supportive press lied about his slaveholding past. A letter to the *Pioneer-Democrat* called any claim of Gen. Lowry's support of slavery a "malicious falsehood." It continued, however, with this untruth: "He never owned a slave, nor had anything to do with slavery." Especially problematic was that the same periodical had printed the Reverend Calhoun's obituary, in which Christopher C. Andrews specifically referred to the African Americans the minister had brought from Tennessee as slaves. Even if Lowry had never brought a slave from the South to St. Cloud, the residency of the Calhouns and their human property on his land implicated him in involvement in slavery.[48]

Gen. Lowry lost by about 3,000 votes statewide to Ignatius Donnelly. The loss of the Reverend Calhoun made Lowry more vulnerable to attacks from Swisshelm, as he became the only living Lowry family member appearing to endorse slavery. Also, for all his federal and state government connections, Lowry was unable to expand his county and city appeal to voters statewide. The state was becoming increasingly Republican. On the other hand, if the state had voted how Stearns County had voted that day, Gen. Lowry would have become lieutenant governor. He won the county's vote by a significant margin. His local victory and the electoral victories of his supporters that year rendered Swisshelm ineffective at crushing his appeal in Stearns County. J. G. Shepley, who had admitted to destroying Swisshelm's press, became the mayor. Louis A. Evans won another office.

The 1859 election was far from a referendum on Lowry's influence or on his practicing of slavery. He maintained his lavish lifestyle to an extent. He traveled through the city with his "colored waiter," according to Swisshelm. In the following year's national census, he listed an African American boy of sixteen years in his household. The new slave was William Butler of Washington, D.C., and Lowry most likely acquired him after having traveled to the nation's capital in 1859 to negotiate another federal agreement with the Ho-Chunk people. Thus, Lowry's federal appeal did not diminish after his electoral defeat. More importantly, the federal government, in appointing him for work, continued its six-decade policy of overlooking the disobedience of federal antislavery laws in order to assign illegal slaveholders to particular tasks. In addition to offering interpreting skills to the federal government, he served as a member of the Board of Visitors at West Point in 1859. It was an ironic appointment that seemed to bring the federal government full circle on upriver slavery from a military standpoint. Lowry's father was a slaveholder appointed by President Jackson to serve in an Upper Mississippi fort, but now the General, who spent his childhood at that fort, was himself a slaveholder helping determine how future soldiers were to serve.

Even outside of politics, Lowry's friends continued to advance in the community. William Caruthers passed the bar in Stearns County on September 19, 1859. He was one of only two people admitted there before the end of the Civil War. William Mitchell, who disagreed politically with Lowry, at least complimented Caruthers on his professionalism. Mitchell described him as a "very ready speaker" who once "became so eloquent in the defense of his client in a criminal case that the defendant took advantage of the spellbound attention of the Court, the auditors, and the sheriff, and made his 'getaway.'"[49]

Proslavery politics in central Minnesota significantly shifted in the meantime. Lowry was relatively inactive in 1860 yet remained in the public eye. He still held no public office and did not run for another one that year. Correspondingly, Swisshelm wrote less about him in her periodical. Hays, on the other hand, had effectively replaced Lowry as central Minnesota's most active advocate of slavery. He remained politically outspoken in 1860. Like other Democrats that year, he struggled with the party's split. He publicly supported John Breckinridge for president. He was willing, however, to vote for Stephen Douglas for practicality's sake; he believed that Abraham Lincoln could lose only if Douglas were the candidate. He yelled at a meeting of Douglas' local supporters, "If the South would, in the case of Lincoln's election, wish to remain in the Union, they deserve to be kicked out and should be kicked out!"[50]

Other Minnesotans joined Hays in publicly vocalizing support for slavery. One of them had preceded Hays as Benton County's land office receiver. In January 1860 state legislator and ex-receiver George W. Sweet of Sauk Rapids introduced a bill calling for the permitting of slavery. The legislature voted against the measure, fifty-seven to twelve. The *St. Paul Minnesotan*, however, took exception to the nearly one-sixth who had approved it. The periodical wanted the identities of the dozen voters in favor of the "atrocious proposition" and referred to them damningly as "the enemies of liberty and humanity." The story developed national readership, providing a perfect challenge to the previous reports that had contributed to Minnesota's reputation for encouraging slavery.[51]

Ironically, neither Sweet nor fellow legislator Daniel A. Robertson, who supported Sweet's bill in the legislature, were southerners but rather hailed from the East Coast. Born in Connecticut, Sweet had arrived in Minnesota in 1849 at age twenty-six. Late in the following year, he bought land that fur traders who had migrated with the Ho-Chunk had deserted. The home he completed for himself in 1851 became one of Sauk Rapids' first dwellings by a European American.[52]

Originally from Pennsylvania, Robertson gained much more prominence as both a Minnesotan and a Democrat in the same amount of time that Sweet had spent in the state by 1860. Like Sweet, Robertson came to the state in 1849. He started the newspaper *Minnesota Democrat* the following year and operated it until 1853. In addition, he served as St. Paul's mayor before his election to the legislature. As with most Upper Mississippi residents, he employed European immigrants for household labor and owned no slaves in Minnesota. On the other hand, as a loyal Democrat, he followed the party's platform of refraining from agitation against legal slavery.[53]

The rest of proslavery Minnesota did not thrive as well as St. Cloud. James Winslow wrote of his recent business woes to Alfred B. Cassell of Minneapolis in June 1859. On hotel letterhead he complained that "money is very scarce and what we have is not very good." The Winslow, however, continued to attract southern vacationers. In 1858 the hotel welcomed 150 guests, and in each of the next two years, twice as many stayed there.[54]

In 1860 the Winslow was the setting for a major turning point in slavery in the Upper Mississippi. The slave of a guest tried to escape from her master but was caught. Colonel Christmas claimed to have brought Eliza Winston to Minnesota only because of the illness of his wife. A court declared her free, however. The verdict settled the legal dispute about Upper Mississippi slavery once and for all. It reversed the *Dred Scott* decision on the state level. A slave became emancipated on free soil in Minnesota instead of remaining the property of the owner. The court decision had an immediate impact that other antislavery laws and verdicts had lacked. Most Minnesotans opposed slavery, and protests against the presence of slaveholding migrants had become more frequent and had grown more intense. Southern guests left the Winslow in droves.[55]

Notwithstanding the court's emancipating of Eliza Winston, slaveholders continued to travel to Minnesota with their slaves. The International — formerly the Fuller House — experienced its own slavery-related trauma that summer. A Mrs. Prince of New Orleans stayed at the hotel with her slave, but he escaped from her by sneaking out of the building. The Lowry-friendly St. Paul *Pioneer* newspaper expressed sympathy for the owner. In response, Swisshelm's periodical added the *Pioneer*'s editor Earle S. Goodman — a friend of Lowry's — to her list of targets, savagely portraying him as just another proslavery puppet of the Democratic Party: "We would respectfully suggest that some one should give the Earle a negro. It would give him much happiness to own a fellow-creature — body and soul — even as the Douglass leaders own him."[56]

In St. Cloud African American slaves stayed at the Stearns House without arousing controversy. In fact, the *Democrat* noted their arrivals without any comment about the presence of slaves in town. That fall H. P. Johnson of Mississippi lodged in the hotel with his two slaves. Meanwhile, in September and October 1860, traveling southerners and three servants, as the *Democrat* called them, met in St. Cloud for an expedition to hunt buffalo. Arriving at the Stearns House in early September, the European American hunters came from four slave states: Col. Henry S. Dawson of Louisiana — home state of the Forstalls; W. C. Smedes from the Caruthers brothers' native Tennessee; Albert G. Bacon of Kentucky, where Lowry was born; and Thomas Kershaw, T. L. Clarke, and V. H. Rhodes of Mississippi. Kentuckian A. T. Burnby also came with a slave but did not participate in the hunt. For four weeks the hunters conducted a round trip to Elk River and collectively killed fourteen buffalo. Dawson's slave named Fielding, however, struck down four of them — more than any of the European Americans had slain during the excursion.[57]

Among the hunters were very wealthy planters who owned large plantations. The 1860 census priced the worth of Kershaw's real estate at $50,000 and his personal estate at $10,000 more. Two overseers lived and worked on his land to supervise his two slaves. Dawson, meanwhile, enjoyed more valuable land and a larger African American labor force. His plantation was worth $80,000 that year. Moreover, he held sixty-five slaves there. Their ages ranged from one to sixty-five; Fielding, at age forty-five, was one of the oldest of Col. Dawson's human chattel.

Swisshelm's paper covered the hunt, as recalled by participant Mark Ledbeater, whom the periodical identified as "our informant." No fiery editorial comments from the abolitionist accompanied the story. Unlike T. P. Calhoun and Gen. Lowry, the hunters received no condemnation from Swisshelm for holding slaves in Minnesota. In contrast to Mary Butler, Chloe Darkey, and their respective children, neither Fielding nor the other two slaves inspired the journalist to plead for their freedom. The hunting party had come to the state on a temporary basis, and none of the members had plans to try to become political forces there. Swisshelm's silence suggested either defeatism to the persistence of temporary slavery by vacationers or assurance that vacation-based slavery in Minnesota was in its death throes. Regardless, she gave the part-time slavery of guests less importance than the full-time slavery of Lowry and St. Cloud's other "Moccasin Democrats."[58]

Ledbeater's story failed to note that Col. Dawson and company had broken Minnesota law. After the hunting expedition ended, the southerners returned to their respective states with their slaves. According to the Eliza Winston case, a slave became free upon reaching Minnesota soil. The hunters, however, considered their servants their property and treated them as such by not emancipating them during their stay in the state. Still, the masters suffered no legal repercussions or local harassment for keeping them in bondage. Enforcement of the law was not likely on the local level, because J. C. Shepley—a close friend to Gen. Lowry—was the mayor of St. Cloud. And on the federal level, Democrat James Buchanan was still president, although not for long.

Even in St. Cloud, however, the proslavery climate had begun to weaken. The change in politics came in part from the dissolution of the city's slave power that year. Col. Hays left his receiver position in 1860, with slightly less than one year remaining in the Buchanan administration. Swisshelm alleged that Hays had pocketed money from transactions with pre-emptors. She debunked the popular assumption that he had lost the job for failing to support Stephen Douglas for president. "A more ultra, unscrupulous, unconscientious Pro-Slavery Democratic-tool than Col. Hays could not be found," she declared.[59]

Gen. Lowry's inner circle suffered further losses that year. After at least three years in St. Cloud, William Caruthers left the register office on February 15, 1860. Like Hays, Caruthers did not survive the entirety of the Buchanan presidency. Unlike Hays, however, Caruthers did not remain in town to create a new life for himself outside of the patronage of Buchanan and Lowry. Rather, he left St. Cloud for Tennessee for good on March 22, 1860. He received favorable press coverage from Swisshelm for the occasion. Her remarks gave no hint that only months had passed since she had last teased him with the epithets "pet darkey" and "Jeemes." She identified him merely as the former register instead of a member of the "Moccasin Democrats." Implying that their feud had indeed ended, she called him an "ancient enemy" who "has left only friends in St. Cloud."[60]

The former register immediately resumed the way of life he had experienced in the South before his time in the Upper Mississippi. On March 30, he returned to Tennessee. Like John Hays before him, Caruthers ended his law practice in St. Cloud before leaving the Midwest. He and his brother Samuel relocated to Smith County in that state by the summer of 1860. They lived with a relative named Mary Allen, and they held slaves there.

The dissolution of Lowry's proslavery inner circle that year also included a fatality. U.S. Willey contracted tuberculosis and suffered quickly and intensely from the illness. As with the departure of Caruthers, Swisshelm addressed Willey's illness with sensitivity and without partisan diatribes. Willey died before the end of the year.[61]

Republican presidential candidate Abraham Lincoln's election that November effectively and irreversibly blocked the Democrat Lowry from access to the White House. No longer was the slaveholder able to influence federal appointees to Minnesota-based offices. He did not even serve as interpreter for any further treaty negotiations between the government and the Ho-Chunk.

As Minnesota transformed from a popular sovereignty territory to a free state, slavery in the Upper Mississippi nearly became the first casualty. As long as local proslavery officials retained political power and continued to overlook the presence of bonded people for the sake of tourism revenue, the peculiar institution survived. Minnesota's communities, however, had grown increasingly intolerant of slavery, and now both a president and a governor shared their antislavery politics. Very few Minnesota towns kept slavery alive at the end of 1860. The challenge for these communities in the new decade lay in how well and how long they could swim against a strong antislavery tide.

The tide was just as strong if not stronger in Wisconsin. Slaveholders were not relocating there nearly as often as in the 1840s. One of the more remarkable aspects of slavery in the state was the consistency maintained in the households concerning membership. A few of the remaining masters from the 1840s managed to retain the services of their slaves well into the 1850s and '60s. Moreover, despite the strength of the abolition movement against slavery in Wisconsin, Grant County and Dane County were the last strongholds of bonded labor in the state.

The Rountree family of Grant County, for example, kept their slave from at least the 1830s to the 1850s. However, they used her disappearance from the household to end their practicing of slavery rather than acquiring another one from the nearby slave states such as Kentucky or Missouri. By 1860, neither she nor any other African American slave remained in the household. On the other hand, neither did any free African Americans live there. The Rountrees kept an all–European American home for the first time since their arrival from Kentucky three decades earlier.

By 1860 the ownership of human beings had crossed gender boundaries in the Upper Mississippi. The last slaveholder in Grant County was a young woman who had inherited her slave from her husband — an elderly, longtime resident there. After Tyree Oldham's death, his widow, Mary, continued to live in Grant County. As a result, she became one of the few women who became the head of a household while enslaving an African American in Wisconsin. Slave Eliza Oldham disappeared from the household as of 1860, but Tom Oldham remained Mary's slave. By this time Black Tom was the only Wisconsin slave of the 1840s to remain human chattel two decades later.

Meanwhile, abolitionists did not completely squelch proslavery politics in the state. As in Stearns County, Minnesota, in the mid–1850s, a proslavery press emerged in La Crosse County, Wisconsin, at the end of the decade. Supporters of President Buchanan established the La Crosse *Daily Union* on October 15, 1859. The editorial management fell not to a southerner but to A. P. Swineford, who had previously published papers at the Minnesota towns of Albert Lea, and, later, La Crescent. Also working as a publisher, Swineford's co-publishers were U. P. Olin, who supervised the printing office, and business manager C. P. Sykes. Local residents considered the team "energetic, industrious and plucky men," but they suffered the misfortune of setting up shop when La Crosse was too poor to support it. "The business condition of the country at large, of the State, of the county or of the city, did not justify such bold enterprises as daily newspapers in so small a city as La Crosse, only one-half of whose population required newspapers published in the English language," he claimed before adding that anyone wanting to start a paper there had to now intensely fight for readership. An unhealthy business community added insult to the periodical's injury, for people making little money because of poor crop seasons in 1858 and 1859 had little to spare to support the venture.[62]

In addition, constant turnover among the Democratic Party's supportive newspapers helped to speedily weaken the party's voice to the public. The *Daily Independent Republican* first appeared on October 25, 1859. The next day publication of the La Crosse *Daily Democrat* began. The next month C. P. Sykes, on November 10, 1859, bought a publisher's interest in the *Weekly National Democrat* and *Daily Democrat*. Then a former employee of the *National Democrat* took control of the *Union*. Finally the new firm Swineford, Sykes & Moore consolidated the *Union* and the *Democrat* into the *Daily and Weekly Union and Democrat*. As the decade ended, readers consequently had one less option for information — La Crosse having gone from three daily newspapers to two.[63]

Meanwhile, in 1860, slavery persisted throughout the state of Iowa. Several of the people who had conditioned sections of the state to tolerate slavery still held positions of power there. In Monroe County Judge John Townsend continued to use thirteen-year-old Catharine's services as the domestic of the household. She no longer shared the surname of the minister who had taken her from Tennessee to Iowa. The federal census of that year identified her as Catharine Wood, instead. It also listed her birthplace as Iowa, although no African Americans named Wood had lived in the state at the time of her birth.

As for her former owners, life went on without controversy. The Elberts were still in neighboring Van Buren County, as was their African American domestic Ellen. In addition to similar labor, she and Catharine shared the fate of having a new surname. Ellen, however, was called Woods instead of Wood. Meanwhile, Elbert still practiced medicine and remained in demand, thus assuring his continued high standing in the county as well as in their hometown of Des Moines. More importantly, the transfer of Catharine away from Ellen did not hinder Elbert's professional ascendancy.

Another wealthy southerner relocating with slaves joined and an acquaintance of the Waples family joined them in Dubuque County at the close of the decade. John T. Lovell of Franklin County, Virginia, had just married Lucy Ann Williams of Shenandoah Valley, Virginia, when they moved to Iowa in 1859. With them was Lucy's relative James H. Williams—a lawyer and a member of the Iowa Legislature. Also in the Lovell household were two African Americans from the newlyweds' home state — Nancy Smith and Arthur Smith.[64]

The political activism of the southern migrants there caused a stir. The local response to their support for proslavery Democrats brought previously unaddressed tension over the issue of slavery to the surface in Dubuque County. On July 7, 1860, the county's supporters of the Breckinridge-Lane ticket for president of the United States met. John Lovell and James Williams were among the speakers. In response, the local newspaper, the _Herald_, exhibiting its political bias, called the participants "secessionists." Such rhetoric was as passionate as the content of the abolitionist press in St. Cloud, and perhaps even more so. Indeed, as inflammatory a manner as Swisshelm wrote about Lowry and his supporters, she did not question his loyalty to the federal government, as the _Herald_ did to Lovell and Williams.[65]

As Dubuque County broke new political ground in Iowa, Henry County experienced new family situations influenced by slavery. The latter county became the home of two slaveholding families by 1860. The Richardses had lost their slave Kate Madison by this time. According to the census, however, her eight-year-old daughter, Rose Madison, remained with the family and continued to perform as the family domestic. The household structure was unique among Upper Mississippi slaveholders, because the only members were a European American family and a mulatto child born in the Upper Mississippi. Regardless of whether Elijah Richards was Rose's biological father or not, the European American adults of the home became the African American slave's _de facto_ guardians.

The county's other slaveholding family had arrived there more recently than the Richardses. Cummins Brown was a Kentuckian who had owned a sixteen-year-old male mulatto slave in his home state in 1850. Ten years later, however, he and his family shared their house with another Kentuckian: a sixty-year-old female domestic slave named Jimmy. The family gave her their surname, thereby reinforcing the similarity of the household living and work arrangements with southern slavery.

One of the state's more dramatic incidents involving slavery took place in Johnson County in 1860. The situation that transpired had yet again to do with interstate transit and sale of slaves but with a unique twist. An auctioneer named John L. Curtis had lived there since 1855 and married his wife, Nancy, in the county on July 2, 1856. Three years later they welcomed daughter Mattie. The household members had diverse geographic heritages; John had moved from Connecticut, Nancy came from Tennessee, and Mattie was born in Iowa. The Curtises differed from previous Upper Mississippi slaveholders in how they responded to a community backlash against the selling of humans. Sharing Nancy's birthplace were the two African American slave girls of the Curtis household. Mary was in her teenage years, and Vessey was four years younger.

Although a wealthy farming family, the Curtises had begun to suffer financial hardship, according to the local press. Their drastic measure to resolve it led only to legal hardship as well. John and Nancy took the girls on a trip to Missouri in February 1860. Some of the locals acquainted with them thought that the couple intended to sell Mary and Vessey upon arriving in the South. A pursuit immediately ensued. The authorities stopped John and Nancy and arrested them. They were charged with kidnapping.

Part of the novelty of the incident lay in the legal outcome. Instead of suffering a trial, the Curtises received the option of legally adopting the slave girls. The couple applied, and Iowa City's mayor granted the adoption. The other unique aspect of this story was that after the adoption, John and Nancy still went south and successfully sold their new children for a total of $1,300. They earned $500 for one child and $800 for the other. Most likely, Mary garnered the higher price because of her probable fertility as an adolescent girl.

To outsiders like Henry Seward, these slaveholders were working against the national interest. He came to Iowa to celebrate its status as a free state. Speaking in Dubuque, he noted that only free people produce true wealth and that slaves make poor businesspeople. Bringing local relevance to his remarks, he said that "there is not a slave engaged in a quarry in the United States. Have you any slaves down your shafts in your lead mines here? Not one. Have you any slaves in your coal mines? Not one. Any in your iron mines? Not one." Concerning local agriculture, he rhetorically asked, "Could a man subsist in Iowa by cultivating wheat or corn with slave-labor?"[66]

Seward's discouragement of the use of slave labor by Iowans had roots not only in economic impracticality but also in ethnic stereotypes. To him, slaves were incapable of performing the labor necessary for trading, manufacturing, and agriculture. He offered as proof the generalization that "on all the oceans there is not a slave engaged in commerce." His glaring inaccuracy, however, was his comment on local slave labor: "No man has ever brought or ever thinks of bringing an African slave here; the reason is a moral one; that slave-labor don't pay, and only free-labor will."[67]

Slavery persisted in Illinois as well, and proslavery sentiment was strong. The arrival of new African Americans into the state violated the state law that had prohibited their immigration since 1853. The state government enforced the law in some areas better than in others. In many of the areas where African Americans continued to filter into the state, they lived with European Americans who had brought them into Illinois when they left the South. The willingness of the European Americans to document the African Americans who shared their households in state and federal censuses demonstrated their confidence in the federal government's protection of their right to disobey the state law banning African Americans.

Hancock County, Illinois, was one such location along the Mississippi River that continued to allow new African Americans to arrive with European Americans during the new decade. In some respects little had changed concerning the implementation of slavery there over the past ten years. For example, new residents Rezin K. Shinn, his wife, Susan, and their family in 1860 shared much in common with the Groves of 1850. In both cases the families had just moved to Hancock County, and they both had left Virginia to do so. Each family also brought one female slave in her late twenties. On the other hand, some differences between the two situations existed. The Shinns' domestic Silva had the surname Bohanah instead of Shinn, unlike the Groves name given to the family servant Elizabeth.

Within Hancock County, the town of Chili proved an especially formidable proslavery community. It was one of the few places in the Upper Mississippi that experienced an increase in the number of masters throughout the late 1850s, instead of a decrease. As of 1860 the Dickersons had fellow slaveholding neighbors in the Forsythe family of Kentucky and the Owen family of Maryland. For the Owens and Dickersons, their coexistence in Hancock signified a reunion of sorts, because many members of both families had intermarried in Maryland. Like the Dickersons, the Owens and Forsythes took female slaves with them to Illinois. Moreover, the Forsythes' home community had procured an African American as a departing gift for the family. They had enough isolation from the rest of Illinois and sufficient prestige as well-to-do landowners to bring African Americans into the state — a violation of local anti-slavery laws and anti–African American immigration laws — without any fear of legal reprisals.[68]

The labor that Esther Hull performed in the Forsythe household was only the latest manifestation of slavery for that family. Alpha Forsythe had inherited her from the previous Forsythe patriarch, Oliver, three decades earlier. Although the census called her Esther, the family occasionally identified her as Hester. Appearing in the 1860 census as part of Alpha's residence, the thirty-eight-year-old Alabamian had been with the family for at least five years by then. She was legally too old to be indentured, according to the state constitution, but she remained the family servant for several years.

By 1860 five decades had passed since the arrival of Ninian Edwards to govern Illinois Territory, and nearly forty years had transpired since entrepreneurs brought slaves to the state of Illinois to work Galena's mines. But the passage of time and the installment of a prohibition of African American immigration did not prevent the entrances of wealthy, well-educated and powerful southerners and their slaves into the state. In Rock Island County along the Mississippi, a rich slaveholder from the South brought many aspects of southern plantation life with him to his new Illinois home. Born in 1797 to a former Continental Army officer of the Revolutionary War, Charles Buford spent the majority of his life in Scott County, Kentucky, but his upper-class status allowed him to travel more than many of his contemporaries. A family history book describes him as "a man of genius, literary and mechanical, sweet-tempered ... with a charming and refined manner." He received his college education at Yale University. He had owned forty-one slaves in his home state in 1850.[69]

He recreated as much of his Scott County lifestyle as possible in Rock Island County upon his arrival in the late 1850s. With real estate worth $100,000 and a personal estate of $50,000 in 1860, he could certainly afford to do so. He built a house in the Greco-Roman style of the plantation homes of the South. Most importantly, he brought a female African American slave named Kitty Johnson from his state to his Upper Mississippi residence. He likely had the ability to enslave because of the county's isolation as well as his wealth and prestige, not unlike the masters of Hancock County.

Johnson worked alongside people who were neither African Americans nor slaves, but she still suffered the standard trauma associated with enslavement. To be sure, she was not the only person who was not a relative in the Buford household. Two other people lived there, and they were immigrants from Sweden and Prussia. In addition, all three were teenage girls. The Europeans, however, were sixteen years old. Johnson, at fourteen, was the youngest of the three. Also, the Bufords, by bringing her with them from Kentucky, separated her not only from her slave family but also from her large community of forty-one slaves on the Buford plantation. In Illinois she had neither such a sizable African American community nor potential for one, because she was now the only African American among the Bufords in a land with few others of her ethnicity.

When Buchanan left office, all of his appointees who had helped preserve slavery in the Upper Mississippi Valley vacated their positions, too. The new president appointed people who shared his views about slavery, and the presence of the appointees in the Midwest emboldened local abolitionists to push harder for the end of slavery. Local slaveholders, on the other hand, now had fewer people in the federal and state governments to advocate for them. Only the strongest proslavery communities could keep the institution alive. Even then, they could only do so on the inertia of the institution in each individual locality. Even in Kansas, antislavery forces prevailed, for Buchanan himself signed the law admitting the territory into the Union as a free state on January 29, 1861. It was one of the last accomplishments of his soon-ending presidency, and it reflected how much his politics on slavery had changed since he had appointed slaveholders and approved the Lecompton Constitution in the early years of his term.

Buchanan, however, left a legacy of national discord. His vagueness on the issue of slavery brought to a national scale the confusion over the institution that had taken place on a local scale in counties and towns all over the Upper Mississippi. The divisions in upriver communities concerning slavery, already firmly entrenched before *Dred Scott*, became increasingly exacerbated as more people learned about federal permissiveness toward slavery in the Midwest and swarmed into the region to test the enforcement of the Supreme Court case. By the time the Civil War erupted, the Upper Mississippi's residents had been in the throes of a cold civil war for years and made the transition into a hot war by choosing either the Union or the Confederacy. Slaves had more complex choices such as whether to stay with their owners in bondage; to become free by serving Union soldiers, some of whom were hostile to African Americans; to stay in the Midwest; or to return to the South when their masters became Confederates. The diverse choices African Americans and European Americans made in response to the war irreversibly affected upriver slavery.

Chapter Seven

Upper Mississippi Slavery in the Civil War Years

W HEN THE CIVIL WAR ERUPTED IN 1861, two people who had spent significant time in the Upper Mississippi Valley became America's two presidents. Even before then, both Abraham Lincoln of the Union and Jefferson Davis of the Confederacy had in common the state of Kentucky as their birthplace. Lincoln left the South during his childhood, spending most of his youth in Illinois. Davis, meanwhile, stayed in the South well into adulthood. The two eventually spent time in the Midwest together in 1832, because they both fought in the Black Hawk War. Although they had shared the experience of militarily securing new land for extralegal slavery, they now battled each other during the Civil War in part because of the institution's existence. Both men were the last veterans of the Black Hawk War to attain the highest executive office, and through the Civil War they settled, once and for all, the question of the legality of the extension of slavery — an extension made possible largely through the conflict in which both presidents had served three decades earlier.

During the Black Hawk War, Lincoln had difficulty adjusting to military life and, unlike Davis, owned no slaves to help him adjust to his new responsibilities. The company to which he belonged consisted of somewhat jaded, undisciplined men who focused only on the mission of driving out the indigenous. They did not care about how they physically looked, and they booed at orders that they considered tangential to their mission. The inconsistency of their resources may have influenced the company's lack of unity. Each soldier had to scavenge for parts for his uniform, and no two men equipped themselves the same way. They tended to wear buckskin breeches and coonskin caps, and they slept with blankets of rough fabric.[1]

Through his wartime service in the Upper Mississippi, the future president likely gained early experience in commanding both slaveholding and non-slaveholding soldiers in a land where the institution had a vulnerable existence — a situation which he again entered as president during the Civil War. In his presidency, however, slavery was weakened in the South as well as the Midwest. Lincoln's leadership skills developed slowly and haphazardly, which did not help during his time in the Black Hawk War. He made many mistakes while adjusting to military life. Early in his career as an officer he led over twenty men across a field before arriving at a gateway. "I could not for the life of me," he began, "remember the proper word of command for getting my company *endwise,* so that it could get through the gate; so, as we came near I shouted: 'This company is dismissed for two minutes, when it will fall in again on the other side of the gate!'" He soon gained their admiration, however, because he proved himself a strong, quick-thinking leader. Through his character he won their obedience.[2]

Upon becoming president of the Confederacy in 1861, Jefferson Davis showed that he had come a long way in public service from his days as a soldier at Prairie du Chien. His inauguration day consisted of splendor that represented his rise in stature. He arrived at the Confederate Capitol with his vice president and a minister in an attractive coach from Montgomery, Alabama, which displayed saffron linings and white silk hangings. Six gray horses pulled the coach. As an unwitting symbol of how deeply slavery affected Davis's career from a Wisconsin soldier to the highest southern office, an African American drove the president's coach.[3]

Davis saw a parallel in the story of Upper Mississippi slavery to that of the Confederacy. He later wrote, "Virginia, in 1784, ceded to the United States the vast territory out of which the great States of Ohio, Indiana, Michigan, Illinois, Wisconsin, and part of Minnesota were subsequently formed. In 1787, at the express instance of Virginia, Congress adopted the celebrated ordinance for the government of this vast domain." After noting that the sixth article of the Northwest Ordinance prohibited slavery, he discussed how upriver settlers had wanted the institution. He recalled that in 1805, territorial legislators of the area had asked Congress to suspend that article. He remembered that Governor William Henry Harrison had made a similar request on behalf of some of the settlers. To demonstrate that the nation once had sectional unity about slavery, he reminisced, "The Select Committee of seven members — representing Virginia, Ohio, Pennsylvania, South Carolina, Kentucky, and New York, with the delegate from the Territory — reported in February, 1806, in favor of the petitioners, and recommended a suspension of the prohibitory article for ten years." Showing that the government had been in agreement with the will of the residents, he continued, "They reported that the suspension was 'almost universally desired in the Territory,' and recorded it as their opinion that the suspension would be a measure alike in the interests of the Territory, the slave-holders, and the slaves." He did not think the legal permitting of upriver slavery would draw controversy, but rather "it would merely occasion the removal of persons already slaves from one part of the country to another." Connecting the extension of slavery then to the institution's struggle for existence in the 1860s, he bitterly wrote of the hypocrisy of the vilification of southern slavery decades after the endorsement of upriver slavery: "It is noteworthy that these dispassionate utterances of representatives of every part of the Union, by men contemporary with the origin of the Constitution, when repeated fifty years later, came to be denounced and repudiated as partisan and sectional."[4]

Davis saw other ways that the history of upriver slavery contributed to the forming of the Confederacy. He blamed the backlash of the North against the Supreme Court's decision in the *Dred Scott* case for goading southerners to secede. To him, the case "involved the question of the status of the African race and the rights of citizens of the Southern States to migrate to the Territories, temporarily or permanently, with their slave property, on a footing of equality with the citizens of other States with *their* property." He acknowledged that confusion reigned regarding territorial slavery by complaining, "The long discussion of this question had been without any satisfactory conclusion." He had assumed that his fellow government officials would accept the Supreme Court's decision as final. To his annoyance, "it was flouted, denounced, and utterly disregarded by the Northern agitators, and served only to stimulate the intensity of their sectional hostility." Expressing futility for sectional unity, he lamented, "What resource for justice, what assurance of tranquility, what guarantee of safety, now remained for the South?" From then onward, secession was inevitable. "No alternative remained," he concluded, "except to seek, out of the Union, that security which they had vainly endeavored to obtain within it. The hope of our people may be stated in a sentence: it was to escape from injury and strife within the Union; to find prosperity and peace out of it."[5]

Based on Davis's writings, the antislavery shift among federal officials caught him off guard. He had, after all, been allowed to bring his slave anywhere he was stationed while in the military, whether the land allowed or forbade slavery. Presidents routinely sent slaveholders upriver, and the land attracted masters like his commanding officer Zachary Taylor. Thus, Davis knew that residents there supported the institution. He did not see opposition to Upper Mississippi slavery coming from anywhere but the North. In an ironic twist, as president of the Confederacy, he now led a nation of people who had seceded from the very government that had *paid* him to care for his slave in the Upper Mississippi. That slave, James Pemberton, remained with Davis until his death in 1852.

In the 1860s national politics still affected Upper Mississippi slavery. However, the beginning of the Civil War meant a military resolution to the issue of upriver slavery because the federal and state branches had developed

Seven. Upper Mississippi Slavery in the Civil War Years

173

both proslavery and antislavery policies and had failed to collectively settle on one side of the debate. Moreover, the nation's preoccupation with the war meant that it would not prioritize the debate over slavery. Northerners and southerners took up arms against each other, starting in April 1861. The Union fought to force the seceded states—the Confederate States of America—to return to the United States. Meanwhile, the Confederacy battled to remain independent of the Union. In the first two years of the war, President Lincoln kept ex-slaves from enlisting in the Union Army in order to continue making slavery a low priority and to prevent slavery from becoming a central issue in the war.

Some people from the Upper Mississippi disagreed with Lincoln's avoidance of the issue of slavery during wartime and took him to task for it. The president had the primary war objectives of having the seceded states return and, therefore, restoring the Union. He did not want abolition of slavery as a goal. On the other hand, James W. Grimes, now a senator from Iowa instead of the state's governor, became an early advocate for the use of African Americans in Union military service. He wrote of the Union states, of which he was a part, "It is because they desire to prevent the recurrence of the rebellion that they demand that it shall now be thoroughly crushed out. Among things necessary to be done to fully accomplish this purpose, we must conquer and hold all the forts and strong positions on the South Atlantic and Gulf coasts." After asking, "How shall they be garrisoned when captured?" he responded to his own question by suggesting that "we should garrison them, in whole or in part, by soldiers of African descent; that instead of returning slaves to their rebel masters to fight against us, we should employ them in our own military service."[6]

In an official sense, the states of the Upper Mississippi supported the Union. New fighting outfits formed there and engaged in combat with the Confederacy. Meanwhile, many of the region's southern-born immigrants opposed the Union. Several residents of the region relocated to the South to join the Confederacy. In central Minnesota, for example, Theodore Barrett and Stephen Miller fought for the Union, and Leonard Jones and William Caruthers became Confederate soldiers.

Because the Upper Mississippi's population consisted of a mixture of northern and southern, the region was especially divided by the war. When people left the area for the South, the Upper Mississippi lost prominent politicians and businesspeople that both northern and southern migrants had supported. Moreover, the region's residents who remained there and joined the Union Army were likely to eventually fight in battle against their former state legislators and land registers, among other leaders.

Even after the first shots of the Civil War, slavery continued in several isolated communities of the Upper Mississippi. To be sure, not as many southerners traveled upriver as before wartime. However, southern entrepreneurs kept employing slaves to operate the boats, wagons, and other modes of interstate transportation. For the first few years of the war, interstate commerce kept the institution viable upriver as well as in the South. At least one slave had a job of regularly transporting grit from his home state of Missouri across the border to Iowa. Employers could not afford to pick random slaves for these trips. The job required their slaves to leave a slave state for a free state, withstand the temptation to attempt to remain in the free state as a free person, and then voluntarily return to the slave state. The bosses did not consider the chosen slaves as flight risks. The haulers tended to have earned the most trust from their bosses through prolonged faithful service. In addition, the companies hired slaves who had families, because those laborers were not as likely as slaves without dependents to leave their family members in bondage.[7]

Anthony Trollope was a passenger in a steamboat traveling through Minnesota in 1861. While aboard, he was able to escape from the upheaval of the war and enjoy the usual sights and African American service of the upriver vessels. "To my taste the finest stretch of the river was that immediately above Lake Pepin; but then, at this point, we had all the glory of the setting sun," he marveled "It was like fairy land, so bright were the golden hues, so fantastic were the shapes of the hills, so broken and twisted the course of the waters! But the noisy steamer went groaning up the narrow passages with almost unabated speed, and left the fairy land behind all too quickly." He remembered mealtimes vividly, "Then the bell would ring for tea, and the children with the beef-steaks, the pickled onions, and the light fixings would all come over again." He recalled that the African Americans performed with humility to even the youngest of passengers, noting that "some embryo senator of four years old would listen with concentrated attention, while the negro servant recapitulated to him the delicacies of the supper-table, in order that he might make his choice with due consideration." The children, in turn, took advantage of such service with enthusiasm, "'Beef-steak,' the embryo four-year old senator would lisp, 'and stewed potato, and buttered toast, and corn cake, and coffee, — and — and — and —; mother, mind you get me the pickles.'"[8]

As the war began, some entrepreneurs felt confidently enough about the status of the southern tourism industry that they decided to invest heavily in it. By that time Stephen Long had taken over the Winslow. He had spent eight years at the International before departing for his new venture. In an advertisement for a St. Cloud newspaper, he announced his new management of the hotel and bragged of the "newly remodeled and renovated" interior. He dubbed it "The Model Hotel of the North West."[9]

Unfortunately for Long and other optimistic upriver hoteliers during wartime, such efforts at attracting customers ultimately became exercises in

Seven. Upper Mississippi Slavery in the Civil War Years

175

futility. The hotels that catered to vacationing southerners lost business and went into decline. After more Upper Mississippi communities harassed tourists and made attempts to free their slaves, slaveholders simply stopped visiting the area in order to avoid trouble and keep their human property. Meanwhile, as southerners defended the Confederacy, they had little time or inclination to venture to the northwest.

On the one hand, Iowa's vague policies on slavery and the state's poor enforcement of antislavery laws worked to the advantage of the southern entrepreneurs of interstate commerce. Slaveholding travelers counted upon the federal laws preserving interstate slavery to trump any local antislavery laws. For example, some slaveholders were still bringing slaves into their households in Iowa without incident, although the state's prohibition of African American immigration was at that point one decade old. The state had even less inclination to prosecute slaveholders who were not remaining permanently in Iowa with their human chattel.

On the other hand, the practical measures taken by the employers concerning the selection of their enslaved workforce demonstrated that the Fugitive Slave Law and the *Dred Scott* decision held little sway in wartime Iowa. To be sure, fugitive slaves in northern areas not under the control of Union soldiers were still susceptible to capture and return to slavery. However, ever since slave Ralph's successful emancipation through the courts twenty years earlier, an increasing number of African American fugitive slaves sued for and won their freedom when challenged by alleged owners. Southern-based interstate companies stood to suffer great financial loss not only from the departure of an expensive slave but also in legal fees they paid to persuade the courts to return their human property.

As the war progressed, interstate commerce between the slave South and the free Midwest became an increasingly insecure means for masters to exploit slave labor. One slave played the soldiers of the war against each other. He hid his family in a wagon to give his cargo the appearance of a covered load of grit. Ignorant of the true contents of the wagon, Confederate soldiers along the Missouri-Iowa border allowed him to cross into Iowa. Upon reaching the free state, he informed a Union soldier, who then protected the family and prohibited their former owner from returning them to Missouri. The ex-slaves subsequently settled in Mount Pleasant, Iowa.[10]

Meanwhile, the slavery debate in Dubuque County, Iowa, had come to a head. On July 4, 1861, at a meeting in the town of Zwingle, the community discussed the Civil War and Iowa's loyalty to the Union. Opposed to the Union's stance, local slaveholder John T. Lovell declared that "no power on earth, in heaven or hell" could force him to fight against his "brothers in Virginia." The others in the meeting quickly silenced him. The Dubuque *Weekly Times* stated, "We have some very bold rebels in this country."[11]

Although glib in its statement, the *Weekly Times* was also somewhat prescient. By the end of the year, Lovell and his family had departed from Iowa for Virginia. Lovell then joined the Confederate Army. His in-law James Williams had already left Iowa when Virginia seceded from the Union. Like Lovell, he also became a Confederate soldier, serving in Chew's Battery. Williams rose in the ranks to lieutenant and eventually to captain.[12]

Slavery had become extremely pervasive in Illinois at this time. It was the only upriver state whose number of slaveholders seemed to increase, whereas those in Wisconsin, Iowa and Minnesota had decreased. The institution in Illinois extended well beyond the counties bordering the Mississippi River, reaching the eastern side of the state. In Vermilion County, near the state of Indiana, a slave was born in the town of Danville. He and his family were later given, however, to a southern slaveholding woman, and they all relocated to the South.[13]

Although Wisconsin was a free state in the 1860s, some of its families still experienced bitter division among themselves when supporting different sides during the Civil War. The 1860 Federal Census was the first to document that John Rountree held no slaves in his Grant County home. In fact no African Americans worked at his homestead; all three of his servants were designated white and had been born in Germany. On the other hand, his brother-in-law, the Rev. James Mitchell, still owned slaves over a decade after having moved south to Missouri. Still a minister in the Methodist Church, his holdings in human chattel had increased from three women in 1850 to four men and a woman the following decade. He then served as a colonel of a Confederate regiment during the war. Nevertheless, abolitionism was so strong in some parts that residents of a town named Buchanan in the upriver county of La Crosse requested to have its name changed to Washington, because they were ashamed at having the name of the proslavery president as the town name. In so doing, they failed to take into account that Washington himself was a slaveholder and, while president, had also contributed to the upriver expansion of slavery. Regardless, the petitioners were successful.[14]

A few resistant southerners who stayed in the Upper Mississippi went against the trend of disavowing their homeland's heritage of slavery. They instead held onto slavery traditions for as long as possible. In St. Cloud, four months after the Civil War had commenced, Samuel Hays hosted a slave wedding on August 25, 1861. His slave Chloe Darkey married Gen. Lowry's slave William Butler that day. The ceremony attracted considerable attention for two main reasons. First, the servants of the two most powerful southern migrants in central Minnesota were scheduled to wed; slave weddings, in general, rarely took place in the state. Second, no two African Americans had previously married in central Minnesota. In either case, the ceremony was a novelty to most residents of the state.

Seven. Upper Mississippi Slavery in the Civil War Years

177

The wedding had potential to benefit Hays in several ways. It linked his business with slavery, because he hosted the festivities at Sauk City Mills. He was able, therefore, to publicize his enterprise to the large number of wedding guests. The new marriage provided another bond between him and Gen. Lowry, who married off a slave of his household to Hays' slave. The ceremony also showed the host's willingness to change under extensive scrutiny, for he permitted his slave to have a last name that was not an ethnic slur. Stearns County recorded the bride as Chloe Topsail instead of Chloe Darkey on the wedding certificate. As a result, he had the means to counter bad press from Swisshelm and publicize how humanely he treated his servants— not merely by giving them respectful surnames but also by going through the trouble of throwing a ceremony for one of them.

The new couple had little in common. Chloe and William shared only their status as Upper Mississippi slaves and their skin color. At age forty-one in 1860, Chloe was more than twice William's age. William was childless and a child himself, but Chloe had not only Ellen but also other children who remained in Virginia. Still, William and Chloe started a relationship. They may have visited each other constantly; Hays was Lowry's friend, and when the General traveled to the congressman's home, William, as the driver, would have had opportunities to see Chloe.

The two slaves received the blessings of their masters to get married. Hays coordinated the wedding. He hosted the ceremony at his home in Sauk City, described by stepson William Fletcher as "a dwelling house on the flat above the [saw and grist] mill building." Either he or Gen. Lowry arranged for an esteemed missionary, the Rev. Sherman Hall, to officiate the service. Hays also served as one of the official witnesses to the marriage, when the Reverend Hall recorded it for the county on August 25, 1861.[15]

Despite Hays's provisions the bride still had a tremendous amount of work to do for her own wedding. She was, after all, a slave. According to Fletcher, "While Chloie [sic] was the principal actress in this drama of life, she still continued to be cook. She prepared a huge feast: "roast pig, turkeys and chickens, and southern dinner in profusion." After cooking she "disappeared into some hidden recess and soon appeared arrayed as a bride." Then the wedding took on the element of an ethnic novelty act of a circus. The attendees treated William and Chloe as an impersonal exhibit — made for the audience to see but not touch. Fletcher recalled, "Many white persons were invited, and everyone was eager to be present, as, despite the disparity in the ages of the contracting parties, they were the only representatives of their race and color living in this part of the country." However, the white men "lack[ed] the inclination" to salute the African American bride.[16]

The county recognized the Topsail-Butler marriage as legally binding, but no immediate changes occurred in the lives of the bride and groom when the wedding ended. On the day both parties exchanged vows, they still lived with their masters; the official county record of the marriage listed Chloe's home as Sauk City Mills. Fletcher noted that when the ceremony and repast ended, "the party broke up and wended their way to their respective homes." Apparently, neither Gen. Lowry nor Congressman Hays saw the joining of two lovers in a free state as just cause to emancipate them.[17]

The Hays family split during the war. Patriarch Samuel and the family members who were in Minnesota when the conflict had begun remained there for the duration. For example, Calhoun, Samuel's youngest son, resided in his father's household when the war began because he was still a teenager at the time. At the end of the war, he was still in the state but had moved out of central Minnesota to Morrison County. Meanwhile, Samuel's sons who lived in Virginia in 1861 not only stayed there but joined the Confederate States of America (CSA) Army. John E. Hays, who had lived in St. Cloud briefly in 1857, fought in the Gilmer Rangers out of western Virginia for the CSA. His brother Peregrine, who joined a different unit of Virginia's CSA, had never moved to Minnesota with his family. Fortunately for the family, Calhoun did not join the military, which meant that the Union did not require him to take up arms against his brothers.

In an ironic turn of events, John E. Hays—a lawyer who had set up a practice during his stay in central Minnesota—now started causing unlawful, terroristic mayhem in Virginia and led people to do the same at his bidding. Union colonel T. M. Harris wrote to the state's governor, F.H. Pierpoint, in November 1861, reporting that Hays was now a leader of "bands of lawless marauders, who are robbing the Union men of all their property, clothing, beds, bed clothing, even down to the children's clothing, little shoes & stockings." He marveled, "They have even gone so far as to take strings of beads off the necks of little children." Hays and company also held four Glenville citizens hostage for two to three days, releasing them only after they pledged loyalty to the Confederacy.[18]

Hays' vigilantism only intensified that first year of the war. On New Year's Eve 1861, Harris wrote to Governor Pierpoint of more discord in western Virginia. Hays and the other Gilmer Rangers seemed "desperate" to him because they had not seen their family or property for over six months. They believed that they could defeat and drive out the Union troops from Glenville and torch their buildings. "Jno. E. Hays swore that if I wintered any forces there, I would winter them on the ashes of Glenville," Harris recalled of Hays' threat.[19]

Like the Hayses, the Caruthers family split to both sides of the war. Abraham and William sided with Confederacy. The elder Caruthers became a fugitive and then died in 1862. William, however, had little time to grieve, because he began fighting in Morgan's Cavalry out of Tennessee for the CSA as of

Seven. Upper Mississippi Slavery in the Civil War Years

179

May 22, 1862. For a brief time, the entire family seemed to side with the Confederacy, because William's brother Samuel lived with the rest of the family in Smith County, Tennessee, as of the June 12, 1860, census. When he moved slightly farther north to Kentucky shortly afterward, the family unity in the South ceased.

Still, Samuel Caruthers relocated more for personal reasons than political ones. He married Cassie C. Campbell in Todd County, Kentucky, on August 24, 1861. The new couple moved to the pro–Union state and started a family there. But like the Hays brothers, the Caruthers brothers never had to fight each other on the battlefield because Samuel did not participate in the war.

The Willey family also fell apart during the war. After U. S. Willey's death in 1860, his widow remained in the state and eventually remarried. His father, on the other hand, had little time to grieve. One year after his son's death, the elder Willey joined the Confederacy. Not too long afterward, Union forces captured him at the Battle of Philippi on July 3, 1861. He spent a year in incarceration until the Union paroled him.

Unlike the other families, the free European American members of the Forstall household remained intact during the war — united in their opposition to the Union. They had left Minnesota to return south before the war began. Theobald started a business in New Orleans, and his nuclear and extended family and slaves went with him. By the time of their departure, the town of Stillwater had become very unfriendly to slaveholders like them. However, life back in the South offered its own share of hardships; Theobald became bankrupt in New Orleans because of the Civil War.

The war was the greatest hardship for the Forstalls. Both Theobald and Numa served in the CSA but were still separated due to their placements in different outfits. Theobald fought out of Louisiana for the CSA in the Garde D'Orleans. Numa, meanwhile, was still in Stillwater when joining the CSA in 1861, and he fought in Beauregard's outfit out of Louisiana for the CSA. The brothers both fought in the Battle of Shiloh in April 1862.

Another figurative casualty from within the Forstall household was the family slave Rosina. Despite the emancipation Eliza Winston had won in a Minnesota court, the Forstalls were able to take Rosina to Louisiana in bondage when they returned south. By this time she was an elderly woman, and as such she would not have had significant monetary value on any auction block. Her owners may have kept her either for sentimental reasons or to retain the high social status of slaveholders in the South. Regardless, four years after the *Dred Scott* decision, Minnesota's lack of enforcement of the *Eliza Winston* decision gave southerners like the Forstalls a license to travel to the free state with slaves and keep them enslaved. Like Scott before her, Rosina's time in Minnesota did not emancipate her.

Not every former slaveholder or supporter of slavery in the Upper

Mississippi fought for the Confederacy. Former governor Willis A. Gorman, who had voted in favor of the Fugitive Slave Bill in 1850, fought for the Union. Albert G. Bacon of Franklin County, Kentucky, enrolled in Union Army on September 4, 1861 — one year to the day of the start of his hunting trip in St. Cloud. In the war he was a captain of the 3rd Kentucky Cavalry. He didn't live beyond the conflict's first year. He was killed in the battle of Sacramento on December 28, 1861. He was forty-five years and twenty days old.

Meanwhile, at least one person tried to promote the Confederacy without leaving the Upper Mississippi. In order to promote political views different from those of Swisshelm in central Minnesota, Sylvanus Lowry founded the ironically-named St. Cloud *Union* newspaper in the summer of 1861 — only two months into the Civil War. Initially giving no hint as to the pro-slavery and pro–Confederacy content to come, he and longtime friend Christopher Columbus Andrews presented the *Union* as a local periodical with an alternative political point of view. "We intend to discuss public questions with fairness and moderation; but without fear or fervor," Andrews promised the readers.[20]

A suspect Swisshelm welcomed the new competing periodical more on the merits of Andrews than of Lowry. She guardedly congratulated them both, saying, "We very nearly wish the *Union* success." Despite the friendship Andrews enjoyed with Lowry, she praised Andrews for his writing and his being a "courteous gentleman." She considered the *Union* as "honorable opposition" to her paper but only "in so far as the *Union* is under [Andrews'] control." In contrast, she made no mention of any journalistic qualities of Lowry, nor did she speak of any favorable anticipation of his written views.[21]

The *Union* soon became exactly the kind of newspaper against which Swisshelm did not want to compete. Lowry severed his partnership with longtime friend C. C. Andrews over slavery in the summer of 1861. Swisshelm immediately defended Andrews, calling him "a fine scholar and fine writer" but "no match for Lowry on a Moccasin trail." She accused Lowry of using Andrews to get support to weaken the Minnesota governor and President Lincoln and to support Henry Rice. She believed that Lowry had never intended to give Andrews any control over the periodical. Her respect for Andrews, however, remained steadfast.[22]

The *Union* became a forum for Lowry's proslavery views, for he now had complete editorial control of the newspaper. The issues now featured more content from supporters of African American slavery. The periodical published quotations from elected officials who, whether vocally or in print, called for the preservation and protection of slavery. As a result, the press in St. Cloud was now more polarized than at any previous point in its brief existence — Swisshelm's vehement abolition versus the General's defense of slavery.

Seven. Upper Mississippi Slavery in the Civil War Years

181

Despite the shift in tone, the new *Union* survived the departure of Andrews. Lowry catered to the segment of the town that held sympathetic views to slaveholders or to the Democratic Party, and the support of that segment kept the newspaper afloat. The people of Upper Town comprised the bulk of his proslavery readership, but the population of that village was dramatically shrinking. On the other hand, the German American population of St. Cloud was largely a Democratic one and a rapidly increasing one. By promoting party politics as well as slavery, Lowry managed to keep from alienating any German American readership repulsed by favorable language about the ownership of people.

The impact of the existence of a Minnesota newspaper run by a slaveholder extended well beyond Minnesota itself. Lowry almost immediately received national attention with the *Union* for its proslavery content. The periodical served as a resource by which people informed themselves of the news about those who supported the Confederacy. Edward Everett, a prominent educator and former politician from Massachusetts, mentioned two passages from the *Union* in order to prove his thesis that abolitionist activism and rhetoric had strengthened slavery. In his own newspaper *The Rebellion Record*, he referred to the *Union* as a "spirited paper" and quoted from two southern senators whose speeches Lowry's newspaper had printed.[23]

The success of the *Union* coincided with the rises of Gen. Lowry's financial and political fortunes. Businessmen continued to set up shop in his Upper Town in the early 1860s. For example, John A. Willis took over the hotel in Upper St. Cloud — Miles Brown's Exchange — and renamed it the New Willis House. In addition, Lowry decided to reenter politics and successfully ran for state legislator in 1861. He started his service as a Minnesota state legislator on January 7, 1862. His victory proved that his political clout, however diminished, still existed in St. Cloud.[24]

Swisshelm's failure to thwart his political aspirations marked the end of an era in both politics and journalism in central Minnesota. Almost immediately after the General had announced his candidacy, the reporter renewed her dispute with him. When he suffered a road accident in the fall of 1861, she expressed delight at the news, for the mishap had involved the same carriage that the Reverend Calhoun had allegedly purchased after having returned to Tennessee to sell his slave. She likened the destruction of the vehicle to divine retribution. Her attacks, however, did not sway local voters against him. She occasionally threw barbs at him after he won the election, but she no longer used the press or any other vehicle to attempt to sabotage the candidacies of proslavery politicians of the area.

The final end to Lowry's career in politics neither came from Swisshelm's propaganda nor had anything to do with the General's proslavery feelings. Rather, the illness that had forced him to forgo a second consecutive term as St. Cloud's mayor in 1857 returned to haunt him five years later. Swisshelm delivered her speech "Woman's Legal Disabilities" before the State Senate in early 1862, and State Senator Sylvanus Lowry attended it. She immediately noticed his despondency: "He sat and looked at me like one in a dream, and I could not but see that he was breaking." She reasoned that he had, after all, taken "a great fall" from undisputed ruler of central Minnesota to a state senator.[25]

Days later, the General's illness debilitated him severely, and he left St. Cloud for a prolonged period for a second time. This time, however, he stayed in the country instead of going overseas for medical attention. On May 22, 1862, Lowry boarded the *Cutter* to a mental institution in Cincinnati. He was out of central Minnesota for fifteen months. During that time the Upper Mississippi began to grapple with the question of whether to make slavery an issue of the Union effort, but central Minnesota's most infamous slaveholder had no say in the matter because of his institutionalization.[26]

The city of St. Cloud moved on without him. His brother-in-law William Wood replaced him as editor of the *Union*. His wife, parents, and sister continued to oversee his land. Samuel Hays and his household remained neighbors and friends of the Lowry household. A replacement completed the General's term in the state legislature. Swisshelm continued to attack slavery but without local people to serve as her targets.

In the fall of 1862, slavery became the least of central Minnesota's problems. The uprising of the Sioux people there irreversibly destroyed the southern settlements of Minnesota such as Breckenridge, Toombs, and Irving. The proslavery migrants who had founded the communities generally lost interest in maintaining them, and they deserted their settlements within a year or two of having started them. Meanwhile, few new southerners went up the Mississippi to colonize the state for slavery after the Civil War erupted. The Sioux then obliterated what little remained of the proslavery communities. Many of the new antislavery settlers who entered the vacated proslavery communities actively sought to erase the proslavery heritage of the settlements. They succeeded in renaming counties and towns that had originally honored politicians who had since entered the Confederate States of America, not unlike the name change from Buchanan, Wisconsin, to Washington, Wisconsin.

The proslavery forces never regained their momentum there, especially because fewer slaveholders lived in the area to push for African American bondage. William Caruthers resettled in Tennessee after having served in the war, never looking back at Minnesota. He married Fannie McCall, daughter of a wealthy Smith County, Tennessee, slaveholder, on December 22, 1862. Not unlike Caruthers' father owning sixteen slaves in 1850, his new father-in-law John A. McCall owned fifteen slaves in 1860. Immediately starting a

Seven. Upper Mississippi Slavery in the Civil War Years

183

family, the newlyweds welcomed son Reid on September 28, 1863 — nine months and six days after their union.

The Forstall family endured great personal hardship in Louisiana during the Civil War, but they too decided to remain in the South for the duration. Theobald was not a physically strong individual, and although he entered the Confederate Army in the New Orleans Guards, he was soon discharged as an invalid. In addition, the extended family had become a collective casualty of the war, because while brothers Theobald and Numa fought for the CSA, their Uncle Morgan May remained in Minnesota.[27]

Along with the sufferings, the Forstalls also experienced a rise in their professional lives during the war. After having fought together, the brothers remained close as they returned to civilian life. Theobald started working at the New Orleans Gas Company after having left the CSA. He served as a bookkeeper for the company. The efficiency of his work and his quick grasp of scientific facts soon brought him into prominence there, and in a comparatively short time he was made general manager. The company employed Numa as well, and he worked as a collector there. Theobald, as a result, became his younger brother's boss.[28]

The year 1863 marked the beginning of the end of slavery in the Upper Mississippi Valley. One major contributor to this shift was a federal mandate. President Lincoln's Emancipation Proclamation declared free the slaves of the Confederate States on the first day of that year. Many of them fled the South and fought for the Union, and some of the divisions that subsequently formed for colored troops came from the Upper Mississippi states. As a result, many Midwesterners who had seen local African Americans only as chattel in transit with their owners now saw freed colored people in their midst. The upriver presence of African Americans as emancipated soldiers was a far cry from the previous six decades of the former Northwest Territory, when the federal government had encouraged southern soldiers to bring their slaves northwest with them as property. Now, the same government invited slaves to the Northwest but to conduct the fighting with European Americans and to become emancipated in the process.

Moreover, most of the states of the Upper Mississippi were among the most willing to recruit African Americans. Free states that bordered the slave states experienced the greatest influx of fugitive slaves into their armies. Consequently, Iowa, bordering Missouri to the north, had 440 African American troops, although only about half the number of official African American residents in the state (249) was of age to serve in the military. Minnesota boasted a smaller but still significant discrepancy of 61 of age but 104 who served. The gap in Illinois was even smaller, with 1,622 of age and 1,811 serving.[29]

Only in Wisconsin did fewer African Americans serve (165) than were eligible (292). However, geography played a significant role for those numbers.

Wisconsin, as the furthest north of the Upper Mississippi states, did not attract as many fugitive slaves as the other states of that region, which were closer to slave states. As a result, runaway slaves did not swell the numbers of African Americans in the military. In addition, the State of Wisconsin had more intensely enforced antislavery laws than the other Upper Mississippi states, which meant that the state's African American population was a free one. Free African Americans were much less inclined to volunteer to serve in the armed forces than runaway slaves were, because unlike slaves, the free people did not have to fight to become free. Consequently, the lack of runaways and the absence of free volunteers caused Wisconsin's numbers of eligible-to-enlisted to decrease instead of increase.

The admission of African Americans into the Union Army did not result in the absence of discrimination. Among the Iowa troops, a color-based division of labor took place, and the acts of service the African American officers performed were similar to those that slaves had performed for their military masters in Upper Mississippi forts over the past few decades. "My line was thinner than I wished, and every man who could discharge a gun was very precious," General John M. Corse remembered. "I remember, I sent my negro servant to carry boxes of ammunition along the line, as I did not wish to use a man who could shoot. The servant afterward got a musket and took his place in the trenches."[30]

Another Union soldier revealed that slaves suffered similar physical abuse within the military. The punishment they received bore similarities to what many slaves received from masters or overseers on plantations. As a result, the Union Army behaved similarly to the state of Illinois as well as the legal slave states in the administering of discipline to African Americans. "Our horses have been two days at a time without scarcely an ear of corn [sic]," the soldier noted. "Officers were thus compelled to purchase corn at their own expense for their private horses—that, too, in violation of paragraph ten, general order No. 15, for the violation of which Captain Dilley's negro servant boy had his head shaved, and in addition thereto received twenty-five lashes on his bare back with a mule whip."[31]

Despite the strong legacy of slavery in the Upper Mississippi, progress towards abolition still happened. Another manifestation of the end of slavery in the Midwest took place with the rise of Republican politicians in formerly strong pro–Democrat, pro-slavery communities. People who had once opposed Minnesota's slave power came into their own political power in the later years of the war. Stephen Miller, who had spoken against Col. Hays' proslavery speeches, returned home from the war with his own military rank of colonel. He successfully ran for governor of Minnesota in 1863, thus surpassing any of the offices won by the state's slave power.

Some of the former pro-slavery leaders struggled to redefine themselves

Seven. Upper Mississippi Slavery in the Civil War Years

185

and their political careers amid new antislavery leadership. Gen. Lowry returned to St. Cloud, Minnesota, in August 1863 from his institutionalization. By this time he had deteriorated into a shell of his former self. His friend Julia Wood later remembered, "Though he partially recovered, and at intervals was his own bright self again, he was more or less under a cloud which never quite lifted." Swisshelm, meanwhile, expressed not so much sympathy for him as for his family. "He was confined in his own house," she began, "and his much envied young wife, with her two babies, had become an object of pity."[32]

One stroke of fortune for Lowry was that he no longer had to fight his strongest political foe in his diminished mental capacity. Seven months before his return, Jane Swisshelm had left St. Cloud for an assignment in Washington, D.C. She had lost all of her prime targets of attack over the past two years. William Mitchell assumed the editorship of her newspaper and continued it for several years.

Swisshelm's departure from the state was a tacit admission that she had done all she could to promote abolition there. She had witnessed the removal of Caruthers and Hays from their positions of political power. After Gen. Lowry's hiatus from the legislature, she had no more local enemies to fight. Meanwhile, the people of St. Cloud continued to elect candidates with ties to the General to political offices. They had only guilt by association, however, for they neither owned slaves nor publicly promoted slavery. In addition, they had removed themselves from Upper Town, physically separating themselves from the General and his fellow slaveholders.

The disclosure of Lowry's illness the previous year had effectively ended the feud between them. She regretted that she had not demonstrated "deep commiseration" for him because of his insanity. She believed that people would have offered him help if they had known earlier. "We recognize now," she wrote, "the secret of that strange mesmeric influence he has exercised over those with whom he came in personal contact. It was the fitful self-assertion of a large, generous, genial soul, which has gone haltingly through this life, crippled by its clay fetters."

Lowry and Swisshelm saw each other one last time in September 1863. Instead of discussing slavery, they talked about their individual personalities. In the process Lowry disclosed how the intensity he and his rival brought to their separate pursuits influenced how he related to her. He did not even mention slavery as the root of their longstanding quarrel. Rather, he offered his theory on their common ground: "I am the only person who ever understood you," he began. "People now think that you go into the hospitals from a sense of duty; from benevolence, like those good people who expect to get to heaven by doing disagreeable things on earth; but I know you go because you must; go for your own pleasure; you do not care for heaven or anything but yourself." Using his alcoholism to prove his notion that they shared a pursuit of pleasure, he theorized, "You take care of the sick and wounded, go into all those dreadful places just as I used to drink brandy — for sake of the exhileration [sic] it brings you."[33]

On occasion, the hostility of European Americans toward African Americans extended beyond the removal of such privileges as the ability to live in a state. The new anti-slavery climate in parts of the Upper Mississippi sometimes did not ensure the safety of African Americans. In 1863 Professor Cromwell's business was burned that year in St. Cloud. He left town soon afterward. As a result, central Minnesota no longer had a free African American citizen. In addition, no one documented the arrival of new African Americans to the city until well after the end of the war.

Some European American residents, on the other hand, were willing to go to the South specifically to liberate slaves. Another major change in local ethnic relations took place when a St. Cloudite not only fought for the Union but helped train African American fugitive slaves to fight to end the very system of slavery that had oppressed them. In February 1864 Col. Theodore Barrett left St. Cloud to lead the 1st Missouri Colored Infantry. As a result, he was responsible for making sure that the ex-slaves remained with him and were not recaptured by their former owners, and he was to enlarge his force by freeing slaves at the places where he and his troops battled.[34]

Slavery further deteriorated in central Minnesota when the primary slaveholding family disintegrated that same year. For all of the General's ability to understand and make peace with his former rival, he lacked the same ability to restore relationships in his own family. In April the Reverend Lowry put Acadia up for sale. Gen. Lowry sued his father and sister over the Acadia deed, which Thomas Calhoun had owned before his death. That same month, Matthew Wright began leasing Lowry's Ferry, which added some income to the family. Unfortunately, the conflict among the Lowrys came to a violent head that summer. On July 22, Gen. Lowry tried to shoot his sister but was stopped by their father. Gen. Lowry had been at his father's and sister's house three previous times that day. The General had violated the law — a far cry from nearly a decade earlier when the city had charged him with the responsibility of enforcing the law by making him the mayor. To be sure, he had broken federal laws while mayor by keeping slaves, but the townspeople did not react as strongly to that infraction as to an alleged attempted murder. The next day Gen. Lowry was arrested. He paid $300 bail. Even at this late date, he retained some of his old proslavery associations. The lawyer for his case was George W. Sweet, who had unsuccessfully tried to pass a bill through the state legislature to legalize slavery four years earlier.

The family of Samuel Hays also experienced disruption but not through internal conflict or anything having to do with slavery. In fact, as the war ended,

Seven. Upper Mississippi Slavery in the Civil War Years

187

he held no slaves at all. He had altered his household so dramatically that none of the residents besides himself were socialized in the ownership of African Americans. Moreover, his family became so large that plenty of people were on hand to perform household chores. On September 14, 1864, Hays married Emma Fletcher, the widow of Hays' partner at Sauk City Mills. Hays' previous wife, Nancy, had died on August 13, 1863. With his new wife having come from England and his new stepchildren having been born in the Midwest, he was now the only southerner in his household. In the meantime, he expanded beyond his milling enterprise and started a new retail business, S. L. Hays & Company.

One part of central Minnesota that remained constant was the acrimonious political divide there. It exhibited itself especially vividly in the local press. Although Swisshelm and Lowry were long departed from the helms of their newspapers in 1864, their successors continued to differ in politics, especially concerning slavery and civil rights. For the new reporters, the local political polarization continued as if Swisshelm had never left and Lowry had never fallen ill.

The *Union*, now renamed the St. Cloud *Times*, was now even more expressively proslavery, anti–Republican and anti–African American than it had been under Gen. Lowry's tenure. R. Channing Moore had taken control of the newspaper by 1864 and gave it a considerable pro–Democrat slant. Ironically, St. Cloud did not contain any African Americans which the paper so vehemently denounced as a general ethnic group. By the next year's state census, both Lowry and Hays had stopped holding slaves. By mid-summer 1864, Moore, unlike his predecessor, had begun using crude epithets to denounce people who supported abolition. On July 30, the *Times* denounced a local speech by a Mr. Hewlett, calling him a "Niggerite" preaching "rum and Niggerism," and "humbugging the people" into reelecting President Lincoln that year. The rhetoric was as vile and ethnically inflammatory as that of any pro–Confederacy newspaper of that period.

On October 29 the *Times* issued more of a manifesto than an editorial. The newspaper declared African Americans inferior to European Americans and not worthy of legal powers. The issue's column, "The White Man First — the Nigger Afterwards," practiced divisive politics, referring to white supremacists as "we" and to the activists for equal rights across ethnic groups as "they." The periodical's staff then proceeded to publicly and proudly align themselves to the cause of repressing the voting rights of African Americans in the name of protecting white sovereignty. The manifesto claimed that Republicans did not like that the United States had a "white man's government"—"made by the white man for the benefit of the white man," as the editor put it — and that they sought to change it to a "nigger's government." The periodical argued that Republicans believed African Americans superior to white people "in some respects," in contrast to the Democrats' embracing of white superiority. Expressing concern for a possible government takeover, the newspaper declared, "We deny that it is proper for negroes to make laws to govern white men. They believe the Government would be better and the white man happier if the negroes could make the laws and administer the government."[35]

The race-baiting articles from the *Times* did not address any relevant concerns to the people of St. Cloud, now that the town had no African Americans against whom to discriminate. African American migrants from the South tended to travel no further north than to either Minneapolis or St. Paul at this time. As slaves disappeared from St. Cloud, ex-slaves and other free African Americans were not immediately forthcoming.

Moore not only approved of African American repression but also of illegal slavery in Minnesota. On June 11, 1864, his *Times* paper reprinted a story from the Chatfield *Democrat* about a Minnesota-based train conductor keeping an African American sent to him from the South. George Shannon, conductor of the Winona and St. Peter railroad, traveled with a slave named Little Abe aboard the train. During trips Shannon ordered his human property to entertain the passengers in different ways. "At the bidding of his 'massa George,'" said the reporter, "come the 'double-shuffle' or rather of a 'break down' equal to an old 'un' and in regular plantation style." The journalist referred to the slave by various patronizing, ethnic epithets, as if overwhelmed by the novelty of reporting about African American property in Minnesota. The article identified Abe as a "little joker," "lively little 'cuss,'" "little darkey," "little nig," and "little nigger."[36]

The Chatfield journalist reported the story with a proslavery slant, despite the avoidance of the words "slave" or "slavery." The article designated Abe "contraband" and noted that "he belonged to the conductor of the train." The main part of the story, however, was not the existence of the slave in Minnesota after three years of Civil War but rather of his abduction. The reporter called Abe's captor a "thief" and a "John Brownite"—inappropriately likening Abe's capture to Brown's deadly slave revolts. Referring to the captor's multiethnic parentage, the Chatfield *Democrat* warned, "We pity that Miscegen if he ever falls into the hands of the railroad boys." The article concluded, "We deeply sympathise with 'George' over his loss, and trust he may yet succeed in finding 'Little Abe' alive and well, as also the scape-grace who stole him away." As a story reprinted without any editorial comment from Moore, the St. Cloud newspaper implicitly shared in the Chatfield periodical's support of the peculiar institution—a direct legacy of Lowry's early work for the Union.[37]

As 1864 drew to a close, Gen. Lowry became the last man standing in central Minnesota in favor of slavery. His support had dwindled over the years

Seven. Upper Mississippi Slavery in the Civil War Years

189

for reasons varying from his politics to his financial controversies and his illness-related erratic behavior. Upper St. Cloud was a deserted area because its residents had either moved farther south in the city or had moved to the South. Samuel Hays stayed in Upper Town but no longer spoke publicly about slavery's virtues. Then on October 9, the Reverend Lowry preached in St. Cloud for the last time before he, his wife, his daughter and her children left town for good. By November they were gone, leaving the General without the extended family who had taken him to Minnesota from Iowa nearly two decades earlier. Now, only he and his nuclear family remained.[38]

By this time slavery in Illinois had come full circle. In 1818 it was the first of the new territories from the Northwest Ordinance to become a proslavery free state. In 1864 — despite the antislavery shifts in Wisconsin, Iowa, and Minnesota after brief periods of support for the practice — Illinois was the last proslavery holdout. That year the state's judicial branch provided a latter-day complement to the legislation and governorships that had enabled slavery's extralegal presence. In December 1862, a judge in Hancock County had convicted a mulatto named Nelson of disobeying the Black Codes. He received the punishment of enslavement. The verdict and sentencing were consistent with the county's tolerance towards slavery, especially because slaveholders like Elijah Richards still lived there. Nelson appealed, however, because he considered unlawful his bondage in a free state, and he considered the state law that called for his enslavement unconstitutional. Two years later, with the case on appeal, the Illinois Supreme Court disagreed with Nelson. According to the court, the statute for slavery was legal, and the state Supreme Court affirmed the lower court's conviction.[39]

The decision meant that Illinois had decided to swim against the antislavery tide sweeping not only the Midwest but also the Union states. Slaveholders and other southern migrants still comprised a sizable portion of the state, even in the upriver counties that bordered Iowa, and the outcome of Nelson's appeal reflected their sensibilities. The verdict not only kept slavery alive in Illinois but also reinforced the strength of the Black Codes' banning of African American immigrants. Therefore, the freeing of slaves in other Upper Mississippi states in recent years and the willingness of the Union to liberate and arm slaves of Confederate states for the past year had very little effect upon slavery in Illinois. On the one hand, the fact that the case existed and went on appeal at all demonstrated that the proslavery *Dred Scott* decision of seven years earlier had not become the final word on slavery that Jefferson Davis had thought it was. On the other hand, the upholding of Nelson's conviction demonstrated that the *Scott* decision had more support in Illinois' judicial branch than the repudiation of *Scott* via *Eliza Winston* in Minnesota did. Although Illinois never tried another case concerning slavery, the decision in Nelson's case left no hint that the institution was on the wane in Illinois.[40]

Despite the antislavery remarks of Iowa' governor, individual counties and communities within the state still quarreled years into the war. Des Moines County, as an upriver county close to the slave state of Missouri, contained proslavery and antislavery residents who argued bitterly with one another. The majority of them put aside their differences to support the Union when the war began. Moreover, they were willing to do so at the expense of the institution of slavery itself. People still debated slavery in the county throughout the course of the war, but whenever they felt threatened because of rumors of an impending Confederate invasion, they prepared for the possibility of having to push back the Confederates.[41]

Meanwhile, the African American demographics of upriver counties in Iowa began to diversify in the wake of the proclamation. For example, African Americans in Van Buren County, Iowa, were no longer exclusively either slaves or servants. At least one of the slaves had gone by the start of the war. Kate McMananey was no longer listed in the county and, indeed, did not live with any McMananeys who still lived there. Even as Dr. Elbert still kept African Americans in his Van Buren household, other African Americans represented the county in the war. S. J. Foutz, Wyatt Jackson, and James Washington joined the Union Army in the fall of 1864. James W. Shepherd of Company K of the Second Colored Cavalry gave his life in the war.[42]

On January 12, 1865, Governor James T. Lewis of Wisconsin joined former Iowa governor Grimes in giving unequivocal support to the Union's emancipation of slaves. He argued that President Lincoln's goal with the Emancipation Proclamation was not the abolition of the institution but rather "the restoration of national authority." Arguing for the proclamation's legality, he declared, "In whatever light, therefore, you may consider the negro slaves, whether property, citizens or enemy, the Government has alike the right to take them, use proper means to get them, and use them in defense of the nation." He also considered the proclamation a crucial means to defeat the Confederacy because of its potential to disrupt the socioeconomic structure of the Confederate states. "It was apparent to all, that the rebel States derived great strength from the labor of their slaves," he noted. "They performed the manual labor of the country, thus leaving all the white population capable of bearing arms, at liberty to join their armies. Any measure, therefore, that would induce these slaves to leave their masters, would tend to weaken the rebellion, as their armies must have food, and if black men did not raise it, white men must." He claimed that about two hundred thousand African American men had migrated from the South and joined the Union Army. Celebrating that their presence "weakened the rebels" and "greatly strengthened the Government," he rhetorically asked if there are "any so shortsighted to-day as to desire to see those black soldiers who are now fighting our battles, who are now holding Southern forts, and otherwise assisting the Government,

Seven. Upper Mississippi Slavery in the Civil War Years

191

returned to their masters to raise bread for the rebel army, and their places filled by a draft from our own citizens?"[43]

To Governor Lewis the benefits of African American armament went beyond the Union. He believed that the proclamation improved the global standing of the United States. "There is no disguising the fact that at the time this proclamation was issued, there was great danger of foreign intervention," he warned. "Foreign nations, particularly England and France, so far as the aristocratic portions of them are concerned, would gladly see this government weakened by disunion." He also observed, however, "that the great mass of the people of England and France are violently opposed to the institution of African slavery." He would not have been surprised if countries hostile to the United States had supported the Confederacy in order to weaken the Union. He acknowledged that most of the nations that knew of the proclamation and its removal of slavery from the Confederacy supported the Union, saying that "their hatred of slavery overcame the jealousy of these governments." Without the proclamation, Lewis considered foreign support of the Confederacy a more likely outcome.[44]

Lewis then made a point of backing his views with quotes from unlikely sources. He cited a similar assessment from the Confederacy's vice president, Alexander H. Stephens: "The silent sympathy of England, France, and other European powers, arises entirely from their mania upon the subject of negro slavery. Lincoln had either to witness our recognition abroad, the moral power of which, alone he saw would break down the war, or make it an emancipation war." He then recalled the words of Andrew Jackson, not when he was expanding upriver slavery as president, but when he had addressed African American soldiers in New Orleans during the War of 1812. "I expected much from you, for I was not uninformed of those qualities which must render you so formidable to an invading foe," he began. "But you surpassed my hopes. I have found in you, united to these qualities, that noble enthusiasm which impels to great deeds." Lewis then disproved any claims that fighting alongside African Americans dishonored European Americans, stating that "Washington, Jackson, Grant and many other great and good men fought beside them, and did not consider themselves dishonored." In other words, if African American soldiers were good enough for Washington, they were to be good enough for Union soldiers.[45]

With Lewis's remarks the governors of the upriver states except for Illinois were unified in their support of the Union's arming of ex-slaves. In addition to the previous affirmation from Iowa's former governor, the governor of Minnesota had also demonstrated his enthusiasm for the Union effort. He had not been in office at the time but rather on the battlefield. Stephen Miller of St. Cloud, however, had served in the Union Army from 1861 to 1863, the year the proclamation went into effect. As a result, from the frontlines he was able to witness the progress of the Union effort after the enlisting of the ex-slaves had begun. By remaining with the Union Army and not withdrawing in protest of the proclamation, he showed that he favored President Lincoln's decision.

In the spring of 1865, the war wound down, and an upriver opponent of slavery gained an unfortunate, dubious distinction. Col. Theodore Barrett of central Minnesota and his troops suffered the Union's last military defeat on the battlefield. The skirmish took place near Boco Chico, Texas. He and his men attacked rebels along the Rio Grande and initially had the upper hand in the conflict. Then, a large Confederate cavalry unit of five hundred soldiers arrived and counterattacked, forcing Barrett and his four hundred soldiers to retreat. Seventy of Barrett's men were killed.[46]

On the other hand, under Barrett's leadership, the quality of the lives of the African American soldiers dramatically improved. He defied the laws of southern states that forbade the teaching of literacy to slaves—an act consistent with his willingness to lead, arm and fight with ex-slaves. Moreover, he went beyond the abolitionist rhetoric of Swisshelm and started activities to improve the lives of the people whose emancipation he monitored as their commanding officer. Whereas his arming of them had enabled them to fight for liberation, his making them literate empowered them to lead new lives on their own after the end of the war. He himself bragged that "of four hundred and thirty-one men, ninety-nine have learned to read and write understandingly, two hundred and eighty-four can read; three hundred and thirty-seven can spell in words of two syllables and are learning to read, not more than ten have failed to learn the alphabet." His track record was impressive and remarkable, considering that he had come from a heavily proslavery environment.[47]

At the same time, politicians in the state of Illinois struggled to redefine its legal treatment of African Americans. They argued over whether to allow African Americans into the state and, if so, which rights to bestow to African Americans. They ultimately decided to repeal the Black Codes. African Americans were no longer officially prohibited from entering the state. The decision marked a stark contrast from the previous year, in which the state's judicial branch had upheld upriver slavery. Still even as late as 1864, the war had no end in sight, and President Lincoln had made no advancement towards abolition in the Upper Mississippi. On the other hand, in 1865, the war was definitely ending, and African Americans had proven invaluable to the preservation of the Union.

Upon the repeal of the Black Codes in Illinois, Iowa remained the only state of the Upper Mississippi Valley to continue to prohibit the immigration of African Americans. The state retained its large southern demographic. Although very few Iowans left the state to join the Confederacy, many of the residents still supported the ethnic stereotypes about African Americans that they had heard as children in the South. In this regard, the state was the last upriver Confederate stand of the Civil War.

Although upriver states and counties remained resistant to extending rights to free African Americans, the politics of some communities along the Mississippi had begun to change in their favor. In the fall of 1865, Wisconsin voted on extending the right to vote to African American men. The measure was defeated. However, not all communities in the state shared the will of the majority of the state's voters. In Trempealeau County, the citizens had voted 319 to 91 in favor of granting suffrage to African Americans. The county's press had also outwardly supported the measure at that time.[48]

While Upper Mississippi residents renamed towns and counties to remove traces of proslavery men, physical symbols of slavery's presence there disappeared, too. On November 2, 1865, Gen. Lowry's dwelling house burned to the ground. Fortunately for them, the Reverend Lowry and the Calhouns had vacated the other house on the land, so the General simply moved himself and his wife and children there. As a symbol of how he had become apolitical and isolated from the community he had once ruled, no one accused any person of setting the structure ablaze in any of the newspapers.[49]

As the year ended, so did legal human bondage in the United States. On December 18, the Thirteenth Amendment to the Constitution became law. The new federal law made all slavery in all states illegal. The amendment provided a mirror image of the recent history of U.S. slavery; states and territories had tried and failed to legally extend slavery beyond the South, but now the amendment extended the emancipation of slaves beyond the Confederate states. The states of the Upper Mississippi Valley had already outlawed the institution in their constitutions. Still, for any southern migrants who had sought loopholes in recent years through visits to certain hotels or isolated towns, the amendment cut off all their options of circumventing emancipation for their chattel. In addition to references to the Northwest Ordinance and the Missouri Compromise, abolitionists now had the amendment to add to their legal arguments for all slavery to cease. However, few arguments were necessary, because with Lincoln and other Republicans claiming the presidency over the next few years, their appointees to upriver federal offices were more likely to enforce the antislavery laws, just as Union troops were doing throughout the South at that time.

Not everyone saw the passage of the amendment as a means of looking forward but rather of waxing nostalgia. Now in Washington, D.C., Swisshelm used the occasion to reminisce about her feud with Gen. Lowry. As with other people with whom she had stopped feuding, she described the General in favorable terms. In her column for the December 21, 1865, issue of the *Reconstructionist* periodical, gone were the names "woman-whipper" and "Moccasin

Democrat." She had, since the more combative years, redubbed his role as "the Southern gentleman who was political dictator in the Northern half of the Territory." Inferring remorse for her remarks about him, she revealed, "He has long since forgiven us and we are good friends now."[50]

Lowry, however, never had the opportunity to read the kind words from his former adversary. Coincidentally, on the day her recollection appeared in the *Reconstructionist*, the General performed his daily routine of sitting by the stove, waiting for his driver to prepare his sleigh for his commute to his office in town. Suddenly Josephine saw him faint and called for a man named Mr. Green, who lived in the Lowry home, to help them. Green quickly came, placed his arm around Gen. Lowry, and sat him up in his chair. Green tried to keep Lowry alive by sprinkling cold water on his face, but with two gasps, he died. The cause was likely heart disease, according to the local press. He barely lived to see a United States without the institution he had seen all over the country for all of his life. Swisshelm's written kind remarks about her former adversary did not circulate in any Minnesota newspapers until exactly one week after his death.[51]

Conclusion

THE CIVIL WAR PROVED THAT African American slavery was integral to the development of the United States. Only through the violence of that conflict did slavery end in the Upper Mississippi as well as in the South. To be sure, Confederate soldiers did not fight Union troops to prevent the emancipation of slaves in Illinois, Wisconsin, Iowa, and Minnesota. On the other hand, the war kept southerners from migrating northwest, because they were needed at home. Also, the Upper Mississippi states continued to overlook violators of the multiple bans on human chattel well into the 1860s. Only after the passage of the Thirteenth Amendment in 1865 did the violations stop; with that amendment and the previous four years of bloody internal warfare, the federal government ended nearly eight decades of undermining its own prohibition of slavery. Now, that restriction applied not only to the Northwest but to the entire nation.

Most of the southern migrants who came to the Upper Mississippi Valley with their slaves remained there after having emancipated them. Some of them had established lucrative businesses or higher social status in the Midwest. Regardless of economic class, southern migrants hardly had incentives to cross the Mason-Dixon Line again. The South, devastated by the war, had little to offer returnees but an opportunity to rebuild the region.

The migrants who returned south as the Civil War erupted remained there after the conflict ended. Some families had more difficulty than others in rebuilding their lives. Some returnees simply resumed the lives they had led before moving northwest. Others struggled to create new lives after the war had ruined their antebellum livelihoods. Regardless of how easily they rebuilt, they shared in common some ambivalence towards returning to the Upper Mississippi.

For African Americans, the opposite effect took place. Very few slaves who had come to the Upper Mississippi states with their owners returned to the South but rather remained in the North. Some of them remained with their former owners after the end of the war. Similarly, most of the slaves who came northward in droves as fugitives and contraband in the decade before emancipation stayed in the Upper Mississippi, found work, and developed their own communities.

The Upper Mississippi did not attract as many African Americans as other regions did immediately after the Civil War. African American migrants tended to travel to the northeast, where slavery had been outlawed the longest. The vast majority of African Americans lived in the South and remained there after emancipation. African American Midwesterners were much smaller in number. The African American communities there were small and offered little by way of institutions such as churches and schools. Most freedmen were employed as barbers or farmers. Most women were domestic servants, as in the antebellum years.

In a sense, the first years after the Civil War for some ex-slaves in the Upper Mississippi were not unlike the same period for ex-slaves in the South. Both groups of people lived similar lives after emancipation to their lives as slaves. In the South, many ex-slaves became sharecroppers. Other ex-slaves there, upon arrests for both legitimate and trumped-up charges, were hired out by law enforcement officials to work in fields, coal mines, factories, and other places. Meanwhile, in the Upper Mississippi, some ex-slaves remained the domestic servants and drivers of their former owners.

The low numbers of African Americans in the region also meant that many unmarried migrants would remain single unless single African Americans lived in the communities to which they migrated. On rare occasion, African Americans married European Americans. Catharine Ewing Wood Townsend remained in Iowa after the end of the Civil War. As unique as her life was as an Iowa-born slave, her immediate years after the war also defied some social conventions of the period. She married Henry Weaver, a European American man from Pennsylvania, and finally left the Townsend household. They settled in the town of Alba in Monroe County, Iowa, and welcomed daughter Georgia in 1874. They were not only one of very few European American–African American married couples in the state at the time but also one of even fewer unions there between a free European American person and a local African American ex-slave. The 1880 census for Iowa listed Georgia as a mulatto.

Catharine's mother, Ellen Woods's life also changed dramatically after the war. Her longtime employer, John Elbert, died in 1865. She relocated to Lee County, also located in Iowa along the Mississippi, and by 1870, she had settled in a rooming house run by an African American family—the Caldwells. For the first time in her life, she was able to experience African American community and to not live in a household among any European Americans at all. At no point in any of the censuses, however, had she reunited with

Catharine in the same household. Their separation remained a tangible legacy of slavery in the Upper Mississippi.

Elsewhere in Iowa, the lives of former slaves hardly improved from the antebellum period. Rose Madison, the mulatto girl born to Kate Madison in Iowa, grew into adulthood without experiencing any other lifestyle besides that of the Richards household's servant. Remarkably, she was allowed to stay in the state despite the fact that until her late teenage years, her presence there was a violation of Iowa's prohibition of African Americans. Before the state lifted the ban, Iowa did not enforce it by exiling her. In the census of 1870, she was mistakenly listed as white. Ten years later she still lived in Iowa with the Richards family.

After the death of Sylvanus Lowry, his widow, Josephine, relocated her family out of St. Cloud. With her parents-in-law and sister-in-law having already left, the town now had no more members of the prominent slaveholding family living there. Moreover, Josephine's departure ended a presence of Lowrys in the Upper Mississippi that had lasted for over three decades.

That presence, however, eventually returned in triumph. David Calhoun, the son of the Rev. Thomas Calhoun and Elizabeth Lowry Calhoun, came with his family to St. Cloud several decades after his father's bringing of slavery into the town. David had barely reached the double-digits in age when his mother removed him and his siblings from there in 1864. Upon his return exactly twenty years later, he ran successfully for mayor—the same office his uncle Sylvanus had held three decades earlier. The victory showed that he was able to extend his appeal throughout the city, as opposed to his

David Calhoun, son of Minnesota slaveholder Thomas Calhoun, nephew of Sylvanus Lowry, and a mayor of St. Cloud, Minnesota. Courtesy Stearns History Museum Archives.

father's limited appeal to only his fellow slaveholders in northern St. Cloud. He also proved he had inherited his uncle's gift of politicking. He ran for reelection two more times and won both contests.

The other slaveholding family of that town did not maintain its presence there for nearly as long a period. Many years after having left his presidential appointment of U.S. receiver, Samuel Lewis Hays returned to public service in 1870 as a probate court judge. The comeback was short-lived, for he died only one year later. It was ironic that a former owner of human property became an authority in a free state about property ownership. By the time he started his new position, he had no African Americans living under his roof. He had instead remarried, and in his new household of his wife and her children, he was now the only southerner in the residence. His son John returned to law in West Virginia. His community appeared to have forgiven his brief time as a renegade during the war. He practiced law in Gilmer County, where he was raised. Like his father, John no longer used the services of African Americans in his household after the war.

The Caruthers brothers also led new lives in the post-bellum era but kept African Americans in their households, as in the antebellum days. Samuel became a Christian minister, and he and his family lived in Columbia, Tennessee. William, meanwhile, farmed and resumed his law practice in Smith County, Tennessee. Both of them employed African Americans as domestic servants.

The Forstalls were among the most successful survivors of the transition from antebellum to post-bellum society. After leaving the Confederate Army, Theobald Forstall became a prominent employee of the New Orleans Gas Company before returning to the Midwest to run a similar enterprise in Chicago. Some of his descendants received an Ivy League education.

Life for the family's former Minnesota slave was not nearly as lucrative. The Forstalls' slave Rosina lived for two more decades after her enslavement in the Upper Mississippi. She remained a domestic servant of the family. Only in the 1880 census was she finally given a surname—Barnett. She died on November 4, 1882, at the age of eighty-seven. Despite having resided temporarily in a free state and living to see her emancipation, she never experienced life beyond the dictates of the Forstalls and Waltons.

In Minnesota, only the Twin Cities retained a significant portion of their antebellum African American population after 1865. Enough ex-slaves had lived there before and during the Civil War to foster several different kinds of African American-run businesses. They tended to set up their own barber shops and shoe-shine stands. Many of them were able to attract customers of diverse ethnic groups and, consequently, remain in business for a lengthy period of time. On the other hand, they performed services that European Americans expected of African Americans at the time, especially the shining of shoes. Some African Americans experimented with more unorthodox business choices such as cloth-dyeing in St. Cloud, but many of the unusual enterprises did not survive for long partly because of their deviance from the traditional African American services.

St. Cloud did not have an African American community until twenty years after the war. The slaves who had lived there disappeared before the end of the conflict. The last local slaveholders were dead by 1871. European American migrants no longer brought servants up with them from the South. African American migrants, meanwhile, tended to travel only as far north as the Twin Cities and settle among other African Americans there. Only in the 1880s did sojourners start moving further northwest to St. Cloud. Even then, the local African American community for the next half-century overwhelmingly consisted of male migrants, and the town discouraged courtships among the ethnic groups. In November 1917 a mob threatened to treat one African American man to a "necktie party" if he did not stop dating a European American woman, and the police exiled him to Minneapolis although the state never officially outlawed such relationships.[1]

The African American community of Galena, Illinois—one of the oldest of the Upper Mississippi—was also one of the socially and economically strongest upriver African American communities, but the people suffered their share of setbacks, too. The former slaves of the miners of the 1820s and the children of those servants acquired a significant amount of property into the 1860s. A man named Thompson Campbell helped facilitate the passage of a law that mandated the funding of a school with the African American residents' taxes on the land they owned in Galena. They raised the money but then lacked a teacher for the school. The problem was not unlike that of southern schools for African Americans, which required benevolent European Americans from the North to relocate to teach ex-slaves. However, the Illinois school was already in the North, but no one immediately expressed willingness to teach Midwestern ex-slaves.[2]

The negative feelings of some European Americans toward African Americans did not quickly abate in Galena after the end of both slavery and the Black Codes. A woman named Hannah Christopher tried to teach at a school for African Americans, but she soon left the job under pressure. Immediately after she had started teaching there, she suffered "slander, abuse ... every thing that prejudice could suggest or hatred of the blacks invent," according to a local historian. The frequency and intensity of the attacks led her to relocate with her family to Abilene, Kansas.[3]

In 1868 separate schools for European Americans and African Americans began in Galena in earnest, and the former students grew to respect the intellectual talents of the latter. Advocates for the African American students pushed for their admittance to high school, but opponents feared for the students' safety in the school. They predicted that their European American schoolmates would kill them for integrating the high school. One advocate declared his willingness to let the African American students take that risk. "If there is any killing to be done," he began, "let them commence by killing some of my children. I am willing to make the sacrifice." The school became integrated shortly afterward, and no killing of any students took place. Galena appeared to break apart from the rest of Illinois in helping African Americans adjust to life after slavery.[4]

The history of slavery in the Upper Mississippi remained in the public eye in the first few years after the Civil War. Discussions of upriver slavery rarely failed to stir old feelings about the slavery debate years after the passage of the Thirteenth Amendment. Author N. Dwight Harris, who wrote *Negro Slavery in Illinois*, simply transferred the stereotyped depictions of abolitionists and slaveholders from the South to the Midwest. As a result, he aroused the defensiveness of the people he unfavorably depicted. "The author is decidedly abolitionist in his sympathies," wrote book reviewer Walter L. Fleming. "For the pro-slavery Democrats and the Southern settlers he shows slight respect. A wealth of adjectives enables him to express his appreciation of the former and his dislike of the latter, yet this feeling seems almost colorless; the dry recital of names, dates, and platforms causes one to welcome these expressions of opinions, which seem rather to be inherited than formed as a result of knowledge." He then juxtaposed Harris's assessments of both sides of the debate. "The spirit displayed by these men was admirable, and worthy of a noble cause," Harris said of abolitionists. "Enough cannot be said in praise of the self sacrifice, the patient perseverance, the conscientious devotion to duty, the high sense of political honor, and withal the genial liberality of these men." On the other hand, Harris described the state's southern migrants as "ignorant, shiftless, and obstinate," as well as "unscrupulous and dishonest" and "as narrow-minded and stubborn as they were kindhearted and hospitable." African Americans suffered in similar ways to what they would have experienced if they had remained in the South, according to Harris.[5]

The reviewer found fault with Harris' work not only for his embracing of stereotypes but also the abolitionist information he neglected to mention. He avoided discussing the "influence of economic forces" that aimed to establish abolition. "The anti-slavery and anti-negro sentiments of the Southern settlers (like Lincoln), who fled from slavery, are not considered important," he complained. Fleming claimed that Harris had attempted to describe "the anti-slavery history of Illinois as a moral and humanitarian movement"—a description the reviewer found inaccurate. "The result is that we have all the facts, but the collector was unable to interpret them," lamented Fleming, who also snidely remarked about the author's ignorance, "Mr. Harris evidently does not know his negro except through documents."[6]

Through fiction authors memorialized upriver African American slavery, too. The title of Phil Stong's 1939 novel *Ivanhoe Keeler* refers to a frontiersman whose adventures in Iowa comprise the book. As he explores the Mississippi Valley, he travels with two people — one of whom is an African American body servant named Samaliel or Sammy. In the novel Sammy is responsible for Ivanhoe's attire and grooming. His constant role of servant to the main character through the book is not unlike the roles played in actuality by York, James Pemberton, Dred Scott and others who served explorers and soldiers in free states but remained slaves.[7]

The effects of slavery linger in several communities of the Upper Mississippi Valley. Although Galena, Illinois, no longer is an important mining center, the community promotes the past national preeminence of its lead mines. Galena's lead-mining district is now a tourist attraction, but it was once populated by African American slaves doing the actual mining. Thus, without slave labor, Galena would not have as much of a mining history to commemorate.

The end of slavery, on the other hand, produced an immediate and significant effect upon the ethnic demographics of Grant County, Wisconsin. Many ex-slaves migrated there from the South immediately after the end of the Civil War. The absence of a large, preexisting African American presence to help them adjust to the Midwest did not prevent the postwar migrants from establishing a new collective settlement. Building their homes near the city of Lancaster, they developed the community known informally as Hurricane. After several prosperous years, the settlement went into decline as residents took jobs on the railroad or in Chicago. Still, Hurricane's fate was not unlike that of Galena, which became overshadowed by the faster and larger growth of nearby Dubuque, Iowa.

The possessions of some of those involved in Midwestern slavery have stood the test of time. Because the states of that region were in the North and supportive of the Union, they never faced attack and devastation as in many of the southern slaveholding communities during the Civil War. For example, in contrast to the decline of Hurricane in Grant County, Wisconsin, one of the county's former slaveholders continues to maintain a strong local cultural presence over one century after his death. The plantation-style mansion of John Rountree still exists in Grant County. His Wisconsin School of Mines evolved into another school facility: Rountree Hall on the campus of the University of Wisconsin at Platteville.

In St. Cloud, Minnesota, a couple of projects begun by local slaveholders remain in operation. First Presbyterian Church evolved from the missionary efforts of ministers David Lowry and Thomas Calhoun. The congregation is multiethnic, and the ministers do not preach on the religious legitimacy of enslaving African Americans. The church has not completely divorced itself from its history, however. Rather, at the bottom of two stained-glass windows in the sanctuary are placards with the names of Lowry and Calhoun.

Gen. Lowry's old *Union* newspaper evolved into the city's only daily newspaper, the *St. Cloud Times*. Nearly every trace of its origins in proslavery sentiment has disappeared. Its editorials no longer espouse white supremacy, nor do they decry niggerism. It still provides a reminder of its heritage in each issue by mentioning somewhere in the front pages that it was established in 1861. Lowry's simultaneous omission and acknowledgment in his own periodical is a fitting metaphor for the history of slavery in the Upper Mississippi Valley — hidden in plain sight.

Chapter Notes

Chapter One

1. Beasley, 22–23.
2. Ibid.
3. Winship et al., 474–475; Blair et al., 169.
4. Woodson, 5.
5. Ibid., 6.
6. Blumrosen and Blumrosen, 159–160.
7. Ibid., 161–162; Moore, 325.
8. Blumrosen and Blumrosen, 165–166.
9. Collier and Collier, 215, 219.
10. Roosevelt, 362; Blumrosen and Blumrosen, 204–206; Moore, 326–327.
11. Moore, 328.
12. Woodson, 8.
13. Wills, 24; Smith, 25.
14. Woodson, 13–14.
15. Wills, 23–24.
16. Middleton, xxvi.
17. Blumrosen and Blumrosen, 87.
18. Cayton, 58; Takaki, 70–71, 75.
19. Cayton, 58.
20. *Moderator-topics*, vol. 12, 490.
21. Fritz, 84–85.
22. Jones, 17, 106.
23. Lewis, *The Journals of the Lewis and Clark Expedition*, vol. 2, 279.
24. Fritz, 84; Lewis, *The Journals of the Lewis and Clark Expedition*, vol. 2, 17.
25. Patrick Gass, journal entry, 8 December 1804, in *The Journals of the Lewis and Clark Expedition*, vol. 10, 65; Joseph Whitehouse, journal entry, 1 July 1805, in *The Journals of the Lewis and Clark Expedition*, vol. 11, 215–216; Patrick Gass, journal entry, 1 September 1805, in *The Journals of the Lewis and Clark Expedition*, vol. 10, 135.
26. Lewis and Clark, 110.
27. Lewis et al., 111, 116–117.
28. Lewis and Clark, 166.
29. Lewis et al., 112.
30. Lewis and Clark, 242.
31. Foley, 158.
32. Ibid., 158.
33. Ibid., 172; Clark and Holmberg, 210.
34. Morris, 144.
35. Kluger, 323–324.
36. Work, 103; Kluger, 323–324.
37. Work, 103.
38. Brawley, 183.
39. George Washington Williams, 28–30.
40. Turner, 116.
41. Ferris Everett Lewis, *Michigan After 1815*, 50.
42. John Fletcher Williams, 183, 186.
43. Woodward, 40–41.
44. Hoffman, 362–363.

Chapter Two

1. Bateman et al., 249.
2. Newton D. Harris, 50–52.
3. Ibid.
4. Ibid.
5. Ibid.
6. McMaster, 521–528.
7. Newton D. Harris, 50–52.
8. N. Dwight Harris, 10–12, 16.
9. Simeone, 24; N. Dwight Harris, 16.
10. Hand, 42–43; Simeone, 21.
11. Ewing, 79–80.
12. Gregg, 59.
13. N. Dwight Harris, 54–55.
14. Newton D. Harris, 50–52.
15. Ewing, 79–80.
16. Simeone, 21.

17. Bateman et al., 259–261.
18. Edwards, *History of Illinois*, 254.
19. Ibid.; N. Dwight Harris, 121.
20. Edwards, *History of Illinois*, 254; Chamberlin, 168; N. Dwight Harris, 29–30.
21. *The Past and Present of Rock Island County*, 127.
22. Newton D. Harris, 50–52.
23. N. Dwight Harris, 260.
24. Simeone, 153.
25. Bateman et al., 259–261.
26. Ibid.
27. Edwards, *The Edwards Papers*, 250.
28. Bateman et al., 259–261.
29. Simeone, 4.
30. Gale, 357.
31. Shoemaker, 83.
32. Meeker, 271–274.
33. Ibid.
34. Ibid.
35. Ibid.
36. Beckwourth, 34.
37. Meeker, 279–281.
38. Ibid.; Beckwourth, 37.
39. Beckwourth, 37.
40. Ibid.
41. Long, 14 May 1823, in *The Northern Expeditions of Stephen H. Long*, 119.
42. Long, 21 May 1823, in *The Northern Expeditions of Stephen H. Long*, 122; Long, 25 June 1823, in *The Northern Expeditions of Stephen H. Long*, 145; Long, 10 September 1823, in *The Northern Expeditions of Stephen H. Long*, 233.
43. *The History of Jo Daviess County*, 257; Gale, 357.
44. *The History of Jo Daviess County*, 257.
45. "History of the Irish in Wisconsin," 249.
46. Gregg, 58.
47. Havighurst, 111–112.
48. Bates et al., 62.
49. Ibid., 65.
50. Havighurst, 96.
51. Ibid., 117.
52. "Literary Notices, No. XXIII," *Railway Locomotives and Cars*, vol. 3, 298.
53. Utley and Cutcheon, 347.
54. Mamie Thompson, interviewed by Miss Irene Robertson, in *Slave Narratives*.
55. N. Dwight Harris, 100.
56. McLean, 205.
57. Ewing, 79–80.
58. Ibid.
59. *The History of Jo Daviess County*, 321.
60. Affidavit, Sarah, 26 October 1830; Order, 4 November 1830; Plea of Trespass, *Matilda vs. Charles St. Vrain*, 9 March 1831; Subpoena, Charles St. Vrain, 9 March 1831; Copy of Order, 4 November 1830; Sheriff's Return, 12 March 1831.
61. *The Governors' Letter-Books*, xix, 203–204; *The Past and Present of Rock Island County*, 127.
62. *The History of Jo Daviess County*, 483.
63. Ibid.
64. Ibid.
65. Ibid.
66. Ibid.
67. Ibid.
68. "Literary Notices, No. XXV," *Railway Locomotives and Cars*, vol. 3, 328.
69. *Dred Scott v. Sanford*, 4.
70. *The History of Jo Daviess County*, 318; Bent, 57.
71. *Jackson Daily News*, 12 September 1926.
72. Hand, 46–47.
73. Cooley, 83.
74. N. Dwight Harris, 116–118; Hand, 46–47.
75. Petersen, 445; Tarver and Cobb, 398.
76. Jakle, 91, 95.
77. Parker, letter to author, 1 July 2010; Burkett and Parker, 261.
78. Gregg, 974.
79. Parker, letter to author, 1 July 2010.
80. Tweet, 32–33.

Chapter Three

1. Thwaites, 209; Legler, 159.
2. Western Historical Co., *The History of Sauk County, Wisconsin*, 320–321.
3. "The Question Box," 226–227.
4. Parish, 281–282.
5. Tuttle, 757.
6. *Journal of the Illinois State Historical Society*, vol. 35, 355.
7. Michigan Pioneer and Historical Society, *Historical Collections*, vol. 37, 328.
8. Dodd, 28–29.
9. Ibid.
10. Gale, 143.
11. John Nelson Davidson, 85.
12. Dodd, 28–29.
13. Bauer, 51; Hamilton, 110.
14. Grignon, 111.
15. Havighurst, 169.
16. Dodd, 28–29.
17. Winston, 14.
18. Gordon, 23.
19. Dodd, 28–29.

20. Cooper, 54; Bradford, 326.
21. Winston, 15.
22. Kennedy and Kennedy, 25.
23. Strong, 250; Wilson, 27.
24. Havighurst, 10.
25. Murphy, 213.
26. Caleb Atwater, 178.
27. Ibid., 180.
28. Ibid.
29. Stevens, 143.
30. Trask, 118.
31. Lorimer, 2; Hinds, 2.
32. Beard, 277.
33. Hamilton, 27; *Todd County Histories*, 376; Fox, 185–188.
34. McDonnold, 413; Abernethy, 219.
35. Bailey, 38; Sparks, 3; Koenig, 8–9.
36. John Nelson Davidson, 129.
37. Ibid.
38. Ibid., 126.
39. "McLean, 205.
40. Ibid.
41. Tuttle, 757; Western Historical Society, *The History of Dubuque County, Iowa*, 464.
42. Western Historical Society, *The History of Dubuque County, Iowa*, 464.
43. Taslitz, 143.
44. *Dred Scott v. Sanford*, 4.
45. Ibid.
46. "The Question Box," 226–227; Featherstonhaugh, 119.
47. Mathews, *Autobiography of Rev. E. Mathews, the Father Dickson of Mrs. Stowe's "Dred,"* 69.
48. Ibid., 68, 70–71.
49. John Nelson Davidson, 120, 122; Mathews, *Autobiography of Rev. E. Mathews, the Father Dickson of Mrs. Stowe's "Dred,"* 71.
50. Mathews, letter to Elder L. C. Matlack, 90.
51. Ibid., 92–96; Federal Writers Project, *Wisconsin*, 42.
52. Strong, 454; Tenney, 253.
53. Schafer, 191–192.
54. John N. Davidson, *Negro Slavery in Wisconsin and the Underground Railroad*, 40.
55. John N. Davidson, "Some Distinctive Characteristics of the History of Our Lead Region," 194.
56. Winchell et al., 113.
57. John N. Davidson, *Negro Slavery in Wisconsin and the Underground Railroad*, 34, 42.
58. Legler, 281; Mouser, 118.
59. Legler, 281; Mouser, 118.
60. Quaife, 214–215.
61. Ibid.
62. John N. Davidson, *Negro Slavery in Wisconsin and the Underground Railroad*, 41.
63. Ibid.
64. Ibid, 35.
65. Curti, 89.

Chapter Four

1. Taylor, 64.
2. Cyrenus Cole, *A History of the People of Iowa*, 44.
3. Ibid.
4. Taylor, 62.
5. Ibid., 63.
6. Ibid.
7. Western Historical Company, *The History of Lee County, Iowa*, 730.
8. Ibid.
9. Ibid.
10. Ibid., 730; Harlan, 631.
11. Harlan, 631.
12. Kearney, 364.
13. *The History of Lee County*, 382.
14. Harlan, 631–632.
15. Petersen, 116.
16. Ibid.
17. Harlan, 631–632; *Memorial and Biographical History of McLennan, Falls, Bell, and Coryell Counties, Texas*, 929–931.
18. Harlan, 631–632.
19. Ibid.
20. Hill, 292.
21. Foss and Mathews, 65.
22. McDonnold, 336; Kempker, 43.
23. McDonnold, 326–327; Burnett, 59.
24. Burnett, 59.
25. Regue, 65; McDonnold, 326–327.
26. Hamilton, 115; Bauer, 66, 68.
27. Kempker, 43.
28. Folsom, 25.
29. Patterson, 131, 133.
30. Arnow, 105, 249; Federal Writers Project, *Tennessee*, 446.
31. Lorimer, 2; Hinds, 2.
32. Federal Writers Project, *Tennessee*, 446.
33. Hale and Merritt, 729.
34. Finger, 316.
35. McMaster, 521–528.
36. Dykstra, 6.
37. *Iowa Citizen*, 26 January 1906, 21.
38. Ibid.
39. Gue, 207; *History of Johnson County, Iowa*, 463; Bailey, 67.
40. Stull, 307–308.

41. Western Historical Company, *The History of Lee County, Iowa*, 592.

42. *Iowa Citizen*, 26 January 1906, 21.

43. Ibid.

44. Harlan, 632.

45. Taylor, 65–72.

46. Annie Elbert Townsend, 16 June 2010.

47. Ibid.

48. Annie Elbert Townsend, 8 July 2010.

49. Ibid.

50. Taylor, 65–72.

51. Annie Elbert Townsend, 16 June 2010.

52. Annie Elbert Townsend, 8 July 2010.

53. Annie Elbert Townsend, 16 June 2010.

54. Senator Townsend, 70–71.

55. Ibid.

56. Ibid.

57. Ibid.

58. Dempsey, 186.

59. Governor James W. Grimes, letter, 46–48.

60. Ibid.

61. Ibid.

62. Ibid.

63. Ibid.

64. Ibid.

65. "The Negro and Slavery in Early Iowa," 479–480.

66. Ibid.

67. Antrobus, 394, 395.

68. Ibid.

69. *Biographies and Portraits of the Progressive Men of Iowa*, 71–72.

70. Ibid.

Chapter Five

1. Bates, 62.

2. Buchanan, 42.

3. Bancfroft et al., 324.

4. Ibid.

5. Clare, 500.

6. Bates, 65; Bond and Belcourt, 193.

7. *The History of Dubuque County, Iowa*, 801.

8. Ibid.

9. McDonnold, 327–328.

10. *Todd County Histories*, 377.

11. Gilman, 113.

12. McDonnold, 324, 327–328; *Todd County Histories*, 377.

13. McDonnold, 599.

14. Ash, 34, 59, 78.

15. Dippel, 220.

16. Lalor, 923.

17. Chapman Bros., *Portrait and Biographical Album of St. Joseph County, Michigan*, 64.

18. Ibid.

19. Isaac Atwater, *History of the City of Minneapolis*, vol. 1, 77.

20. Ibid.

21. Owen W. Muelder, *The Underground Railroad in Western Illinois*.

22. William Kirchner, "Minnesota Revealed as Tourist State in Early Days When California Was Luring Prospectors," *Minneapolis Tribune* (8 October 1922), 8.

23. Thomas McLean Newson, *Pen Pictures of St. Paul, Minnesota, and Biographical Sketches of Old Settlers*, 371.

24. Jack El-Hai, *Lost Minnesota*, 60.

25. The Rev. Frank C. Coolbaugh, "Reminiscences of the Early Days of Minnesota, 1851 to 1861," *Collections of the Minnesota Historical Society*, 484; Frank G. O'Brien, *Minnesota Pioneer Sketches* (Minneapolis: Housekeeper, 1904), 219.

26. Hiram Fairchild Stevens, *History of the Bench and Bar of Minnesota*, vol. 1 , 31–32.

27. Col. A. P. Connolly, quoted in Lucy Leavenworth Wilder Morris, *Old Rail Fence Corners*, 212.

28. Ibid.

29. William Fletcher King, *Reminiscences*, 172.

30. David Empson et al., *The Street Where You Live*, 110.

31. William Bell Mitchell, *The History of Stearns County, Minnesota* (Chicago, 1915), 46, 416.

32. Raymond J. DeMallie, *Documents of American Indian Diplomacy*, 846–847.

33. Boone County, Kentucky Will Book A, 30 December 1806, 41–46.

34. Gertrude Gove, *A History of St. Cloud in the Civil War*, 8.

35. *Long Prairie Leader*, 27 November 1941, in *Todd County Histories*, 376; *Long Prairie Leader*, 4 December 1941, in *Todd County Histories*, 377.

36. Christianson, 246; Delta Kappa Gamma, Eta Chapter, 1, 10.

37. Christopher Columbus Andrews, 141–2, 143–4; Gove, *A History of St. Cloud in the Civil War*, 8.

38. Mitchell, 451; *Todd County Histories*, 377.

39. Mitchell, 451; *Todd County Histories*, 377.

40. Newson, 569; Parker, 27–28.

41. C.C. Andrews, quoted in *History of Stearns County, Minnesota.*
42. Gilman et al., 68.
43. Parker, 27–28.
44. Caruthers, 207.
45. Ibid., 383.
46. Langum and Walthall, 40.
47. Robert, 89, 106–107, 117.
48. Jackson, 82.
49. Royster, 58.
50. Sauk Rapids *Frontiersman*, 15 October 1857.
51. Sauk Rapids *Frontiersman*, 20 August 1857.
52. Chambers, 291.
53. Sauk Rapids *Frontiersman*, 24 September 1857.
54. St. Cloud *Democrat*, 7 April 1859.
55. Finger, 196, 266.
56. Finger, 266, 316; Lamon, 19.
57. Finger, 216; Lamon, 22, 24.
58. Swisshelm, 172–3; Potter, 112.
59. St. Cloud *Democrat*, 3 October 1861, 2; Lamon, 6–7; Abernethy, 331; Calhoun, 11 May 2010.
60. St. Cloud *Democrat*, 3 October 1861, 2; Burnett, 59.
61. Gutman, 75–76.
62. St. Cloud *Democrat*, 3 October 1861, 2. Minnesota's 1857 census, Stearns County, documented John Butler as one month old in September of that year.

Chapter Six

1. Taney, 407.
2. Ibid., 440–441.
3. Ibid., 558.
4. Governor James W. Grimes, 110.
5. Ibid., 110.
6. Merrick, 64–65.
7. Ibid., 250.
8. Ibid., 251–252.
9. Ibid.
10. Ibid., 252.
11. *Chicago Daily Tribune*, 10 June 1857, 2.
12. Dominik, 37.
13. *St. Paul Times* in *Chicago Daily Tribune*, 27 June 1857, 2.
14. Ibid.
15. Ibid.
16. *Hartford Daily Courant*, 6 June 1857, 2.
17. "Slaves Held in Iowa — More Beauties of the Dred Scott Decision," *Chicago Daily Tribune*, 23 November 1857, 2.
18. Nichols and Nichols, 261.

19. "News and Notes," *Minnesota History*, December 1936, 488.
20. Benjamin, 11; William Henry Smith and Whitelaw Reid, 253.
21. Carlyle, "Morgan May."
22. Easton, 230.
23. Bancroft, 315–316.
24. Ibid., 312–313.
25. Sauk Rapids *Frontiersman*, 18 March 1858; Sauk Rapids *Frontiersman*, 1 April 1858, 2.
26. Ibid.
27. Ibid.; St. Cloud *Democrat*, 7 April 1859.
28. St. Cloud *Democrat*, 24 February 1859.
29. C. C. Andrews, letter in *St. Paul Pioneer-Democrat*, 27 February 1859, 2.
30. St. Cloud *Democrat*, 3 October 1861, 2.
31. Swisshelm, 204; St. Cloud *Democrat*, 7 April 1859, 1; St. Cloud *Democrat*, 3 October 1861, 2.
32. Calhoun, letter to author, 11 May 2010.
33. Swisshelm, *Half a Century.*
34. Dominik, 4.
35. C. C. Andrews, *St. Paul Pioneer-Democrat* (27 February 1859).
36. Ibid.
37. St. Cloud *Democrat*, 7 April 1859, 1.
38. St. Cloud *Democrat*, 23 September 1858.
39. St. Cloud *Democrat*, 16 September 1858.
40. St. Cloud *Democrat*, 24 March 1859.
41. Sauk Rapids *Frontiersman*, 17 June 1858; St. Cloud *Democrat*, 21 April 1859.
42. St. Cloud *Democrat*, 7 April 1859.
43. Ibid.
44. St. Cloud *Democrat*, 16 September 1858.
45. St. Cloud *Democrat*, 14 October 1858.
46. Forrest, 261–262.
47. St. Paul *Pioneer-Democrat*, 20 August 1859, 2; St. Paul *Pioneer-Democrat*, 2 September 1859, 1.
48. St. Paul *Pioneer-Democrat*, 27 February 1859; St. Paul *Pioneer-Democrat*, 2 September 1859.
49. Mitchell, 504.
50. St. Cloud *Democrat*, 13 September 1860.
51. St. Paul *Minnesotan*, 5 January 1860, in Chicago *Press and Tribune*, 11 January 1860, 2.
52. Upham, 58.
53. Kelley and Woods, 109.
54. "Minnesota Historical Society Notes," *Minnesota History*, June 1932, 195–196; Parsons, 37.
55. Gilman, *The Story of Minnesota's Past*, 109.
56. St. Cloud *Democrat*, 26 July 1860.
57. St. Cloud *Democrat*, 11 October 1860.

58. Ibid.

59. St. Cloud *Democrat*, 14 September 1860.

60. St. Cloud *Democrat*, 19 April 1860.

61. St. Cloud *Democrat*, 10 May 1860.

62. Consul Willshire Butterfield, *History of La Crosse, Wisconsin*, 540.

63. Ibid.

64. T. K. Cartmell, *Shenandoah Valley Pioneers and Their Descendants*, 501, 504.

65. Ibid., 346.

66. "Mr. Seward in the West," *New York Times*, 27 September 1860.

67. Ibid.

68. Parker, letter to author, 1 July 2010; Burkett and Parker, 261.

69. Buford, 85.

Chapter Seven

1. Tarbell, 76–77.

2. Ibid.

3. Schaff, 125.

4. Davis, 15.

5. Ibid., 46–47.

6. Senator James W. Grimes, "Speech on the Surrender of Slaves by the Army," 14 April 1862, 190.

7. Johnson, Archive of Folk Song.

8. Trollope, 212–213.

9. St. Cloud *Union*, 16 August 1861.

10. Johnson, Archive of Folk Song.

11. Dubuque *Weekly Times*, 11 July 1861.

12. Cartmell, 501.

13. Lawson, 244–245.

14. *Cincinnati Gazette*, 11 December 1860, *The Rebellion Record*, vol. 10, 65.

15. Fletcher, 3; *Stearns County First Book of Marriages*, volume A, 20.

16. Fletcher, 3.

17. *Stearns County First Book of Marriages*, volume A, 20.

18. Marie Mollohan, *By the Banks of the Holly*, 176–177.

19. Ibid., 190.

20. St. Cloud *Union*, 13 June 1861.

21. St. Cloud *Democrat*, 20 June 1861.

22. St. Cloud *Democrat*, 29 August 1861.

23. Everett, 46.

24. Gove, *St. Cloud in the Civil War*, 24.

25. Swisshelm, 217.

26. St. Cloud *Democrat*, 29 May 1862.

27. *Light, Heat and Power*, vol. 8–9, 39.

28. Ibid.

29. Berlin et al., 203.

30. Corse, 288.

31. Lothrop, 251.

32. Swisshelm, 222.

33. *Mississippi Valley Historical Review*, vol. 7, 221–222.

34. Gove, *A History of St. Cloud in the Civil War*, 50.

35. St. Cloud *Times*, 29 October 1864.

36. St. Cloud *Democrat*, 11 June 1864.

37. Ibid.

38. Gove, *A History of St. Cloud*, part II, 8–9; Gove, *A History of St. Cloud in the Civil War*, 63.

39. Hand, 47.

40. Ibid., 47.

41. Western Historical Co., *The History of Des Moines County, Iowa*, 447–448.

42. Ibid., 453, 455.

43. Governor James T. Lewis, 221–222.

44. Ibid.

45. Ibid.

46. J. Matthew Gallman, *The Civil War Chronicle*, 529.

47. Col. Barrett, farewell address to the 62nd, 4 January 1866.

48. Curti, 90.

49. Gove, *A History of St. Cloud in the Civil War*, 63.

50. *Reconstructionist*, 21 December 1865.

51. St. Paul *Pioneer-Democrat*, 28 December 1865.

Conclusion

1. St. Cloud *Times*, 26 November 1917.

2. *The History of Jo Daviess County*, 362.

3. Ibid.

4. Ibid.

5. Fleming, 309.

6. Ibid.

7. Clarence A. Andrews, 17.

Bibliography

Abernethy, Thomas Perkins. *From Frontier to Plantation in Tennessee: A Study in Frontier Democracy*. Tuscaloosa: University of Alabama Press, 1967.

Andrews, Christopher Columbus. *Minnesota and Dacotah*. New York: Arno Press, 1857.

Andrews, Clarence A. *A Literary History of Iowa*. Iowa City: University of Iowa Press, 1972.

Antrobus, Augustine M. *The History of Des Moines County, Iowa*. Chicago: Clarke, 1915.

Arnow, Harriette Simpson. *Seedtime on the Cumberland*. New York: Macmillan, 1960.

Ash, Stephen V. *Middle Tennessee Society Transformed, 1860–1870: War and Peace in the Upper South*. Baton Rouge: Louisiana State University Press, 1988.

Atwater, Caleb. *Remarks Made on a Tour to Prairie du Chien*. Columbus, OH: Whiting, 1831.

Atwater, Isaac. *History of the City of Minneapolis*. Vol. 1. New York: Munsell, 1893.

Bailey, Chris Harvey. *The Stulls of "Millsboro."* Madison: Bailey, 2000.

Bailey, Edwin C. *Past and Present of Winneshiek County*. Chicago: Clarke, 1913.

Baker, T. Lindsay, and Julia Baker, eds. *The WPA Oklahoma Slave Narratives*. Norman: University of Oklahoma Press, 1996.

Bancroft, Frederic. *Slave Trading in the Old South*. New York: Ungar, 1931.

Bancroft, Hubert Howe, et al. *History of Mexico, 1824–1861*. San Francisco: History, 1888.

Barrett, Theodore H. Farewell address to the 62nd United States Colored Infantry. 4 January 1866.

Bateman, Newton, et al. *Historical Encyclopedia of Illinois*. Vol. 1. Chicago: Munsell, 1918.

Bates, George E., Jr., et al. *Historic Lifestyles in the Upper Mississippi River*. Lanham, MD: University Press of America, 1983.

Bauer, K. Jack. *Zachary Taylor: Soldier, Planter, Statesman of the Old Southwest*. Baton Rouge: Louisiana State University Press, 1985.

Beard, Richard. *Brief Biographical Sketches of Some of the Early Ministers of the Cumberland Presbyterian Church*. Nashville: Cumberland Presbyterian Church, 1874.

Beasley, Delilah Leontium. *The Negro Trail Blazers of California*. Los Angeles: Bancroft Library, 1919.

Beck, Catherine, and Gertrude Gove. *St. Cloud, Minnesota Houses from Log Cabin to Mobile Home, 1855–1973*. St. Cloud, MN: Eta Chapter of Delta Kappa Gamma, 1973.

Beckwourth, James P. *The Life and Adventures of James P. Beckwourth*. London: Unwin, 1892.

Benjamin, Judah Philip. *Kansas Bill*, 11.

Bent, Charles. *The History of Whiteside County*. Clinton, IA: Allen, 1877.

Berlin, Ira, et al. *Slaves No More*. Cambridge: Cambridge University Press, 1992.

Blair, Emma Helen, et al. *The Indian Tribes of the Upper Mississippi and Region of the Great Lakes*. Vol. 2. Cleveland: Clark, 1912.

Blumrosen, Alfred W., and Ruth G. Blumrosen. *Slave Nation*. Naperville, IL: Sourcebooks, 2005.

Bond, John Wesley, and George Antoine Belcourt. *Minnesota and Its Resources*. Chicago: Keen & Lee, 1857.

Boone County, Kentucky Will Book A. 30 December 1806.

Brawley, Benjamin Griffith. *A Short History of the American Negro*. New York: Macmillan, 1919.

Buchanan, Thomas C. *Black Life on the Mississippi*. Chapel Hill: University of North Carolina Press, 2004.

Buford, Marcus Bainbridge. *A Genealogy of the Buford Family in America*. San Francisco: n.p., 1903.

Burnett, Mary Wilcox. *Child of the Sun*. Los Altos, CA: Sunreach, 1995.

Burkett, Kathryn Lewis, and Donald Parker. *Hancock County, Illinois*. Virginia Beach, VA: Donning, 2000.

Butterfield, Consul Willshire. *History of La Crosse, Wisconsin*. Chicago: Western Historical, 1881.

Carlyle, Mimi. "Who Was Morgan May?" *Historical Whisperings*, July 1989.

Cartmell, T. K. *Shenandoah Valley Pioneers and Their Descendants*. Winchester, VA: Eddy, 1909.

Cayton, Andrew Robert Lee. *The Frontier Republic*. Kent, OH: Kent State University Press, 1986.

Chamberlin, Henry Barrett. "Elias Kent Kane." In *Transactions of the Illinois State Historical Society for the Year 1908*. Springfield: Illinois State Journal, 1909.

Chambers, Lenoir. *Stonewall Jackson*. Vol. 1. New York: Morrow, 1959.

Chapman Bros. *Portrait and Biographical Album of St. Joseph County, Michigan*. Chicago: Chapman Bros., 1889.

Christianson, Theodore. *Minnesota, the Land of Sky-Tinted Waters*. Chicago: American Historical Society, 1935.

Clare, Israel Smith. *Illustrated Universal History*. Philadelphia: McCurdy, 1881.

Clark, William, and James J. Holmberg. *Dear Brother*. New York: Yale University Press, 2002.

Cole, Cyrenus. *A History of the People of Iowa*. Cedar Rapids, IA: Torch, 1921.

Collier, Christopher, and James Lincoln Collier. *Decision in Philadelphia*. New York: Random House, 1986.

Coolbaugh, The Rev. Frank C. "Reminiscences of the Early Days of Minnesota, 1851 to 1861." In *Collections of the Minnesota Historical Society*. St. Paul: Minnesota Historical Society, 1915.

Cooley, Verna. "Illinois and the Underground Railroad to Canada." In *Publications of the Illinois State Historical Library*, no. 23. Springfield: State of Illinois, 1917.

Cooper, William J. *Jefferson Davis, American*. New York: Vintage, 2000.

Corse, John M. Letter. In *The Annals of Iowa*. Des Moines: Historical Department of Iowa, 1912.

Curti, Merle. *The Making of an American Community*. Palo Alto, CA: Stanford University Press, 1959.

Davidson, John N. *Negro Slavery in Wisconsin and the Underground Railroad*. Milwaukee: Parkman Club, 1897.

_____. "Some Distinctive Characteristics of the History of Our Lead Region." In *Proceedings of the State Historical Society of Wisconsin* 46 (1899).

Davidson, John Nelson. "Negro Slavery in Wisconsin." *Proceedings of the Annual Business Meeting*, State Historical Society of Wisconsin, 1903.

Davis, Jefferson. *A Short History of the Confederate States of America*. New York: Belford, 1890.

DeMallie, Raymond J. *Documents of American Indian Diplomacy*. Norman: University of Oklahoma Press, 1999.

Dempsey, Terrell. *Searching for Jim: Slavery in Sam Clemens's World*. Columbia: University of Missouri Press, 2003.

Dippel, John Van Houten. *Race to the Frontier: "White Flight" and Westward Expansion*. New York: Algora, 2005.

Dodd, William Edward. *Jefferson Davis*. Philadelphia: Jacobs, 1900.

Dominik, John J., Jr. *3 Towns into 1 City*. St. Cloud, MN: St. Cloud Area Bicentennial Commission, 1976.

Dykstra, Robert R. *Bright Radical Star*. Cambridge, MA: Harvard University Press, 1993.

Easton, Augustus B. *History of the Saint*

Croix Valley. Vol. 1. Chicago: Cooper, 1909.

Edwards, Ninian W. *The Edwards Papers.* Chicago: Fergus, 1884.

_____. *History of Illinois.* Springfield: Illinois State Journal, 1870.

El-Hai, Jack. *Lost Minnesota.* Minneapolis: University of Minnesota, 2000.

Empson, Donald, et al. *The Street Where You Live.* Minneapolis: University of Minnesota, 2006.

Everett, Edward. *The Rebellion Record.* Vol. 1. New York: Putnam, 1861.

Ewing, Elbert William Robinson. *Legal and Historical Status of the Dred Scott Decision.* Washington, DC: Cobden, 1909.

Featherstonhaugh, George W. *A Canoe Voyage up the Minnay Sotor.* London: Bentley, 1847.

Federal Writers' Project. *Slave Narratives.* Washington: Works Progress Administration, 1941.

_____. *Tennessee: A Guide to the State.* New York: Viking, 1939.

_____. *Wisconsin: A Guide to the Badger State.* New York: Duell, Sloan and Pearce, 1941.

Finger, John R. *Tennessee Frontiers: Three Regions in Transition.* Bloomington: Indiana University Press, 2001.

Fleming, Walter L. Book review, *Negro Slavery in Illinois,* by N. Dwight Harris, *Dial,* 16 November 1904.

Fletcher, William. "A Few Reminiscences." Sauk Rapids *Sentinel,* 18 August 1927.

Foley, William E. *Wilderness Journey.* Columbia: University of Missouri Press, 2004.

Folsom, William H.C. *Fifty Years in the Northwest.* Taylor Falls, MN: Taylor Falls Historical Society, 1888.

Forrest, Robert J. "Mythical Cities of Southwestern Minnesota." *Minnesota History,* 1933.

Foss, Andrew T., and Edward Mathews. *Facts for Baptist Churches.* Utica, NY: American Baptist Free Mission Society, 1850.

Fox, Early Lee. *The American Colonization Society, 1817–1840.* Baltimore: Johns Hopkins University Press, 1919.

Fritz, Harry W. *The Lewis and Clark Expedition.* Westport, CT: Greenwood Press, 2004.

Gale, George. *Upper Mississippi.* Chicago: Clarke, 1867.

Gallman, J. Matthew. *The Civil War Chronicle.* New York: Crown, 2000.

Gilman, Rhoda R. *Henry Hastings Sibley.* St. Paul: Minnesota Historical Society, 2004.

_____. *The Story of Minnesota's Past.* St. Paul: Minnesota Historical Society, 1991.

Gordon, Armistead Churchill. *Jefferson Davis.* New York: Charles Scribner's Sons, 1918.

Gove, Gertrude B. *A History of St. Cloud.* Part II. St. Cloud, MN: St. Cloud Times, 1935.

_____. *A History of St. Cloud in the Civil War.* St. Cloud, MN: Stearns County Historical Society, 1976.

Gregg, Thomas. *History of Hancock County.* Chicago: Chapman, 1880.

Grignon, Antoine. "Recollections of Antoine Grignon." In *Proceedings of the Annual Meeting of the State Historical Society of Wisconsin.* Madison: State Historical Society of Wisconsin, 1905.

Grimes, Governor James W. Address to General Assembly, 12 January 1858. In William Salter, *The Life of James W. Grimes.* New York: Appleton, 1876.

_____. Letter, 8 April 1854. In William Salter, *The Life of James W. Grimes.* New York: Appleton, 1876.

Grimes, Senator James W. "Speech on the Surrender of Slaves by the Army," 14 April 1862. In William Salter, *The Life of James W. Grimes.* New York: Appleton, 1876.

Gue, Benjamin F. *History of Iowa.* New York: Century History, 1903.

_____, and Benjamin Franklin Shambaugh. *Biographies and Portraits of the Progressive Men of Iowa.* Des Moines, IA: Conaway and Shaw, 1899.

Gutman, Herbert R. *The Black Family in Slavery and Freedom, 1750–1925.* New York: Vintage Books, 1976.

Hale, Will T., and Dixon L. Merritt, *A History of Tennessee and Tennesseans: The Leaders and Representative Men in Commerce, Industry and Modern Activities.* Vol. III. Chicago: Lewis, 1913.

Hamilton, Holman. *Zachary Taylor: Soldier of the Republic.* Hamden, CT: Archon Books, 1966.

Hand, John P. "Negro Slavery in Illinois." In

Publications of the Illinois State Historical Library, no. 15.

Harlan, A. W. "Slavery in Iowa Territory." In *Annals of Iowa*. Des Moines: Historical Department of Iowa, 1912.

Harris, N. Dwight. *The History of Negro Servitude in Illinois*. Chicago: McClurg, 1904.

Harris, Newton D. "Negro Servitude in Illinois." In *Papers in Illinois History and Transactions*. Springfield: Illinois State Historical Library, 1906.

Havighurst, Walter. *Voices on the River*. New York: Macmillan, 1964.

Hill, James J. "Migration of Blacks to Iowa 1820–1960." In *Journal of Negro History* 66, no. 4 (Winter 1981–1982).

Hinds, J. I. D. "Rev. David Lowry, D.D." In *The Cumberland Presbyterian*, 3 May 1877.

Historical Collections. Vol. 37. Detroit: Michigan Pioneer and Historical Society, 1909.

The History of Jo Daviess County. Chicago: Kett, 1878.

History of Johnson County, Iowa. Iowa City: n.p., 1883.

"History of the Irish in Wisconsin." In *The Journal of the American-Irish Historical Society* 13.

Hoffman, C.F. "A Prairie Jumbie." In *The Living Age* 3 (1844).

Jackson, Steven. *The Irish Ancestry of Stonewall Jackson*. Durban, SA: Just Done, 2008.

Jakle, John A. "Towns to Visit: Sights (Sites) to See." In *Grand Excursions on the Upper Mississippi River*, Curtis C. Roseman and Elizabeth M. Roseman, eds. Iowa City: University of Iowa Press, 2004.

Johnson, George. Narrative. In Archive of Folk Song. Music Division. Library of Congress, Washington, DC.

Jones, Landon Y. *William Clark and the Shaping of the West*. New York: Hill and Wang, 2004.

Kearny, Stephen W. Letter, 26 September 1835. *Iowa Journal of History* 7.

Kelley, Oliver H., and Thomas A. Woods. *Knights of the Plow*. Ames: Iowa State University Press, 1991.

Kempker, John F. Document pertaining to Fort Atkinson along the Turkey River in Iowa. 20 September 1916.

Kennedy, James Ronald, and Walter Donald Kennedy. *Was Jefferson Davis Right?* Gretna, LA: Pelican, 1998.

King, William Fletcher. *Reminiscences*. New York: Abingdon, 1915.

Kirchner, William. "Minnesota Revealed as Tourist State in Early Days When California Was Luring Prospectors." *Minneapolis Tribune*, 8 October 1922.

Kluger, Richard. *Seizing Destiny*. New York: Knopf, 2007.

Koenig, Gwen. *History of Twin Springs (Festiva)*. Decorah, IA: Anundsen, 1979.

Lalor, John Joseph. *Cyclopaedia of Political Science, Political Economy, and of the Political History of the United States*. Vol. 3. Chicago: Cary, 1884.

Lamon, Lester. *Blacks in Tennessee*. Knoxville: University of Tennessee Press, 1981.

Langum, David J., and Howard P. Walthall. *From Maverick to Mainstream: Cumberland School of Law, 1847–1997*. Athens: University of Georgia Press, 1997.

Legler, Henry Eduard. *Leading Events of Wisconsin History*. Milwaukee: Sentinel, 1898.

Lewis, Ferris Everett. *Michigan after 1815*. Hillsdale, MI: Hillsdale Educational Publishers, 1973.

Lewis, Governor James T. "Annual Message," 12 January 1865. In *Civil War Messages and Proclamations of Wisconsin War Governors*. Reuben Gold Thwaites, ed. Madison: Wisconsin History Commission, 1912.

Lewis, Meriwether. *The Journals of the Lewis and Clark Expedition*. Vol. 2. Lincoln: University of Nebraska Press, 2001.

_____, and William Clark. *History of the Expedition Under the Command of Captains Lewis and Clark*. New York: Barnes, 1904.

_____, et al., *History of the Expedition of Captains Lewis and Clark*. Chicago: A.C. McClurg, 1902.

Long, Stephen. Document, 14 May 1823. In *The Northern Expeditions of Stephen H. Long*. St. Paul: Minnesota Historical Society Press, 1978.

Lorimer, L. "David Lowry, Cumberland Presbyterian Minister, 1796–1877." In *The Cumberland Presbyterian*, 12 April 1877.

Lothrop, Charles H. *A History of the First Regiment Iowa Cavalry Veteran Volunteers*. Lyons, IA: Beers and Eaton, 1890.

Mathews, Edward. *Autobiography of Rev. E. Mathews, the Father Dickson of Mrs. Stowe's "Dred."* Miami: Mnemosyne, 1969.

_____. Letter to Elder L. C. Matlack, 28 March 1848, in Lucius C. Matlack, *The History of American Slavery and Methodism from 1780 to 1849: and History of the Wesleyan Methodist Connection in America.* New York: No. 5 Spruce Street, 1849.

McDonnold, Benjamin Wilburn. *History of the Cumberland Presbyterian Church.* Nashville: Cumberland Presbyterian Church, 1888.

McLean, Justice John. "Dred Scott Case — Justice McLean's Opinion." *The Political Text-book or Encyclopedia.* Michael W. Cluskey, ed. Philadelphia: Smith, 1860.

McMaster, John Bach. *A History of the People of the United States, from the Revolution to the Civil War.* New York: Appleton, 1913.

Meeker, Moses. "Early History of Lead Region of Wisconsin." In *Collections of the State Historical Society of Wisconsin.* Vol. 6. Madison: Wisconsin History Commission, 1872.

Memorial and Biographical History of McLennan, Falls, Bell, and Coryell Counties, Texas. Lewis: Chicago, 1893.

Merrick, George Byron. *Old Times on the Upper Mississippi.* Cleveland: Clark, 1909.

Middleton, Stephen. *The Black Laws in the Old Northwest.* Westport, CT: Greenwood Press, 1993.

Mitchell, William Bell. *The History of Stearns County, Minnesota.* Chicago: Cooper, 1915.

Mollohan, Marie. *By the Banks of the Holly.* Lincoln, NE: Iuniverse, 2005.

Monroe, Haskell M. Jr., and James T. McIntosh, eds. *The Papers of Jefferson Davis.* Vol. 1. Baton Rouge: Louisiana State University Press, 1981.

Moore, Charles. *The Northwest Under Three Flags, 1635–1796.* New York: Harper & Brothers, 1900.

Morris, Larry E. *The Fate of the Corps.* Chicago: Donnelley, 2004.

Morris, Lucy Leavenworth Wilder. *Old Rail Fence Corners.* Austin, MN: McCulloch, 1914.

Morris, Thomas D. *Southern Slavery and the Law, 1619–1860.* Chapel Hill: University of North Carolina Press, 1996.

Mouser, Bruce L. *Black La Crosse, Wisconsin, 1850–1906.* La Crosse, WI; La Crosse County Historical Society, 2002.

Muelder, Owen W. *The Underground Railroad in Western Illinois.* Jefferson, NC: McFarland, 2008.

Murphy, Lucy Eldersveld. *A Gathering of Rivers.* Lincoln: University of Nebraska Press, 2000.

Newson, Thomas McLean. *Pen Pictures of St. Paul, Minnesota, and Biographical Sketches of Old Settlers.* St. Paul: Newson, 1886.

Nichols, Henry, and Charles W. Nichols. "Henry M. Nichols and Frontier Minnesota." In *Minnesota History*, September 1938.

O'Brien, Frank G. *Minnesota Pioneer Sketches.* Minneapolis: Housekeeper, 1904.

Parish, John Carl. *George Wallace Jones.* Iowa City: Iowa Historical Society, 1912.

Parker, Nathan Howe. "The Minnesota Handbook for 1856–1857." Boston: Jewett, 1857.

Parsons, Ernest Dudley. *The Story of Minneapolis.* Minneapolis: n.p., 1913.

The Past and Present of Rock Island County. Chicago: Kett, 1877.

Patterson, Caleb Perry. *The Negro in Tennessee, 1790–1865.* New York: Negro University, 1922.

Pelzer, Louis. "The Negro and Slavery in Early Iowa." *The Iowa Journal of History and Politics.* Vol. 2. 1940.

Petersen, William J. *Steamboating on the Upper Mississippi.* Iowa City: State Historical Society of Iowa, 1968.

Potter, Merle. *101 Best Stories of Minnesota.* Minneapolis: Schmitt, 1931.

Quaife, Milo Milton. *The Convention of 1846.* Vol. 27. Madison: State Historical Society of Wisconsin, 1919.

"The Question Box." *Wisconsin Magazine of History 2.*

Reque, Sigrud S. *History of Old Fort Atkinson.* Iowa City: State Historical Society of Iowa, 1944.

Robert, Joseph Clarke. *The Road from Monticello: A Study of the Virginia Slavery Debate of 1832.* New York: AMS, 1941.

Roosevelt, Theodore. *The Winning of the West.* New York: G. Putnam's Sons, 1906.

Royster, Charles. *The Destructive War*. New York: Knopf, 1991.

Schafer, Joseph. *The Wisconsin Lead Region*. Madison: State Historical Society of Wisconsin, 1932.

Schaff, Morris. *Jefferson Davis: His Life and Personality*. Boston: Luce, 1922.

Scott, Dred v. Sanford.

Sheets, J., A. Hendrickson, and O. DeLaurier, eds. *Todd County Histories*. Long Prairie, MN: Todd County Bicentennial Committee, 1976.

Shoemaker, Nancy. *Negotiators of Change*. New York: Routledge, 1995.

Simeone, James. *Democracy and Slavery in Frontier Illinois*. DeKalb: Northern Illinois University Press, 2000.

Smith, James Morton. *The Republic of Letters*. New York: Norton, 1995.

Smith, William Henry, and Whitelaw Reid. *A Political History of Slavery*. New York: G.P. Putnam's Sons, 1903.

Sparks, Charles H. *History of Winneshiek County*. Decorah, IA: Leonard, 1876.

Stearns County First Book of Marriages. Vol. A.

Stevens, Frank Everett. *The Black Hawk War*. Chicago: Stevens, 1903.

Stevens, Hiram Fairchild. *History of the Bench and Bar of Minnesota*. Vol. 1. Minneapolis: Legal, 1904.

Strong, Moses M. "The Indian Wars of Wisconsin." *Collections of the State Historical Society of Wisconsin*. Vol. 8. Madison: Wisconsin History Commission, 1908.

Stull, O. H. W. "Proclamation by the Acting Governor of Iowa Territory" (11 May 1842). *The Messages and Proclamations of the Governors of Iowa*. Vol. 1. Iowa City: State Historical Society of Iowa, 1903.

Swisshelm, Jane Grey. *Half a Century*. Chicago: Jensen, McClurg, 1880.

Takaki, Ronald. *A Different Mirror*. Boston: Little, Brown, 1993.

Taney, Chief Justice Roger. *A Report of the Decisions of the Supreme Court of the United States and the Opinions of the Judges Thereof in the Case of Dred Scott versus John F. A. Sanford*. New York: Appleton, 1857.

Tarbell, Ida Minerva. *The Life of Abraham Lincoln*. New York: Lincoln History Society, 1909.

Tarver, Micajah, and H. Cobb. *The Western Journal and Civilian*, Vol. 7. 1851.

Taslitz, Andrew E. *Reconstructing the Fourth Amendment*. New York: New York University Press, 2006.

Taylor, L. L. *Past and Present of Appanoose County, Iowa*. Chicago: Clarke, 1913.

Tenney, Horace A. *Memorial Record of the Fathers of Wisconsin*. Madison: Atwood, 1880.

Thwaites, Reuben Gold. *Wisconsin*. Boston: Houghton Mifflin, 1908.

Townsend, Senator. Address (15 February 1900). In *Pioneer Lawmakers' Association of Iowa: Reunion of 1900*. Des Moines: Conaway, 1900.

Trask, Kerry A. *Black Hawk: the Battle for the Heart of America*. New York: Holt, 2007.

Trollope, Anthony. *North America*. Leipzig: Tauchnitz, 1862.

Turner, Wesley B. *The War of 1812: The War That Both Sides Won*. Toronto: Dundum, 2000.

Tuttle, Charles R. *The State of Wisconsin*. Madison, WI: Russell, 1875.

Tweet, Roald D. "Building a Mighty Fine Line: The Chicago and Rock Island Railroad." In *Grand Excursions on the Upper Mississippi River*, Curtis C. Roseman and Elizabeth M. Roseman, eds. Iowa City: University of Iowa Press, 2004.

Upham, Warren. *Minnesota Place Names*. St. Paul: Minnesota Historical Society, 2001.

Utley, Henry Munson, and Byron M. Cutcheon. *Michigan as a Province, Territory, and State*. Detroit: Publishing Society of Michigan, 1906.

Western Historical Company. *The History of Des Moines County, Iowa*. Chicago: Western Historical, 1879.

_____. *The History of Dubuque County, Iowa*. Chicago: Western Historical, 1879.

_____. *The History of Lee County, Iowa*. Chicago: Western Historical, 1879.

_____. *The History of Sauk County, Wisconsin*. Chicago: Western Historical, 1880.

Williams, George Washington. *History of the Negro Race in America from 1619 to 1880*. New York: G.P. Putnam's Sons, 1883.

Williams, John Fletcher. "Memoir of Capt. Martin Scott." *Collections of the Minne-*

sota Historical. St. Paul: Minnesota Historical Society, 1880.

Wills, Garry. *Negro President.* New York: Houghton Mifflin, 2003.

Wilson, Elinor. *Jim Beckwourth.* Norman: University of Oklahoma Press, 1972.

Winchell, Newton Horace, et al. *History of the Upper Mississippi Valley.* Minneapolis: Minnesota Historical Society, 1881.

Winship, George Parker, et al. *The Coronado Expedition, 1540–1542.* Vol. 14. No. 1. Washington: Smithsonian Institution, 1896.

Winston, Robert W. *High Stakes and Hair-Trigger: The Life of Jefferson Davis.* New York: Holt, 1930.

Woodson, Carter Godwin. *A Century of Negro Migration.* Washington, DC: Association for the Study of Negro Life and History, 1918.

Woodward, William E. *Years of Madness.* Cleveland: Frontier, 1967.

Work, Monroe Nathan. *Negro Year Book and Annual Encyclopedia of the Negro.* Alabama: Tuskegee Institute, 1913.

Periodicals

Chicago *Daily Tribune.*
Chicago *Press and Tribune.*
Cincinnati *Gazette.*
Dubuque *Weekly Times.*
Hartford *Daily Courant.*
Iowa *Citizen.*
Jackson *Daily News.*
Journal of the Illinois State Historical Society.

Light, Heat and Power.
Minnesota History.
Mississippi Valley Historical Review.
Moderator-topics.
New York Times.
Railway Locomotives and Cars.
Rebellion Record.
Reconstructionist.
St. Cloud *Democrat.*
St. Cloud *Times.*
St. Cloud *Union.*
St. Paul *Minnesotan.*
St. Paul *Pioneer-Democrat.*
St. Paul *Times.*
Sauk Rapids *Frontiersman.*

Documents pertaining to *Matilda v. Charles St. Vrain*

Affidavit, Sarah (26 October 1830).
Copy of Order (4 November 1830).
Order (4 November 1830).
Plea of Trespass (9 March 1831).
Subpoena, Charles St. Vrain (9 March 1831).
Sheriff's Return (12 March 1831).

Letters to the author

Calhoun, Andrew (11 May 2010).
Parker, Don (1 July 2010).
Townsend, Annie Elbert. Quoted in Lynne Bie (16 June 2010).
Townsend, Annie Elbert. Quoted in Lynne Bie (8 July 2010).

Index

Index